THE PRESIDENCY AND INFORMATION POLICY

THE PRESIDENCY AND INFORMATION POLICY

Harold C. Relyea
with
Larry S. Berman, John A. Gosden,
Michael Baruch Grossman, Morton H. Halperin,
Martha Joynt Kumar, Arthur S. Miller,
Jon A. Turner, Alexandra K. Wigdor, and David
Wigdor

Foreword by R. Gordon Hoxie

Sponsored by:
CENTER FOR THE STUDY OF THE PRESIDENCY
Proceedings: Volume IV, Number 1, 1981

". . . that government of the people,
by the people, for the people,
shall not perish from the earth."

ABRAHAM   LINCOLN
November 19, 1863

Table of Contents

Selected Reading List

Foreword

A. *The General Issues*

The theme of this volume, *The Presidency and Information Policy*, gets to the heart of our democratic processes and of democracy's dilemma in relating security with freedom of information. The substance of the relationship among Congress, the Presidency, the Courts, and the people is communication based upon *information, understanding,* and *trust*. Each of these three—information, understanding, and trust—constitutes a vital part in an interdependent triad.

Nearing the completion of a life-time of counselling Presidents, the late Professor Adolf Berle, a decade ago, concluded that what was most needed by the American people was *information*. As he expressed it, there needs be "better and more accurate information for the American public, accuracy that American public opinion will function more continuously and more responsibly as it deals with the day to day decisions a President must make. . . ."[1]

It was, in part, such perceptive views that had led to the 1966 enactment of the Freedom of Information Act, during the Johnson Administration and to its subsequent amendments during the Nixon and Ford administrations. Ironically, none of these Presidents exhibited any enthusiasm for this legislation, despite its worthy expressed purposes. For they were witness to what we term "democracy's dilemma." That most astute French observer, Alexis de Tocqueville, writing in 1835 in his *Democracy in America*, recognized that dilemma when he observed that by contrast to a dictatorship, a democratic country like the United States "cannot combine its measures with secrecy or await their consequences with patience."[2] By way of example, Congressional examinations of the intelligence community in the mid-1970s, as observed editorially in *The New York Times*, had been characterized by "a counter productive rash of leaked reports and premature disclosures."[3]

How are matters of security and information balanced off? What are the principles for decisions related to both? These are among the issues explored in the searching essays comprising this volume. The inspiration for this work was in the person of Dr. Harold C. Relyea, member of the Board of Editors, *Presidential Studies Quarterly*. Few other scholars have examined in such depth, as has Dr. Relyea, the subjects of this volume, including the Freedom of Information Act, executive privilege, security classification, Presidential papers, libraries, information management, and the President and the media. Indeed, as a valuable appendix to the volume, Dr. Relyea has provided an extensive reading list on each of these subjects.

These essays were all completed just prior to the 1980 election of President Ronald Reagan, a man particularly alert to the importance of information policy in the formulation of both Congressional and public opinion. It is believed that he and members of his Cabinet and staff, many of whom are members of the Center for the Study of the Presidency, will find interest in this volume, as will Congressmen on both sides of the aisle. For all of them must address the issues contained in this work. Indeed, these issues pose dilemmas which force us to examine anew the fundamentals of our constitutional relationships and our democratic system of government. For example, in their chapter on the media, Professors Michael B. Grossman and Martha Joynt Kumar give us this arresting conclusion: "News organizations have *not* made it more difficult to govern. What has made the exercise of power more difficult are the forces that gave to the media its present status: the diffusion of governmental authority and the breakdown of traditional lines of communication."

Does "the diffusion of governmental authority" mean that our separation of powers system is not working? As was expressed in the Committee on Effectiveness of Governmental Operations, "One of our hangups is to make separation of powers an inflexible barrier between the branches. It is clear that the Framers had in mind something far different. . . . What was emphasized in *The Federalist*," by Hamilton, Madison, and Jay in 1788, "was not just a separation of powers but also a co-mingling of the branches working together."[4]

Moreover, the Framers exhibited considerable common sense on such issues as security, confidentiality, and information when, as members of the first Washington administration, they placed in operation the government under the Constitution. Alexandra R. Wigdor and David Wigdor, in their own essay, include a revealing 1792 interchange between Washington and Gouverneur Morris. The latter, (who had spoken more often than any other delegate at the Constitutional Convention) was concerned with the confidentiality of his diplomatic dispatches from London and Paris to President Washington. Should they be sent through the Department of State? Washington counselled that whereas most matters could "be freely communicated to the Department, he believed Morris should exercise his judgement on sensitive dispatches where "not more than one intermediate person would be entrusted. . . ."[5] This is further mindful of the counsel of Hamilton when he proposed the establishment of an intelligence community. He recognized the necessity for Congressional insight but he contended that it should be limited to "three members of each House of Congress."[6]

Balancing off the requirements of security are the necessities for communications. Much of the difficulties of the 1970s between the Congress and the President resulted from poor communications. The following 1976 interchange in the Committee on Effectiveness of Government Operations between Congressman James R. Mann and the President of this Center is revealing:

> *Hoxie:* Between Congress, and the President, in the final analysis then, isn't much of the difficulty a communications problem?
>
> *Mann:* I would have to endorse what you say 100%. My major frustrations since going to Congress in January 1969 have been the lack of information, the lack of access to information and the lack of investigative staffing to get information.[7]

Another source of strain between the Congress and the Presidents examined in this volume is the doctrine of executive privilege. In a hard hitting essay Professor Arthur S. Miller shoots out of the water Raoul Berger's often quoted contention that executive privilege is "a constitutional myth." In point of fact, Professor Miller asserts privilege "is an indubitable part of the living American Constitution." However, Miller has little empathy for its usage. "It seems," he concludes, "the President is privileged when he can get away with it politically."

During the decade of the 1970s Presidents had difficulties in getting "away with it politically." In 1976, Covey T. Oliver,

Ferdinand Wakeman Hubbell Professor of Law Emeritus, University of Pennsylvania, observed, "I know of no other government in the world in which the legislative branch claims, as Congress seems to be claiming today, that the executive departments are not privileged to keep internal operations communications to themselves [Executive privilege] and that state secrets must be revealed to legislative assemblies."[8]

B. *Highlights and Summaries*

In this volume, the first chapter, by Dr. Relyea, is masterfully divided into two parts. First he traces security policies and then information policies. He asks and answers the question: "How do these security concerns relate to the people's right to know?" He perceives that "the excesses and passions of the Vietnam-Watergate era have now subsided. Nonetheless, the people must forever remain watchful, vigilant, and informed. . . ."

In the second chapter, Jon A. Turner and John A. Gosden examine the Carter White House experiment in information management. With considerable wisdom they conclude that sophisticated hardware is not the basic answer to improved decision-making in the White House or, indeed, in the larger Executive Office of the President. "At this level, the most important skills are political, and the operative mechanisms are persuasion, bargaining, and negotiation."

In Chapter Three, Professor Miller pragmatically concludes, "One can believe that government openness is desirable (functional) and still assert that some secrecy is needed." As for calling upon executive privilege, Presidents from Washington in 1796 (with Hamilton's persuasion) to the present have been doing so.

In Chapter Four, Dr. Morton H. Halperin examines balancing considerations between freedom of information and security. President Carter in 1978 sought to establish by Executive order a system for balancing those considerations. According to Dr. Halperin, ". . . a decision to balance is not a decision to release, but simply a decision to take account of the public value of the information and to test that against the injury to national security which would result from release of the information."

In Chapter Five, Dr. Larry Berman traces the development

of Presidential libraries. He opposes recent proposals to centralize future Presidential library facilities in Washington D.C. "Granted costs of individual libraries, they nonetheless offer distinct advantages which should not be lost." They are sources of inspiration for the citizenry as well as oases for Presidential scholars.

In Chapter Six, on the future of Presidential Papers, Alexandra and David Wigdor express concern with the 1978 Presidential Records Act. "In deciding a President's papers to be public property, the Presidential Records Act reversed long-standing patterns of law and custom." They deplore the fact that the Act is "creating a situation in which the Federal Government is to be the single custodian of its past." While "public papers are extremely important for historians, . . . personal papers are most fruitful for recapturing the human dimension of political leadership."

In the concluding Chapter Seven, Professors Grossman and Kumar examine "the President as he appears through the media." The media, indeed, the people, discern the difference between style and substance. All of the "Rafshooning" only added to the conclusion of the American people that the Carter Administration was more concerned with style than with substance. Grossman and Kumar believe, "the public has a major stake in whether White House reporting is adequate or not. The President's message, as filtered through and interpreted by the media, often determines the role that the public will play in the shaping of policy." They conclude that although some White House reporters "may be unfair or inaccurate, and a large number present a fuzzy image," by and large, "the picture that emerges reflects the tone and substance of the administration and the character of the President."

C. The Eisenhower Test

Dr. Relyea and his co-authors of this volume, in graciously inviting me to write this *Foreword*, encouraged my observations on the Presidency in which I am most familiar, Eisenhower. Further, they suggested I give particular attention to how Eisenhower related information and security. Of recent date, especially since 1977, the Eisenhower Presidency has become increasingly regarded as the most successful politically of our post-World War II administrations. Why was Eisenhower able to have such effective Congressional and press relations and firmly exercise executive privilege? So skillfully did Eisenhower involve the Congress in decision-making in such sensitive areas as Southeast Asia and the Middle East, that Senator William Fulbright lamented that "we snoop and pry," and Speaker Sam Rayburn avowed, "He would have no criticism from me."[9]

There is nothing that frustrated either the Congress or the people more than being willfully cut off from information by the Executive branch. Professors Grossman and Kumar effectively quote the Richard Nixon of 1961 criticizing President Kennedy for a cover-up of the Bay of Pigs fiasco:

> The concept of a return to secrecy in peacetime demonstrates a profound misunderstanding of the role of a free press as opposed to that of a controlled press. The plea for secrecy could become a cloak for errors, misjudgements, and other failings of government.

How different this 1961 Nixon than that of a dozen years later, involved in a far more infamous and more protracted cover-up. And how different was his conduct from that of Eisenhower when faced with the only critical cover-up in his eight years in the Presidency.

The U-2 episode of May 1960 presents in microcosm so many of the issues addressed in this book: the balancing of security and information and relations with the media. In brief, on May Day, 1960, President Eisenhower was advised by his Staff Secretary, General Andrew Goodpaster, that a United States U-2 surveillance aircraft was missing and may have gone down inside the Soviet Union. For five days the Soviets, with their controlled media, made no public announcement of this incident. In the interim, on May 3rd, the National Aeronautics and Space Administration had announced "A NASA U-2 research airplane . . . apparently went down in the Lake Van Turkey area." The report added, "The U-2 program was initiated by NASA in 1956 as a method of making high-altitude weather studies."[10] So well guarded was the mission of these high altitude surveillance aircraft in the four years they had been in operation, that the NASA information officer making this announcement really believed it was a weather plane.[11]

Then, on May 5th, Soviet Premier Khrushchev triumphantly announced the May 1st shooting down of a United States reconnaissance aircraft. Eisenhower acquiesced in a State Department cover-up story purporting that this was a "weather research plane" and that it had "accidentally violated Soviet airspace."[12]

Was this cover-up wise? Diplomats, politicians and intelligence officials at home and abroad had hoped that the President would not involve himself. Khrushchev had not charged Eisenhower with the responsibility. CIA Director Allen Dulles wanted to take the onus. All of this went against the grain of the old soldier. And then, with no warning and to the consternation even of Congressional members of his own party, Eisenhower, on May 11th, convened a press conference in which he took full responsibility. He told the reporters: ". . . ever since the beginning of my administration I have issued directives to gather in every possible way the information required to protect the United States and the free world against surprise attack." Further, he defended "intelligence gathering activities" in general. "These activities have their own rules and methods of concealment which seek to mislead and obscure. . . . It is a distasteful but vital necessity." He added that the goals he was seeking in a summit conference in Paris, in which Khrushchev was to participate a few days hence, included "the reduction of secrecy and suspicion."[13]

What followed was Khrushchev's stalking out of the summit and a responsive strengthening of relationships among the Western allies. Eisenhower, upon his return to the United States, in a radio and television address to the Nation, declared without equivocation, ". . . I take full responsibility for approving all the various programs undertaken by our government to receive and evaluate military intelligence. . . . As to our government's initial statement about the flight, this was issued to protect the pilot, his mission and our intelligence process."[14] As Dr. Herbert S. Parmet has observed, "the President" had taken ". . . a step unprecedented in the annals of espionage" by declaring it was at his personal direction.[15] And what was the public reaction? According to the Gallup Poll his sustained eight years of strong public support moved even higher.[16]

D. *Conclusions*

All of the considerations and principles enumerated in this volume, including the necessity for openness in fundamental policy and secrecy in certain security operations, and the complexity in decision-making in our system, point to the basic necessity to secure more than a modicum of consensus. This can only have its foundation with information, with understanding, with trust. The Presidency, which Theodore Roosevelt liked to refer to as a "bully pulpit" is central to consensus. The President is the sole elected representative of all the people.

Richard Neustadt has suggested in his classic work, *Presidential Power*, that the basic Presidential power is the "power to persuade." The two Roosevelts and Eisenhower were perhaps our most effective twentieth century Presidents because they were the most convincing persuaders. Eight months into the Reagan administration, it appears that the incumbent President may have many of the same persuasive qualities.

But in the final analysis, what is involved is more than persuasion. There are also the matters of knowledge, trust and a due respect for mankind. Knowledge is fundamental to trust which, in turn, is fundamental to our political system. The Freedom of Information Act, to which considerable attention is appropriately given in this volume, is, of course, only applicable to the Executive Branch of our Federal Government. Whereas Constitutional immunities render inapplicable provision of such a law for either the Congress or the courts, we may well inquire whether the spirit of the Freedom of Information Act might not be applicable to the courts and the Congress. Should they have parallel information access standards to those imposed upon the executive branch? Are there lessons to be learned by examining the freedom of information legislation in other democratic societies (as for example Canada)?

Finally, a further word on the subject of trust. Granted all of Congress' inquiries and oversight roles as related to the Executive Branch, the separation of powers system is simply not operable without a spirit of mutual trust. Bryce N. Harlow, Counsellor to three Presidents, was in a very real sense a human engineer seeking to build a bridge across the chasm between Congress and the Presidents. As Harlow expressed it, "The first and paramount requirement is trust."[17] Similar in spirit to this expression from the executive branch is that of a wise United States Senator from Louisiana, who exhorted his colleagues with need for trust a long time ago. As Senator J. S. Johnston asserted in 1829: "No Government can exist without it. And this distrust and jealousy of the Executive will destroy all power to do good and all power to act effectively."[18]

Center for the Study of the Presidency desires to express its appreciation to the Ford Foundation not only for a grant in helping make this volume possible but also for its support for the Center's related conference, convening in Cincinnati, Ohio, October 16-18, 1981, on Government and the Media.

In particular in this volume Dr. Relyea and his colleagues have given us a better understanding of the significance of the Freedom of Information Act, democracy's recent (1966) window for enlightenment, which daily gives new vistas as related to the Executive Branch. To date, there has been surprisingly little acknowledgment of the help this Act has given the media in investigative reporting. A notable exception is *U.S. News & World Report* which, in its recent probe of the General Services Administration, referred to "internal audit reports obtained . . . under the Freedom of Information Act."[19]

It is noteworthy that Dr. Relyea selected as the opening quotation for this volume an excerpt from Lincoln's Gettysburg Address. Lincoln combined statements of fact with enunciations of truths. The American experience has proven that given the facts through a healthy unfettered information policy, not just from the Nation's public servants but also by an inquiring media, the people can determine the instruments, the goals, the ends of policy. Nearly a century ago the British scholar, James Bryce, concluded in his *American Commonwealth* that America's accomplishments will be finally judged not by the "intelligence and happiness . . . of . . . the favoured few for

whose benefits the world seems hitherto to have framed its institutions, but . . . [by] the whole body of the people."[20]

R. GORDON HOXIE
President
Center for the Study of the Presidency
New York City
August 15, 1981

Preface

Almost three decades ago, the late Justice William O. Douglas, agreeing with a majority of his brethren to a limitation on the powers of the Chief Executive in the *Steel Seizure* case, offered a reminder to the American citizenry.

> The great office of President is not a weak and powerless one. The President represents the people and is their spokesman in domestic and foreign affairs. The office is respected more than any other in the land. It gives a position of leadership that is unique. The power to formulate policies and mould opinion inheres in the Presidency and conditions our national life.

This volume is dedicated to a fuller understanding of what Justice Douglas, and others, so poignantly have observed: the President is not weak and powerless, significantly moulds opinion, and profoundly conditions our national life. Our focus here is upon those aspects of national information policy which are intertwined with the Presidential office. Through interdisciplinary analyses, we have sought to portray the breadth and limitations upon the authority of the Chief Executive with regard to certain expressions of information policy emanating from the Oval Office. There is concern here, as well, with the implications of the President's information powers for the citizenry, the press, and other institutions of government in our democratic polity.

The volume opens with an assessment of the Presidency and the people's right to know about the activities and operations of their government. A theme is established here consistent with the observation that the nation's highest office "is not a weak and powerless one." Indeed, the President possesses a considerable amount of autonomy in exercising Executive privilege or in creating and protecting official secrets. Counterbalanced with these authorities is the citizen's right of access to Executive Branch records, expressed in the Freedom of Information Act and, to some extent, in both the Privacy Act and the Presidential Records Act.

This introductory overview is amplified by the next three essays. Together, John Gosden and Jon Turner explain the data management systems being used by the contemporary Presidency to organize information and marshall it for policy decisions. Moving from a housekeeping level to power considerations, Arthur Miller discusses the independent discretion of the President to invoke Executive privilege with decisive effect. Then, Morton Halperin offers some prospects for mitigating the Chief Executive's traditional role in the creation and virtually unchallenged maintenance of official secrets.

Turning from active to retired records, Larry Berman explores the evolution and significance of Presidential libraries; David and Sandy Wigdor comment upon the documentary holdings of these institutions, giving special consideration to what may or may not be found in future collections of records associated with the Chief Executive as a consequence of the Presidential Records Act of 1978.

Finally, in a shift away from purely documentary forms of information, Michael Grossman and Martha Kumar discuss both the current and future operational settings for Presidential press relations. Thus, once again, we arrive at the consideration of an informed public — affected, in this instance, by the "reflecting lens" of the media — relative to the information powers of the Chief Executive.

The views expressed by each author in this volume are entirely their own and are not attributable to any other source. It has been my pleasure to serve as the organizer and editor of this project. I wish to thank each contributor to the symposium and to express my appreciation to Gordon Hoxie and the Center for the Study of the Presidency for sponsoring this undertaking. A selected reading list may be found at the end of the volume following the individual presentations.

Transcending traditional partisan and ideological considerations of political power in America, the cross-currents of tension in information policy and practice seemingly shall remain with us for the immediate future, perhaps intensifying as we venture into the "information age" of post-industrial society. Hopefully the views and analyses presented here will assist in understanding and ameliorating this dynamic competition with its profound implications for democratic government. Indeed, a truth expressed over three and a half centuries ago assumes even greater profundity for the future: knowledge is power.

HAROLD C. RELYEA
Alexandria, Virginia

September 1, 1980

About the Authors*

LARRY S. BERMAN is Assistant Professor of Political Science, University of California at Davis. He received his Ph.D. from Princeton University and is the author of *The Office of Management and Budget and the Presidency, 1921–1979.*

JOHN A. GOSDEN is Vice President for Telecommunications with The Equitable Life Assurance Society where he is responsible for planning, providing, and recommending management policy for all electronic communications, including both voice and data. Prior to joining Equitable in 1970, he served with LEO Computers in London, the Auerback Corporation, and the MITRE Corporation. Mr. Gosden has participated in several special study groups on The National Library of Medicine MEDLARS system, the Manned Orbiting Laboratory Support System, and the Air Traffic Control En Route System. In 1977, he was the chairman of the Federal Advisory Group on White House Information Systems, Office of Science and Technology Policy, Executive Office of the President.

MICHAEL BARUCH GROSSMAN is Professor of Political Science, Towson State University. He received his Ph.D. from The John Hopkins University, has written on various aspects of the government and the news media as well as urban politics and organization, and is the co-author of *Portraying the President.*

MORTON H. HALPERIN is Director of the Center for National Security Studies. He received his Ph.D. from Yale University, served as Deputy Assistant Secretary of Defense (1967-1969), and was a senior staff member of the National Security Council (1969). The author of many articles and books, he recently co-authored *Freedom vs. National Security* and *Top Secret: National Security and the Right to Know.*

R. GORDON HOXIE is the President, Center for the Study of the Presidency; and Editor, *Presidential Studies Quarterly.* He received his Ph.D. from Columbia University, served as Chan-

---

* The views expressed in this volume are those of the individually identified authors and are not attributable to any other source.

cellor of Long Island University and President of C.W. Post College. He has also served as a consultant to both the Department of State and the Department of Defense. His volumes include *The White House: Organization and Operations; The Presidency of the 1970's; Command Decision and the Presidency;* and (with others) *Organizing and Staffing the Presidency.*

MARTHA JOYNT KUMAR is Associate Professor of Political Science, Towson State University. She received her Ph.D. from Columbia University, has written on various aspects of the Presidency and the news media, served as an election consultant to N.B.C. (1968-1974), and is the co-author of *Portraying the President.*

ARTHUR S. MILLER is Professor of Law Emeritus, The George Washington University. He received his J.S.D. from Yale University, has served as an expert constitutional and legal consultant to congressional committees, and is the author of many articles and books on matters of law and public policy, the courts, and presidential power. He is presently completing a study on the Supreme Court.

HAROLD C. RELYEA is a Specialist in American National Government, Congressional Research Service, Library of Congress. He received his Ph.D. from The American University. In addition to his writing on national emergency powers, his research on government information policy and practice has appeared in professional journals and official publications in Australia, Canada, and England, as well as the United States. He is a member of the Board of Editors of *Presidential Studies Quarterly* and is preparing a book on the evolution of Federal information policy.

JON A. TURNER served as a member of the Advisory Group on White House Information Systems, Office of Science and Technology Policy, Executive Office of the President. He received his Ph.D. in information systems (Industrial Engineering and Operations Research) from Columbia University and, from 1968 to 1978, was Director of Advanced Systems at the Columbia University Center for Computing Activities. He is presently an Assistant Professor in the Computer Applications and Information Systems area at the Graduate School of Business Administration of New York University.

ALEXANDRA K. WIGDOR is a member of the research staff of the National Academy of Sciences. Her graduate education was in the field of English legal history and she served on the research staff of the National Study Commission on Records and Documents of Federal Officials where she prepared *Study of the Records of Supreme Court Justices.*

DAVID WIGDOR is an historian with the Manuscripts Division, Library of Congress, where he evaluates new collections in the field of 20th century political history. He received his Ph.D. from the University of Missouri, was an expert contributor to the Conference on the Research Use and Disposition of Senator's Papers (1978), and is the author of *Roscoe Pound: Philosopher of Law.*

CHAPTER ONE

The Presidency and the People's Right to Know

HAROLD C. RELYEA

The legally prescribed and honored procedures whereby an American President arrives at and departs from office alone may save the Nation from a kingship. Monarchs are not elected; they do not serve a fixed term of incumbency; they cannot be impeached. Yet, on occasion, Presidents have exercised power with regal absolutism—perhaps, some would argue, even with dictatorial determination—virtually without restraint by Congress or the courts.[1] Nevertheless, one of the most notable of the wielders of imperial authority, Abraham Lincoln, addressing the populace of Lawrenceburg, Indiana, over a century ago, shortly before his inauguration, offered this highly poignant comment:

> I have been selected to fill an important office for a brief period, and am now, in your eyes, invested with an influence which will soon pass away; but should my administration prove to be a very wicked one, or what is more probable, a very foolish one, if you, the *people*, are but true to yourselves and to the Constitution, there is but little harm I can do, *thank God!*[2]

The citizenry, exercising their sovereign authority through constitutional procedures, must hold their "governors" in check, suggests the sixteenth President, lest these stewards of the people become "rulers." Indeed, at the outset of the American struggle for nationhood, the Declaration of Independence, consistent with the Eighteenth Century suspicion of the state, reflected the Enlightenment assumption that neither society nor government are organic or natural to human existence. In the view of the English philosopher John Locke, whose ideas directly influenced the Founding Fathers, individuals contract with each other to conduct social intercourse and, subsequently, establish a governing institution to protect pre-societal or "natural" rights, as well as to facilitate social affairs. Implied in this arrangement is the right to withdraw from the contract when government does not fulfill its responsibilities.[3]

In this regard, the Declaration, after postulating that governments derive "their just powers from the consent of the governed," recognizes that the state can become destructive of the rights of the citizenry. But, because there is popular "consent" to, but not "submission" to, the government exercising certain powers, such consent or support can be withdrawn when the state assumes non-delegated responsibilities, abuses its authority, or corrupts itself in the exercise of power. In order to judge the propriety of government actions, including those of the President, the citizenry must have, of their own volition, information about the activities and operations of the state. In brief, the people must be watchful of their government in order to preserve popular rule.

Later, with the ratification of the Constitution, this idea of an informed citizenry received further expression in First Amendment guarantees of freedom to discuss public business (a privilege previously reserved for members of the legislature), freedom of the press (to assist the people in maintaining their watchful vigil over the state), and "freedom to petition the Government for a redress of grievances" (which could include presentations against state secrecy or for official records). Indeed, if the people are to meaningfully discuss public business and if the press, or other reporters of government activities, are to be free to function without state interference, each must have direct access to government information at their own request. This understanding of "the people's right to know" perhaps has been expressed best in the often quoted and cherished words of the fourth President, James Madison:

> A popular Government without popular information, or the means of acquiring it, is but a Prologue to a Farce or a Tragedy; or perhaps both. Knowledge will forever govern ignorance: And a people who mean to be their own Governors, must arm themselves with the power which knowledge gives.[4]

Presidential Privilege

The invocation of secrecy occurred early in the development of the Presidency.[5] The action, which would become known as

"Executive privilege" (i.e. the privilege of the Chief Executive not to disclose requested information), seems to have derived in part from both the British doctrine of Crown privilege (i.e. the unchallenged prerogative of the sovereign — the king or his government — to prevent the disclosure of requested information)[6] and the constitutional independence of the Executive Branch (i.e. the separation of powers principle).[7]

In the fourth year of the Federal experiment, the concept of Presidential privilege took formation on the occasion of an investigation by the House of Representatives into an Indian massacre of a military expedition under the command of General Arthur St. Clair. With a troop of approximately 1,500 men, St. Clair had set out in September, 1791, to construct a ring of outposts in the area of northwestern Ohio to provide protection to pioneer settlements against Indian attacks. The expeditionary force was composed of regulars, raw levies, and Kentucky militia. After weeks of cold and wet weather, a band of sixty of the levies declared, on the last day of October, that their term of enlistment had expired and they fled to the rear of the march. To protect his supply wagons and to instill discipline, St. Clair dispatched his best units to round up the deserters. With his forces thus depleted, he then pushed on into the headwaters region of the Wabash River.

On the evening of November 3, the party encamped on high ground near the eastern branch of the upper Wabash. Due to the lateness of the hour and the fatigue of his men, St. Clair did not order the preparation of earthwork defenses that night, but left their construction for the next morning. At daybreak, the camp was attacked by a small but determined Indian band. Not only were they veteran warriors but, according to one authority: "In discipline and leadership this group probably excelled any other the red men ever assembled."[8] Because Indian marksmen killed every artilleryman, the cannon had to be spiked. Major General Richard Butler, second-in-command, was mortally wounded. Raw recruits fled and most of the officers were killed. After three hours of fighting, half of the troop had been lost and the order was given to retreat to Fort Jefferson some thirty miles south. Approximately 600 officers and soldiers were slain in the engagement, half as many were wounded, but fewer than seventy Indians perished.[9]

In March of 1792, an effort was initiated in the House of Representatives to investigate the circumstances surrounding the St. Clair debacle. It was the second such military disaster of its kind, forces under General Josiah Harmar having met a similar, but less overwhelming, defeat in March of 1791. Some Members were concerned about military discipline and precautions, others considered the incidents constitutionally and morally questionable. In dispatching the troops, President Washington was pursuing war with the Indians without a proper declaration from Congress. In addition, the army was invading Indian lands to protect people who had no proper purpose for being there and to seize territory for land speculators. Such campaigns also constituted a serious drain on the Federal treasury.[10] Subsequently, a special committee of seven members under the chairmanship of Representative Thomas Fitzsimmons, a Federalist, was created. In the resolution establishing the panel, it was authorized that "said committee be empowered to call for such persons, papers, and records, as may be necessary to assist their inquiries."[11]

When Secretary of War Henry Knox received the committee's request for the original letters and instructions pertaining to the ill-fated St. Clair party, he referred the matter to President Washington. This led to two discussions of the propriety of the Chief Executive providing information to Congress. On March 31, 1792, at a Cabinet meeting attended by Secretary of State Thomas Jefferson, Secretary of the Treasury Alexander Hamilton, Attorney General Edmund Randolph, and Knox, the President, according to notes kept by Jefferson,

> . . . had called us to consult, merely because it was the first example, and he wished that so far as it should become a precedent, it should be rightly conducted. He neither acknowledged nor denied, nor even doubted the propriety of what the House were doing, for he had not thought upon it, nor was acquainted with subjects of this kind: he could readily conceive there might be papers of so secret a nature, as that they ought not to be given-up. We were not prepared, and wished time to think and inquire.[12]

The Cabinet met again on April 2, with Jefferson recording the following details.

> We had all considered, and were of one mind, first, that the House

was an inquest, and therefore might institute inquiries. Second, that it might call for papers generally. Third, that the Executive ought to communicate such papers as the public good would permit, and ought to refuse those, the disclosure of which would injure the public: consequently were to exercise a discretion. Fourth, that neither the committee nor House had a right to call on the Head of a Department, who and whose papers were under the President alone; but that the committee should instruct their chairman to move the House to address the President. . . . Note; Hamilton agreed with us in all these points, except as to the power of the House to call on Heads of Departments.

He observed that as to his Department, the act constituting it had made it subject to Congress in some points, but he thought himself not so far subject, as to be obliged to produce all the papers they might call for. They might demand secrets of a very mischievous nature. . . . I observed here a difference between the British Parliament and our Congress; that the former was a legislature, an inquest, and a council . . . for the King. The latter was, by the constitution, a legislature and an inquest, but not a council. Finally agreed, to speak separately to the members of the committee, and bring them by persuasion into the right channel. It was agreed in this case, that there was not a paper which might not be properly produced; that copies only should be sent, with an assurance, that if they should desire it, a clerk should attend with the originals to be verified by themselves.[13]

Thus agreed, Secretary Knox transmitted copies of the requested papers to the special investigating committee. The theoretical basis for the doctrine of Presidential privilege, though expressed, had yet to be asserted in practice: when confronted with a *proper* request for information (i.e. one expressly authorized in law), the President should respond in accordance with his view of the "public good," that is, he should exercise a discretion, and this discretion extends to information held within the Executive Branch. In 1796, when the House again sought papers from the President, on this occasion regarding the Jay Treaty, the President formally refused the request.[14] While this incident involved official records, it apparently was not until 1877 that an Executive Branch official declined to appear before a congressional committee.[15]

While certainly not all assertions of Presidential privilege constitute mischief for the democratic prospect or representative government, they soon became pervasive, reaching an extreme during the Eisenhower Administration: virtually any officer of the Executive Branch might claim Executive privilege in his or her own behalf.[16] Responding to a congressional request for a reconsideration of this situation, President Kennedy wrote: "Executive privilege can be invoked only by the President and will not be used without specific Presidential approval." Both Presidents Johnson and Nixon continued this policy.[17] Neither President Ford nor, to date, President Carter, expressed themselves on this matter, though they each were requested to do so.[18]

Building upon the vigorous defense and generous view of Executive privilege advanced by Attorney General William Rogers during the Eisenhower regime, Attorney General Richard Kleindienst, testifying before three Senate subcommittees in joint session during the Watergate inquiry, advanced an absolutist view of Presidential privilege. Acknowledging that the Chief Executive alone could invoke this authority, Kleindienst offered ". . . if the President of the United States should direct me or any other person on his staff not to appear before a congressional committee to testify or bring documents, that he has the constitutional power to do so and that person should not do it."[19] The Attorney General indicated this privilege pertained to any subject, including alleged criminal matters of interest to Congress as these more properly should be treated by the judicial system. Thus, while he did not seem to forsee Executive privilege being invoked against the Judiciary in a criminal trial, no such limitation pertained to Congress. According to Kleindienst:

> If you are conducting an impeachment proceeding based upon high crimes and misdemeanors and you want to subpena someone from the President's staff to give you information, I believe that, based upon the doctrine of separation of powers, the President would have the power to invoke executive privilege with respect to that information.[20]

In addition, the President, according to Kleindienst, might extend the privilege to any officer or employee of the Executive Branch.[21] Twenty days after expounding this bold theory of Executive privilege, the Attorney General resigned; slightly less than a year-and-a-half later, the President whom he served also resigned and the crisis over Presidential privilege subsided.

Today, [early 1980] assertions of Executive privilege against Congress remain in uncertain dispute. Presidents have been successful in these denials as a result of the advantage of physical possession of records being sought together with congressional unwillingness to seek a definitive legal resolution of the issue. Thus, the "discretion" remains.

In 1974, the Supreme Court ruled against the Chief Executive in his claim of Presidential privilege against the Special Prosecutor, an Executive Branch official, who was seeking certain evidence by subpoena for criminal proceedings.[22] In its opinion, the Court noted the President's counsel cited two grounds for the Chief Executive's claim of "absolute privilege:" "the valid need for protection of communications between high government officials and those who advise and assist them in the performance of their manifold duties" and "that the independence of the Executive Branch within its own sphere . . . insulates a president from a judicial subpoena in an ongoing criminal prosecution, and thereby protects confidential presidential communication." In ruling on these points, the Court offered this engaging judgment:

> . . . neither the doctrine of separation of powers, nor the need for confidentiality of high level communications, without more, can sustain an absolute, unqualified presidential privilege of immunity from judicial process under all circumstances. The President's need for complete candor and objectivity from advisers calls for great deference from the courts. However, when the privilege depends solely on the broad, undifferentiated claim of public interest in the confidentiality of such conversations, a confrontation with other values arises. Absent a claim of need to protect military, diplomatic or sensitive national security secrets, we find it difficult to accept the argument that even the very important interest in confidentiality or presidential communications is significantly diminished by production of such material for *in camera* inspection with all the protection that a district court will be obliged to provide.[23]

Thus, the Court, for the first time, directly recognized the

President's authority to assert Executive privilege but, in doing so, established that the privilege is a qualified one when invoked against a Federal prosecutor seeking evidence through the subpoena process for a criminal proceeding.[24]

Three years later, in deciding the constitutionality of the Presidential Recordings and Materials Preservation Act (88 Stat. 1695) giving the Federal Government custody over certain papers and tape recordings from the Nixon White House, the Court ruled more generally as to the qualified nature of an Executive privilege claim,[25] indicated that it was available to an ex-Chief Executive although "a former President is in less need of it than an incumbent,"[26] and suggested that a former occupant of the Oval Office, for purposes of protecting the records of his administration, might make use of an Executive privilege plea in a judicial proceeding involving such materials or to offset a plea from the public for access to some portion of them.[27]

Recently, the Court added a temporal dimension to the concept, saying "that documents shielded by executive privilege remain privileged even after the decision to which they pertain may have been effected, since disclosure at any time could inhibit the free flow of advice, including analysis, reports and expression of opinion. . . ."[28]

The exercise of Executive privilege remains a Presidential discretion which militates against the people's right to know as a consequence of its applicability to virtually any policy subject and certain practical problems it presents in terms of legal redress by the citizenry, not the least of which are standing and cost considerations. Ground rules on the nature and use of Executive privilege, begun by President Kennedy and continued by Presidents Johnson and Nixon through letters of agreement with Congress, but vacated by Presidents Ford and Carter, should be instituted. Some effort was made by the Carter Administration to draft an Executive order on this matter, but the fruits of that labor have not publicly appeared. An enduring Presidential pronouncement on the expression of this privilege, regarding its form, delegation to or invocation by officials other than the Chief Executive, public expression, and justification, would appear to be warranted.[29] Of course, it also is hoped that the President will exercise restraint in resorting to claiming this privilege and will seek alternatives short of an absolute denial of information to the people or their representatives.

Official Secrecy

"Absent a claim of a need to protect military, diplomatic or sensitive national security matters," said the Court in *United States* v. *Nixon*, a President's argument for strict confidentiality is "difficult to accept."[30] The implication here is that special considerations of secrecy attach to military, diplomatic, and "national security" matters. To maintain information protection in these areas, Presidents have established procedures for creating an "official secret." Developed without direct statutory authorization, these arrangements for restricting access to information began with nineteenth century military orders and evolved into the present Presidentially mandated security classification system.

Although members of the armed forces of the United States, since the time of the Revolution, were prohibited from communicating with the enemy, no directives regarding the protection of information or guarding against foreign or unfriendly intelligence operatives were issued until after the Civil War. During the time of the rebellion, President Lincoln placed strict government controls upon communications via the telegraph, the mail, and, to a somewhat lesser extent, even the press. The military controlled communications and civilian activities within the shifting war zones.[31]

A few years after the cessation of hostilities, the War Department turned its attention to security procedures for peacetime. General Orders No. 35, Headquarters of the Army, Adjutant General's Office, issued April 13, 1869, read: "Commanding officers of troops occupying the regular forts built by the Engineer Department will permit no photographic or other views of the same to be taken without the permission of the War Department." Such language placed limited information control within the discretion of the War Department. The substance of this order was continued in Army regulations of 1881, 1889, and 1895.[32]

Deteriorating relations with Spain and the possibility of open warfare subsequently prompted more stringent security precautions. A portion of General Orders No. 9, Headquarters of the Army, Adjutant General's Office, issued March 1, 1897, directed:

> No persons, except officers of the Army and Navy of the United States, and persons in the service of the United States employed in direct connection with the use, construction or care of these works, will be allowed to visit any portion of the lake and coast defenses of the United States without the written authority of the Commanding Officer in charge.
>
> Neither written nor pictorial descriptions of these works will be made for publication without the authority of the Secretary of War, nor will any information be given concerning them which is not contained in the printed reports and documents of the War Department.

Revised for inclusion in General Orders No. 52, War Department, issued August 24, 1897, "the principal change was insertion of a paragraph indicating that the Secretary of War would grant special permission to visit these defenses only to the United States Senators and Representatives in Congress who were officially concerned therewith and to the Governor or Adjutant General of the State where such defenses were located."[33] That the War Department did not want to extend special defense facilities visitation permission to the entire membership of Congress is evident. This policy of selective congressional access to secret defense matters has continued, in various forms, into the present period.

Army regulations of 1901 continued the language of the 1897 order with its provision for granting certain Members of Congress special access to the coastal and lake defenses. New regulations in 1908 omitted specific mention of congressional visitors and said:

> Commanding officers of posts at which are located lake or coastal defenses are charged with the responsibility of preventing, as far as practicable, visitors from obtaining information relative to such defenses which would probably be communicated to a foreign power, and to this end may prescribe and enforce appropriate regulations governing visitors to their posts.
>
> American citizens whose loyalty to their Government is unques-

tioned may be permitted to visit such portions of the defenses as the commanding officer deems proper.

The taking of photographic or other views of permanent works of defense will not be permitted. Neither written nor pictorial descriptions of these works will be made for publication without the authority of the Secretary of War, nor will any information be given concerning them which is not contained in the printed reports and documents of the War Department.

These portions of the 1908 regulations were continued in subsequent issuances of 1910 and 1917. All of these information control regulations pertained to defense facilities.

The first system for the protection of national defense documents and papers was promulgated in General Orders No. 3, War Department, of February 16, 1912. This directive identified certain classes of records which were to be regarded as "confidential" and, therefore, kept under lock, "accessible only to the officer to whom intrusted." Those materials falling into this category included submarine mine projects and land defense plans. "Trusted employees" of the War Department, as well as "the officer to whom intrusted," might have access to "maps and charts showing locations on the ground of the elements of defense, of number of guns, and of the character of the armament" and "tables giving data with reference to the number of guns, the character of the armament, and the war supply of ammunition."

Serial numbers were to be issued for all such "confidential" information with the number marked on the document(s) and lists of the records kept at the office from which they emanated. No security labels were used. Within one year's time, officers responsible for the safekeeping of these materials were to check on their location and existence. While available to all commissioned officers at all times, "confidential" information was not to be copied except at the office of issue.

On April 6, 1917, the United States declared war on Germany (40 Stat. 1). This action prompted new regulations to protect national defense information. Mobilization was begun immediately and the first American troops arrived in France in late June. It was also at this juncture that the American military, working with their French and British allies, had an opportunity to observe the information security arrangements of other armies.

On November 22, 1917, General Orders No. 64, General Headquarters, American Expeditionary Force, was issued on the matter of the protection of official information. This directive established three markings for safeguarded records, saying:

> "Confidential" matter is restricted for use and knowledge to a necessary minimum of persons, either members of this Expedition or its employees.
>
> The word "Secret" on a communication is intended to limit the use or sight of it to the officer into whose hands it is delivered by proper authority, and, when necessary, a confidential clerk. With such a document no discretion lies with the officer or clerk to whom it is delivered, except to guard it as SECRET in the most complete understanding of that term. There are no degrees of secrecy in the handling of documents so marked. Such documents are completely secret.
>
> Secret matter will be kept under lock and key subject to use only by the officers to whom it has been transmitted. Confidential matter will be similarly cared for unless it be a part of officer records, and necessary to the entirety of such records. Papers of this class will be kept in the office files, and the confidential clerk responsible for the same shall be given definite instructions that they are to be shown to no one but his immediate official superiors, and that the file shall be locked except during office hours.
>
> Orders, pamphlets of instructions, maps, diagrams, intelligence publications, etc., from these headquarters . . . which are for ordinary official circulation and not intended for the public, but the accidental possession of which by the enemy would result in no harm to the Allied cause; these will have printed in the upper left hand corner, "For Official Circulation Only."

The directive also specified:

> Where circulation is to be indicated otherwise than is indicated [above] . . . there will be added limitation in similar type, as:
>
> Not to be taken into Front Line Trenches.
> Not to be Reproduced.
> Not to go below Division Headquarters.
> Not to go below Regimental Headquarters.

Commenting on this prescription, one authority has noted:

> This order itself makes clear that the markings "Confidential" and "Secret" were already in use, for it says "There appears to be some carelessness in the indiscriminate use of the terms 'Confidential' and 'Secret'." This previous usage was undoubtedly taken over from the French, who used these two markings, often with added injunctions such as "not to be taken into the first line." The British also had a marking "For official use only."[34]

During the final weeks of 1917, at the initiative of the Acting Chief of the War College, military regulations on the use of information control markings once again were modified. The action was taken to insure that protective labels being used by the A.E.F. were officially authorized and supervised within units under War Department jurisdiction apart from the Expeditionary Force. New instructions, issued December 14, 1917, outlined the conditions under which "Secret," "Confidential," and "For Official Use Only" were to be utilized. Records designated "Secret" would not have their existence disclosed, but those marked "Confidential" might circulate to "persons known to be authorized to receive them." The third label was designed to restrict information from the public or the press.[35] In addition, the new order contained the following proviso: "Publishing official documents or information, or using them for personal controversy, or for private purpose without due authority, will be treated as a breach of official trust, and may be punished under the Articles of War, or under Section 1, Title I, of the Espionage Act approved June 15, 1917."

> This reference to both the Articles of War and the Espionage Act thoroughly confuses the purpose of the issuance. While the Articles of War contained provisions against corresponding with the enemy and against spying, the reference here can only be to the provisions of the Articles of War against disobedience of orders and miscellaneous misconduct. Section 1, Title I, of the Espionage Act, on the other hand, was very comprehensive with respect to any mishandling of "information respecting the national defense." If that section alone had been referred to, the implication would have been that the new issuance related entirely to defense information. In-

clusion of the reference to the Articles of War makes it possible to argue that the marking "For official use only" was not intended to apply exclusively to defense information and that the intention with respect to the marking is hardly clear.[36]

The thrusts of the Espionage Act of 1917 (40 Stat. 217) and an earlier statute of 1911 (36 Stat. 1084) prohibiting the disclosure of national defense secrets were toward the regulation and punishment of espionage. Neither law specifically sanctioned the information protection practices of the War Department or the armed forces, nor were the orders and directives of these entities promulgated pursuant to these statutes. The markings prescribed for the use of the military were designed for utilization on internal communiques and records. With the passage of the Trading With the Enemy Act (40 Stat. 411), provision was made for the President to designate patents, the publication of which might "be detrimental to the public safety or defense, or may assist the enemy or endanger the successful prosecution of the war," to be kept secret (40 Stat. 422, Section 10(i)). No label was devised for this action. Quite the contrary, the means provided for maintaining this secrecy was to "withhold the grant of a patent until the end of the war." This would appear to be the first direct statutory grant of authority to the Chief Executive to declare a type of information officially secret. Also, although the provision pertained to defense policy, utilization of this authority was placed in civilian, not military, hands.

There is speculation that reference to the Espionage Act was made in the new War Department regulations of December, 1917, to emphasize the precautions for safegarding defense information upon a wartime army composed of new recruits at all ranks.

There is no indication that there was any realization at this time that difficulties could arise in enforcing the Espionage Act if official information relating to the national defense was not marked as such, insofar as it was intended to be protected from unauthorized dissemination. Violations of the first three subsections of Section 1, Title I, of the act depended in the one case on material relating to the national defense having been turned over to someone "not entitled to receive it" and in the other case on such material having been lost or compromised through "gross negligence." Since the expression "relating to the national defense" was nowhere defined the possibility of the public being permitted to have any authenticated knowledge whatever about the national defense, even the fact that Congress had passed certain legislation related thereto, depended on application of the expressions "not entitled to receive it" and "gross negligence."

In any prosecution for violation of either of the last two subsections the burden of proving that one or the other key expression had application in the case would rest on the prosecution, and proof would be difficult unless clear evidence could be adduced that authority had communicated its intention that the specific material involved should be protected or unless that material was of such a nature that common sense would indicate that it should be protected. For purposes of administering these two subsections of the Espionage Act the marking of defense information that is to be protected is almost essential, and its marking can also be of great assistance for purposes of administering the preceding three subsections.

It would be logical to suppose that the marking of defense information began out of legal necessities for administering the Espionage Act, but the indications are that such was not the case. The establishment of three grades of official information to be protected by markings was apparently something copied from the A.E.F., which had borrowed the use of such marking from the French and British.[37]

Changes in military regulations governing the protection of sensitive information did not occur until well after the armistice and return of American troops from Europe. On January 22, 1921, the War Department issued Army Regulation No. 330-5 which, with slight modification, constituted a compilation of the wartime information procedures which were to remain in force during peacetime. The essential provisions, with regard to the utilization of classification markings, were that "Secret" was to be used on information "of great importance and when the safeguarding of that information from actual or potential enemies is of prime necessity;" "Confidential" pertained to material "of less importance and of less secret nature than one requiring the mark of 'Secret', but which must, nevertheless, be guarded from hostile or indiscreet persons;" and "For official use only" had reference to "information which is not to be communicated to the public or to the press, but which may be communicated to any person known to be in the service of the

United States whose duty it concerns, or to persons of un-
doubted loyalty and discretion who are cooperating with Government work."

A basic shortcoming of these regulations seemed to be the in-
ferred, unspecific qualitative nature of the instruction pertaining to the use of "Confidential." The presumption was that regulations pertaining to the application of the "Secret" marking
were sufficiently clear that records warranting this designation
might be easily distinguished from those in the "Confidential"
category and that the individual affixing "Confidential" to a
document had some qualitative familiarity with "Secret" information.

Another fault in the issuance was

. . . its failure to relate itself to the Espionage Act of 1917 or to limit
itself to defense information. It merely provided for the continua-
tion of a system of markings that had been established in wartime.
This system was not a product of any thoughtful consideration of
the general problem of protecting defense information and other
official information. It was a result of reflex response to immediate
necessities arising in the prosecution of the war.[38]

Between 1921 and 1937 the regulation underwent various
modifications and changes. Only two major policy shifts appear
to have occurred during these revisions. A 1935 issuance introduced "Restricted," a fourth marking designed to protect "research work or the design, development, test, production, or
use of a unit of military equipment or a component thereof
which it is desired to keep secret." The provision further noted
that the class of information which this new label was designed
to safeguard "is considered as affecting the national defense of
the United States within the meaning of the Espionage Act
(U.S.C. 59:32)." The instructions regarding the other three information markings still contained no reference to the Espionage Act.

New Army regulations of the following year omitted "For official use only" and redefined the other markings. Of particular
interest is the broadened understandings of the type of information to which the security labels might be applied, including
foreign policy material and what might be properly called "political" data. "Secret" referred to information "of such nature

that its disclosure might endanger the national security, or cause serious injury to the interests or prestige of the Nation, an individual, or any government activity, or be of great advantage to a foreign nation." Similarly, "Confidential" could be applied to material "of such a nature that its disclosure, although not endangering the national security, might be prejudicial to the interests or prestige of the Nation, an individual, or any government activity, or be of advantage to a foreign nation." And "Restricted" could be used in instances where information "is for official use only or of such a nature that its disclosure should be limited for reasons of administrative privacy, or should be denied the general public." The outstanding characteristic of these provisions is their broad discretionary nature with regard to subjects of application. While initial regulations had been created to safeguard coastal defense facility information, 1936 saw the possibility of information restriction policy extending to almost any area of governmental activity within the purview of the military. Such regulations were promulgated without any clear statutory authority. Even the Espionage Act was designed for wartime use. Yet, under armed forces directives governing information protection during the late 1930s, "to reveal secret, confidential, or restricted matter pertaining to the national defense is a violation of the Espionage Act," according to Army regulations of 1937.

In Changes in Navy Regulations and Naval Instructions No. 7 of 1916, that service had gone so far as to prescribe that "Officers resigning are warned of the provision of the national defense secrets act," implying that former Navy personnel returned to civilian life could not, without subjecting themselves to prosecution, discuss information which had been protected under Navy regulations. The violation in question would involve the 1911 secrets law (36 Stat. 1084), not the Navy's directives on the matter. The point is of interest in that it illustrates how armed forces regulations pertaining to the protection of information, though not promulgated in accordance with a statute—i.e. law created by Congress—enjoyed the color of statutory law for their enforcement.

If, in terms of the multiplicity of policy areas to which they could be applied, the significance of a system of information protection markings came to be realized within the higher reaches of government leadership, it is not surprising that the management of these matters should be seized by the very highest level of authority within the Executive Branch. The first Presidential directive, issued March 22, 1940, as E.O. 8381, purportedly was promulgated in accordance with a provision of a 1938 law (52 Stat. 3) which read:

> Whenever, in the interests of national defense, the President defines certain vital military and naval installations or equipment as requiring protection against the general dissemination of information thereto, it shall be unlawful to make any photograph, sketch, picture, drawing, map, or graphical representation of such vital military and naval installation or equipment without first obtaining permission of the commanding officer.

Utilizing the clause regarding "information relative thereto," the President authorized the use of security labels on "all official military or naval books, pamphlets, documents, reports, maps, charts, plans, designs, models, drawings, photographs, contracts or specifications which are now marked under the authority of the Secretary of War or the Secretary of the Navy as 'secret,' 'confidential,' or 'restricted,' and all such articles or equipment which may hereafter be so marked with the approval or at the direction of the President." Commenting on this situation, one authority has observed:

> Congress, in passing the act of January 12, 1938 [52 Stat. 3], can hardly have expected that it would be interpreted to be applicable to documentary materials as "equipment." . . . The provisions of the Executive order were probably a substitute for equivalent express provisions of law that Congress could not be expected to enact. Mention may be made in this connection of the refusal of Congress, long after the attack of Pearl Harbor, to pass the proposed War Security Act submitted to Congress by Attorney General Francis Biddle on October 17, 1942 (H.R. 1205, 78th Congress, 1st session).[39]

Noteworthy, as well, is the wholesale adoption of the broad definitions, suggested by armed forces regulations, of the types of policy to which these markings might be applied. Revision or modification of these jurisdictions or the scope of label applications remained, essentially, with the officers of the War and Navy Departments. Little civilian control was provided over the frequency or appropriate use of the labels. It apparently was presumed that the markings would be utilized chiefly by the armed services.

E.O. 8381 was the principal Presidential directive on security classification until 1950 when a new order was promulgated. Prior to the issuance of the new directive, two additional special types of officially secret information were created. With the enactment of the Atomic Energy Act in 1946 (60 Stat. 755) so-called "Restricted Data" — sensitive material pertaining to atomic energy production — was established (60 Stat. 766). The following year, the newly adopted National Security Act (61 Stat. 495), which provided a unified administrative structure for the defense establishment and mandated the National Security Council and the Central Intelligence Agency, explicitly charged the Director of Central Intelligence with responsibility of protecting intelligence sources and methods (61 Stat. 498).[40] However, Executive Branch records containing either of these types of information — "Restricted Data" or intelligence material — are marked and managed largely in accordance with the procedures specified in the prevailing Presidential security classification order.

In 1950, President Truman, relying upon the 1938 defense installations protection law (52 Stat. 3), promulgated E.O. 10104 which replaced E.O. 8381 issued by his predecessor. Authorization for the same three security classification markings was continued and the new instrument also "formalized the designation 'Top Secret', which had been added to military regulations during the latter part of World War I to coincide with classification levels of our allies."[41] Supervisory authority for carrying out the provisions of the order was vested in the Secretary of Defense and the three armed services secretaries.

> It is important to emphasize that through the historical period of the use of classification markings described thus far until 1950, such formal directives, regulations, or Executive orders applied to the protection of military secrets, rarely extending into either those affecting nonmilitary agencies or those involving foreign policy or diplomatic relations. One exception is in the area of communications secrecy, governed by section 798 of the Espionage Act. This law, which protects cryptographic systems, communications intelligence information, and similar matters, applies, of course, to

both military and non-military Federal agencies such as the State Department. Aside from more restrictive war-time regulations, non-military agencies had, until 1958, relied generally on the 1789 "housekeeping" statute . . . as the basis for withholding vast amounts of information from public disclosure.[42]

Then, on September 24, 1951, with the issuance of E.O. 10290, the Chief Executive extended the coverage of the classification system to non-military agencies involved in "national security" matters. The order cited no express constitutional or statutory authority for its promulgation. Instead, the President seems to have relied upon implied powers such as the "faithful execution of the laws" clause. Although these postures for the order generally were recognized and accepted as a legitimate basis for issuing such an instrument, the President's role in the matter was felt to have limitations as well.[43] In this regard, one congressional committee observed:

Foremost among these is the well settled ruled that an Executive order, or any other Executive action, whether by formal order or by regulation, cannot contravene an act of Congress which is constitutional. Thus, when an Executive order collides with a statute which is enacted pursuant to the constitutional authority of the Congress, the statute will prevail [*Kendall v. United States,* 12 Peters 524 (1838)]. This rule, in turn, gives rise to a further limitation which finds its source in the power of the Congress to set forth specifically the duties of various officers and employees of the executive branch. Since the President can control only those duties of his subordinates which are discretionary, to the extent that the Congress prescribes these duties in detail, these officials can exercise no discretion and their actions cannot be controlled by the President. In other words, if the Congress enacts a statute which is constitutionally within its authority, the President cannot lawfully, either by Executive order, regulation, or any other means, direct his subordinates to disobey that statute, regardless of whether it affects third persons or whether it is only a directive concerning the management of the executive branch of the Government.[44]

Congress might attempt to overturn an Exeutive order by rescinding it or by possibly offering alternative language supplanting or amending the directive, though there would seem to be a constitutional conflict in such a course of action in the particular case of E.O. 10290. Thus, on September 28, 1951,

Senator John W. Bricker introduced S. 2190 which provided for the repeal of the President's directive, but the bill failed to receive consideration.[45] The order thus remained in effect until 1953.

When President Eisenhower took office in January 1953, he took notice of the widespread criticism of Executive Order 10290 and requested Attorney General Brownell for advice concerning its recission or revision. On June 15, 1953, the Attorney General recommended recission of the Executive order and the issuance of a new order which would "protect every requirement of national safety and at the same time, honor the basic tenets of freedom of information."

That fall, President Eisenhower replaced the controversial Truman order with Executive Order No. 10501, "Safeguarding Official Information in the Interests of the Defense of the United States." This order, issued on November 5, 1953, became effective on December 15, 1953; it was amended several times in the succeeding years, but for almost twenty years served as the basis for the security classification system until it was superceded in March 1972.[46]

Although E.O. 10501 was issued to improve the classification system in operation at the time, the directive also presented certain problems of its own. In promulgating the order, the President "was apparently relying primarily on implied constitutional powers of his office and statutes claimed to afford a basis on which to justify the issuance."[47] A search of the statutes does not reveal specific provisions directly sanctioning such a policy instrument.

The order provided nothing with regard to the prosecution of individuals mishandling or improperly disclosing classified information. An automatic declassification and security downgrading procedure was not part of the E.O. 10501 system until 1961 when a special amendment (E.O. 10964) added such arrangements.

With regard to the administration of the order, apparently no actions were taken against known cases of over-classification.[48] One expert, a retired Air Force official having many years of experience with E.O. 10501 operations, told a congressional subcommittee in 1972:

There is a massive wastage of money and manpower involved in protecting this mountainous volume of material with unwarranted classification markings. Last year, I estimated that about $50 million was being spent on protective measures for classified documents which were unnecessarily classified. After further observation and inquiry, and including expenditures for the useless clearances granted people for access to classified material, it is my calculation that the annual wastage for safeguarding documents and equipment with counterfeit classification markings is over $100 million.[49]

A General Accounting Office analysis at this time reported that four Federal agencies—the Departments of Defense and State, the Atomic Energy Commission, and the National Aeronautics and Space Administration—spent $126,322,394 annually on various activities related to the security classification system. This was thought to be slightly less than twice the amount of money spent by these same entities for their public information programs.[50]

It also was discovered that E.O. 10501 had little effect upon the creation of special secrecy arrangements. In combination with the three labels authorized by the order, Executive Branch departments and agencies were found utilizing some 62 different information control markings to limit the distribution and dissemination of documents upon which they appeared. In almost every case, they were promulgated and used without any statutory authority.[51] It was not known how many such additional markings might exist to effect special secrecy systems and there was no assurance from Executive Branch officials at the time of this revelation that any better management or elimination of these record control labels would be undertaken.

Shortly, however, another Presidential initiative in security classification policy soon became apparent.

After the eruption of the controversy over the publication of parts of the "Pentagon Papers" by the New York Times, Washington Post, and other newspapers, it was revealed that President Nixon had, on January 15, 1971, directed that "a review be made of security classification procedures now in effect." He established an "interagency committee to study the existing system, to make recommendations with respect to its operation and to propose steps that might be taken to provide speedier declassification." He later directed that "the scope of the review be expanded to cover all aspects of information security."[52]

The President's interagency committee initially was headed by William H. Rehnquist, Assistant Attorney General, Office of Legal Counsel, and included representatives from the National Security Council, the Central Intelligence Agency, the Atomic Energy Commission, and the Departments of State and Defense. With Rehnquist's appointment to the Supreme Court in late 1971, David R. Young, Special Assistant to the National Security Council, assumed the chairmanship of the panel. Simultaneously,

> . . . the White House on June 30, 1971, issued an "administratively confidential" memorandum to all Federal agencies signed by Brig. Gen. Alexander M. Haig, Jr., Deputy Assistant to the President for National Security Affairs, ordering each agency to submit lists of the Government employees, outside consultants, and private contractors who hold clearances for access to top secret and secret information.
>
> Several days later, President Nixon then asked Congress to approve a $636,000 supplemental appropriation for the General Services Administration to assist the National Archives in the declassification of World War II records, which he estimated to total "nearly 160 million pages of classified documents."[53]

Meeting through the summer and autumn of 1971, the interagency committee, under Rehnquist's leadership, incorporated its recommendations into a draft revision of E.O. 10501. This document was circulated in January, 1972, to relevant departments and agencies by the National Security Council. Ultimately, on March 8, 1972, President Nixon released what the Executive Branch considered to be an improved instrument, complete with revisions offered during its circulation in draft, as E.O. 11652.

Entitled "Classification and Declassification of National Security Information," the new order substantially reduced the number of personnel who review government information for classification while certain substantive aspects of the directive suggested significant policy shifts. Curiously, it was promulgated in consonance with the permissive exemption clause of the Freedom of Information Act (5 U.S.C. 552(b)(1)). The thrust of the statute is that government records, upon request, should be made available to the public and, with specified exception, nothing should be withheld. The order utilized the Act's justification for the permissive withholding of records to suggest a more absolute basis for denying access to classified materials.

While E.O. 10501 contained the reference "interests of national defense" to specify its policy sphere, the new order utilized "interests of national defense or foreign relations" which collectively refer to "national security."[54] Not only was this a broadening of the policy sphere of application, but the phrase in E.O. 11652 was not harmonious with the statutory provision upon which it allegedly was based. The Freedom of Information Act clause uses the term "interest of national defense or foreign *policy*." Said one authority:

> In addition to putting the language of the new Executive order at variance with the language of the Freedom of Information Act on which it relies for application of the exemption, the semantic and legal differences between the terms "national defense" and "national security" and the terms "foreign policy" and "foreign relations" weaken the entire foundations of Executive Order 11652, while failing to correct a basic defect in Executive Order 10501 — namely, its lack of a definition for the term "national defense." For example, "relations" is a much broader word than "policy" because it includes all operational matters, no matter how insignificant.[55]

Congress seems to have affirmed this view in adopting the 1974 amendments to the Freedom of Information Act (88 Stat. 1561) which provide the courts with authority to examine classified documents *in camera* to determine whether or not material is classified properly and, accordingly, withheld justifiably from public inspection.

Other defects in the order were noted by a congressional oversight committee:

> (1) Totally misconstrues the basic meaning of the Freedom of Information Act (5 U.S.C. 552);
> (2) Confuses the sanctions of the Criminal Code that apply to the wrongful disclosure of classified information;
> (3) Confuses the legal meaning of the terms "national defense"

and "national security" while failing to provide an adequate definition for any of the terms;

(4) Increases (not reduces) the limitation on the number of persons who can wield classification stamps and restricts public access to lists of persons having such authority;

(5) Provides no specific penalties for overclassification or misclassification of information or material;

(6) Permits executive departments to hide the identity of classifiers of specific documents;

(7) Contains no requirement to depart from the general declassification rules, even when classified information no longer requires protection;

(8) Permits full details of major defense or foreign policy errors of an administration to be cloaked for a minimum of three 4-year Presidential terms, but loopholes could extend this secrecy for 30 years or longer;

(9) Provides no public accountability to Congress for the actions of the newly created Interagency Classification Review Committee;

(10) Legitimizes and broadens authority for the use of special categories of "classification" governing access and distribution of classified information and material beyond the three specified categories—top secret, secret, and confidential; and

(11) Creates a "special privilege" for former Presidential appointees for access to certain papers that could serve as the basis for their private profit through the sale of articles, books, memoirs to publishing houses.[56]

With regard to actual operations under E.O. 11652, the panel (1) reiterated certain defects within the directive which its analysis had revealed, (2) lamented that "appropriate committees of the Congress having extensive experience and expertise in the oversight of the security classification system were not given the opportunity by the Executive Branch to comment on the design of the new Executive order," (3) criticized the President for releasing the new classification directive without giving the agencies ample opportunity to prepare implementing regulations and otherwise "provide for the orderly transition from the old system to the new," (4) pointed out conflicting statements by Executive Branch witnesses and demonstrated lack of clarity regarding "the extent to which 'domestic surveillance' activities by Federal agencies involving American citizens are subject to classification under the new Executive order," (5) disapproved of the limitations the new order placed on classified data of the World War II era which "fall far short of the policies necessary to permit the Congress or the public to benefit from historical insights into defense and foreign policy decisions of this crucial period of U.S. involvement in global crises," and (6) praised the statutorily based information protection program of the Atomic Energy Commission.[57] Ultimately, the panel recommended

> . . . that legislation providing for a statutory security classification system should be considered and enacted by the Congress. It should apply to all executive departments and agencies responsible for the classification, protection, and ultimate declassification of sensitive information vital to our Nation's defense and foreign policy interests. Such a law should clearly reaffirm the right of committees of Congress to obtain all classified information held by the executive branch when, in the judgment of the committee such information is relevant to its legislative or investigation jurisdiction. The law should also make certain that committees of Congress will not be impeded in the full exercise of their oversight responsibilities over the administration and operation of the classification system.[58]

Three years later, in 1976, another congressional committee urged that legislation be enacted to provide for the classification and declassification of Federal records.[59] However, no such statute was produced. Instead, the new President, Jimmy Carter, elected on pledges of "sunshine" and "broad public access" in government, "maximum security declassification," and "minimum secrecy" in the Executive Branch, issued still another new classification directive, E.O. 12065, in July, 1978.[60]

The pattern was familiar. Shortly after assuming office, President Carter created a committee, with leadership from the Domestic Policy Staff, to prepare an improved classification order. First drafts were greeted with considerable opposition from civil liberties organizations.[61] Ironically, the day before the White House released the text of the order, its contents were disclosed by *The New York Times*.[62] Shortly after this incident, the President complained to congressional leaders that leaks of classified information from Capitol Hill were adversely effecting intelligence sources and damaging the nation's security.

However, the Chief Executive provided neither examples of the indiscretions concerning him nor any indication of the types of negative effects suffered by the intelligence community.[63]

While generally acknowledging that the Carter classification directive "is an improvement over Executive Order 11652," a House oversight subcommittee concluded it also "is nonetheless weighted toward secrecy, and does not adequately balance, as it purports to do, the competing interest of public access." Further, with regard to the allocation of classification authority, the subcommittee found "it is not clear that the order will result in fewer officials exercising such authority, or will result in less information being classified, or will result in earlier declassification than under the existing order." It also was thought that the directive's "oversight and control mechanisms, in particular, are notably deficient in detecting and correcting abuses of the system."[64]

Other weaknesses attributed to the new order included "no general declassification schedule" and "no requirement that the classifier mark the document he is classifying to show which of the criteria he is relying upon."[65] It was felt that the directive "should expressly direct that classifiers take the public's need for the information in question into account at the time the classification decision is made."[66] Concern was expressed that the procedures of the new order "could easily result . . . in more information being kept secret longer than is the case under the existing order, despite the fact that the maximum period of classification prior to review has been shortened from 30 years to 29 years."[67] Although records classified for more than a decade would be required to undergo a review every ten years, the new directive allowed the head of an agency or the Director of Central Intelligence to obtain a "waiver" of this obligation, providing a means, in the assessment of the subcommittee, "where the head of an agency could prevent declassification review at any time."[68] And, in another area, the subcommittee noted:

> . . . the fact that the proposed order permits an unlimited delegation of "Secret" and "Confidential" classification authority from one level of officials to a subordinate level may well result in a significantly greater number of officials with the power to keep information secret than we have under the present order. There is no requirement in the proposed order that the head of an agency ap-

27

prove such delegation of authority, and no provision that lists of such delegations be published or even transmitted to the Oversight Office [within the General Services Administration].[69]

With regard to the Oversight Office created by the new order, the subcommittee commented: "Given GSA's lack of political or economic leverage over most agencies with classification authority, placing the Oversight Office within GSA does not seem to portend particularly vigorous enforcement of the order."[70] In addition, the new directive classifies information for purposes of "national security," a policy problem discussed earlier, and allows the creation of "special access programs of ultra-secret materials apart from the categories prescribed by the order. Finally, E.O. 12065 provides that when "inspection, or access to specific categories of classified information would pose an exceptional national security risk," the director of the Information Security Oversight Office may be denied the opportunity to scrutinize some security systems, thus weakening the role of this administrative accountability monitor.

Because E.O. 12065 was not implemented until very late in 1978, an evaluation of operations under the new directive has been possible only of late. However, an assessment of the administration of the order by the General Accounting Office reported various disturbing conditions. Based upon an examination of 23 installations and offices of the Department of Defense which were located in the continental United States, Hawaii, Europe, and the Canal Zone, the G.A.O. study found that "information was originally classified by individuals who were not authorized classifiers; individuals with top secret classification authority improperly delegated authority to subordinates to extend classification for more than six years; and sections of some classification guides did not specify the level of classification to be used in classifying information on a derivative basis which, in effect, allows unauthorized individuals to make classification decisions."[71] In addition, of 556 sample classified documents reviewed by G.A.O. personnel, 133, or approximately 24 percent, "contained information that had been improperly classified" and the agency "identified one or more marking errors on 33 percent of the documents it reviewed."[72]

Although the Carter regime's security classification system

appeared to be in need of further refinement, the White House did not limit its efforts at perfecting official secrecy to this one policy area. Carter Administration attorneys successfully pursued former C.I.A. officer Frank Snepp to discourage other ex-agents from publishing their memoirs, even though the Government admitted that his critical account of the Agency's role in Vietnam contained no classified information and disclosed no secrets.[73] In March 1979 Administration lawyers succeeded in obtaining a prior restraint of a publisher's First Amendment rights when they obtained an injunction against *The Progressive* magazine for attempting to print an article allegedly containing "Restricted Data" on the manufacture of an atomic bomb.[74] In January 1980, in his State of the Union address before Congress, President Carter said:

> We also need quick passage of a new charter to define clearly the legal authority and accountability of our intelligence agencies. While guaranteeing that abuses will not recur, we need to remove unwarranted restraints on our ability to collect intelligence and to tighten our controls on sensitive intelligence information.[75]

The Administration's objectives in this regard included extensive immunity for the Central Intelligence Agency, if not the entire intelligence community, from the requirements of the Freedom of Information Act and establishing criminal penalties to be applied to anyone convicted of improperly disclosing the identity of intelligence operatives.[76] How do these security concerns relate to "the people's right to know"?

Freedom of Information

Consistent with the Constitution's First Amendment guarantee of the right of petition, which traces its origin to Magna Carta, the Freedom of Information Act (5 U.S.C. 552) provides procedures whereby the citizenry, of their own volition, may directly request a document from an Executive Branch entity. If denied access to the item(s) sought, redress in the courts ultimately is available. Such a request, however, is limited to existing records: the agency is under no compulsion to prepare an item if the requested information is not readily available in documentary form. Prior to the 1966 enactment of the F.O.I. Act,

Federal public records law was devoid of a clear petition procedure for obtaining documents.

Another innovation achieved with the adoption of the F.O.I. Act—perhaps the most revolutionary and sweeping change—was a reversal in policy presumption. Prior law indicated the Executive Branch departments and agencies would decide who could have access to records and, thereby, fostered a "need to know" policy, but the Freedom of Information Act presumes these records are available to the public unless a particular document qualifies for exemption from disclosure under the precise terms of the F.O.I. statute. However, even then, the nine exemptions of the law (5 U.S.C. 552(b)(1)-(9)) are to be applied permissively; every effort is to be made by bureaucrats to facilitate disclosure. In this regard, the F.O.I. Act is an embodiment and a manifestation of the unwritten "right to know."

The "need to know" policy preceding the Freedom of Information Act derived from a variety of sources. Conditioned by the official secrecy experience of World War II and the subsequent Cold War, the tirades of the early 1950s by the witch-hunting Senator Joseph R. McCarthy, and the various workforce reductions which accompanied the arrivals of the Eisenhower and Kennedy Administrations, the Federal bureaucracy was not eager to have its activities and operations disclosed to the public, the press, or other Government entities. The prevailing law tolerated this situation, offering citizens no clear avenue to government information: the housekeeping statute of 1789 (formerly codified at 5 U.S.C. 22 and now found at 5 U.S.C. 301) authorized agency heads to prescribe regulations regarding the custody, use, and preservation of the records, papers, and property of their unit and a provision of the Administrative Procedure Act of 1946 (codified at 5 U.S.C. 1002 before being displaced by the F.O.I. Act) indicated that matters of official record should be made available to the public, but added that an agency could restrict access to its documents "for good cause found" or "in the public interest." Such provisions did not so much foster the "need to know" policy but, rather, justified it.

With the adoption of the Freedom of Information Act in 1966 (80 Stat. 250), "need to know" was replaced by a policy of presumptive public access to Executive Branch records. Deriving from some eleven years of investigative hearings by the Special Subcommittee on Government Information of the House Committee on Government Operations,[77] the statute was the product of additional legislative deliberations before the successor House Foreign Operations and Government Information Subcommittee and the Subcommittee on Administrative Practice and Procedure of the Senate Committee on the Judiciary.[78]

During the legislative hearings on the Freedom of Information bill, neither the White House nor any Executive Branch department or agency voiced support for the proposal. In terms of drafting, the statute came into existence handicapped by political compromise and a mixture of interpretations. Initial problems derived from the differences in House and Senate reports on the legislation. After the Senate approved the F.O.I. bill in 1965, President Johnson sought to blunt the impact of the proposal by pressuring the House Committee on Government Operations into producing a much more limited and antithetic report than the Senate counterpart.[79]

Further, certain language, even when subjected to judicial interpretation, has been misunderstood[80] or is of unclear meaning on its face.[81] In part, this interpretation quandary, as noted above, devolves from the legislative history of the law — in particular, the politics of the reports on the bill — but other influences also must be acknowledged: the Executive Branch agencies did not support the proposal and had it forced upon them; the President reluctantly signed the bill, indicating to top administrators a lack of sympathy for the statute's requirements; the Attorney General's memorandum interpreting the Act reflected a bias against the true spirit of the law; and the departments and agencies, in allocating resources for the administration of the Act, failed to seriously regard its dictates.[82]

This lack of good faith on the part of the Executive Branch, which some characterized as contempt for the F.O.I. Act, was readily identified in 1972 when the first oversight hearings were held on the statute by the House Foreign Operations and Government Information Subcommittee.[83] Reporting on findings deriving from these proceedings, the panel's parent committee concluded: "The efficient operation of the Freedom of Information Act has been hindered by 5 years of foot-dragging by the Federal bureaucracy, . . . obvious in parts of two administrations."[84]

As a consequence of these findings, vigorous efforts were undertaken during the 93rd Congress to amend the F.O.I. Act to improve its administration and expedite operations pursuant to its provisions. A bi-partisan reform proposal moved through the legislative maze during the early months of 1974 with little opposition from any congressional source, but also without any Executive Branch support. The legislation was ready for the President's signature in early October. Arguing that the proposal would adversely affect the retention of military or intelligence secrets, would compromise the confidentiality of investigatory law enforcement files, would unreasonably burden agencies by imposing specific response times, and was otherwise "unconstitutional and unworkable," the Chief Executive vetoed the measure on October 17. On November 20, the House voted 371-31 for override and, with two-thirds of the membership expressing favor, the President's objections were rejected. The Senate completed action on the matter the following day, voting 65-27 for override. The bill thereby became law (88 Stat. 1561).[85]

No Chief Executive has given direct support to the Freedom of Information Act. President Johnson seemingly disliked the original legislation and reluctantly signed it into law at the last moment. President Ford vetoed the decisive 1974 amendments to the statute and President Carter has sought to provide special favor for the Central Intelligence Agency, by shielding it from the provisions of the F.O.I. Act. The Justice Department assumed government-wide supervision of the administration of the Freedom of Information Act, but has never exerted vigorous leadership in this policy area.[86] A recommendation in a 1977 report of the Commission on Federal Paperwork, a Presidential study panel, that the President "promptly issue a directive to the heads of all executive branch departments and agencies reaffirming the public disclosure policy of the Freedom of Information Act and the need for fuller disclosure not only to the public but among Federal agencies as well" has fallen upon deaf ears.[87] Indeed, President Carter carefully avoided any significant comment upon the F.O.I. Act, other than to endorse and seek C.I.A. immunity from its provisions, and his White House staff, like that of his predecessors, have publicly relished their exemption from the reach of the statute.[88]

The Freedom of Information Act is a poignant reminder to occupants of the Oval Office and its servants of the sovereignty of the people, providing both a legal declaration of the citizen's right to know about the activities and operations of government while offering procedures for realizing this just claim. The American public has been much forewarned of late against the "Imperial Presidency," but perhaps the corruption is better understood as an arrogance of power. Some may be tempted by the potential for kingship. The Supreme Court put it well over a century ago:

> This nation . . . has no right to expect that it will always have wise and humane rulers, sincerely attached to the principles of the Constitution. Wicked men, ambitious of power, with hatred of liberty and contempt of law, may fill the place once occupied by Washington and Lincoln.[89]

The people must forever remain watchful, vigilant, and informed in order to safeguard their sovereignty. No quarter of the government can afford to frustrate the exercise of the popular right to know for long without some consequential cost — the farce, tragedy, or both against which Madison so eloquently warned long ago.

The President and Information Management: An Experiment in the Carter White House

JON A. TURNER and JOHN A. GOSDEN

It is popularly accepted that the role of the President of the United States has become so complicated that successful performance is almost beyond human ability. No other executive constantly faces so many decisions, over so wide a range of topics, with such potentially grave consequences, and subject to so much scrutiny. This is compounded by the fact that any one decision has ripple effects into many other areas, some foreseen and many that are not. Given this situation, it is reasonable to make use of any technique or device that has the potential of improving executive performance.

An interesting facet of the Carter Administration has been its effort to use information systems technology to improve the decisionmaking process in the White House, or more correctly, in the Executive Office of the President (E.O.P.). There are two major reasons for this development. First, President Carter seemed favorably disposed to technology. With his rational decisionmaking style and his background in nuclear engineering, the President was probably aware of the potential of technology and is comfortable with it.

Second, one of the staff members President Carter brought with him from Georgia, Richard Harden, was keenly interested in information technology. Harden, who has a background in accounting, is interested in ways in which information systems could alter the roles and performance of Presidential assistants.[1]

Harden's concept was that the performance of Presidential assistants and their staffs could be improved through changes in organization and support systems. The support systems would emerge from using a network of terminals and computers to provide better control of, and access to, data. Such systems are known colloquially as "office automation."

Along with the desire to improve the performance of Presidential assistants, Harden also appeared to want to free the President from some of the constraints imposed by the Washington information and decisionmaking establishment. As outsiders without prior Washington experience, the advisors around President Carter resented, often with justification, their dependency on the Washington bureaucracy. The thought that communication and information technology might enlarge the circle of Presidential advisors and provide new sources of information is, on the surface, an appealing one. This could be done by developing resource networks. One network linked to many outside experts across the country could be used to poll selective relevant experts for additional data or opinions on particular topics as they arise. Another network might be developed to provide direct access to various data bases, avoiding the delays and distortions inherent in conventional access via intermediaries.

At the beginning of the Carter Administration, there was relatively little information processing in the E.O.P. The applications which existed were fragmented and uncoordinated. One cluster of systems, developed by the Office of Management and Budget (O.M.B.), centered around Federal Government budget preparation and analysis and the administration of certain Federal regulations (for instance, those pertaining to the Freedom of Information Act). Another group of systems supported the National Security Council (N.S.C.), and a third group had been developed by the U.S. Representative for Trade Negotiations (S.T.R.) as part of the GATT and multinational trade negotiations. A fourth cluster, much less homogenous, supported the White House staff. Other agencies or groups within the E.O.P. that needed applications developed or needed access to a computer, made do on an "ad hoc" basis, using services provided by Federal data centers or commercial service bureaus.

For the most part, the hardware and operating system software installed in these four clusters were relatively antiquated. Except for the N.S.C. and the S.T.R., adequate capacity during peak loading was always a problem. When needed, additional capacity was obtained from the departments or other Federal data processing centers, with the result that, over time, it seemed that more application systems were being run on computers outside the E.O.P. than within it. Although, in a restrictive sense, this may be considered "cost effective," a considerable price was paid in application system staff productivity, operational complexity, maintenance support, and in a lack of control. The technical staff had to be familiar with many environments, and there were too many events beyond staff control that influenced their ability to meet scheduled commitments.

Three other factors tended to influence this environment. The White House frequently usurped staff and equipment capacity. Because these requests came from staff that worked closely with the President, the requests tended to be given a higher priority than was warranted on the content of the application alone.

Second, there was no formal mechanism for resolving resource or application development conflicts among E.O.P. units. In practice the relative power of the units or principals involved tended to be the governing factor.

Third, a conflict existed within O.M.B. The Information Systems Division provided both data processing facilities and applications development services, *as well as* being responsible for establishing government-wide Automatic Data Processing (A.D.P.) policy. In order to protect itself from criticism, this group tended to be conservative in its facilities and application development role. That is, they operated with little slack capacity and they were followers rather than innovators in the design and use of information systems.[2]

Several additional characteristics of the E.O.P. environment compounded the difficulty of the situation. The nature of the work within the E.O.P. is highly pressured and always important. The range in power between individuals at the top and the bottom of the organizational structure is so great that communication frequently breaks down and, as service requests are transmitted from one organizational level to another, considerable distortion is introduced. The workload is so heavy and the deadline pressures are so intense that it is almost impossible to establish priorities: sometimes it seems that *everything is an emergency and every request is in the name of the President.*

Furthermore, within the E.O.P., the primary orientation is external. The E.O.P.'s advertised function is to support the President directly in his day to day activities and, in the name of the President, to provide overall guidance to the Executive Branch departments. The staff's attention is so constantly fixed on the outside world, and on the President, that they have no time to consider their own operations. Unfortunately, almost no one within the E.O.P. is concerned with internal operations and this results in serious coordination and management problems. One of the consequences of the external orientation is that little guidance and direction is given to the information systems staff. Except for the budget systems that were developed over a ten year period, few long term projects have been completed.

The E.O.P. is not an environment that is conducive to thoughtful planning, carefully reasoned strategies, or long term development projects. Rather, it tends to be forced to react to crisis situations, to favor short term stop-gap measures, and arbitrary deadlines. Deferring for a moment the question of the appropriateness of using computer based application systems as decision aids in this environment, it was clear that the EOP was, in 1977, not even making effective use of information systems for routine data processing activities, where their value has been repeatedly demonstrated. The resources that were being allocated to information systems mostly were being used for maintenance of the Federal budget systems. There were few, if any, new development projects in process and there were no resources available for building new application systems.

Clearly this was not a satisfactory base upon which to build decision support systems in the E.O.P. Harden wanted to remedy this situation by building application systems that could be used by future administrations. If sufficient resources are allocated, a nucleus of operational level systems might be formed that embody the procedures necessary to run the E.O.P. These systems would be a legacy for future administrations. To achieve the Administration's goals, the resources devoted to information systems development and operation would have to be increased. Accomplishing this would involve obtaining the funding for new equipment and staff, procuring the equipment, modifying the physical plant, hiring additional staff, and making organizational changes.

Reorganization of the E.O.P.

In March, 1977, President Carter created a special reorganization task group to study the E.O.P. and recommend changes that would improve performance. The reorganization study made three recommendations designed to encourage the use of information systems and to make system development easier. The first was to place the O.M.B. automatic data processing policy function in a separate organization from information systems development and computer facilities management activities. The existing dual mission created conflicts that were not being resolved within the common structure. The recommendation was to separate the policy activity and relocate it elsewhere within O.M.B.

Second, if O.M.B. computer facilities were to serve the whole of the E.O.P., they should be part of a unit that has E.O.P.-wide service as its primary mission. Third, there should be sufficient financial resources applied to E.O.P. information systems to automate the major operational activities of the various E.O.P. units, to develop modern support systems, and to pursue decision support systems. This implies some reserve capacity in computing facilities and in development staff.

As a result of other recommendations of the reorganization study, an Office of Administration (O.A.) was created to provide E.O.P. administrative services. Richard Harden, Special Assistant to the President for Organization and Management, was appointed director of O.A. Given this management structure, it seemed reasonable to consolidate the computer facilities and the systems development staff for the E.O.P. in O.A. With the exception of a unit serving the immediate needs of senior Presidential advisors, this was done. It was a crucial move that made it possible to consider exploiting the potential benefits of information technology.

An Advisory Group on White House Information Systems was established in August, 1977, to review the reorganization study recommendations and to provide more specific advice. While the original intent of the group was to assess the information system needs of the White House and the E.O.P., the scope became more broadly defined as the study progressed. Two factors contributed to this. First, no part-time committee could determine the information system needs of the White House and related units, especially when its input was based upon limited testimony from busy staff representatives. Considerably more field work would be needed. Second, discussions with several principals indicated that the White House desired general rather than specific direction.[3] The Advisory Group concluded that there was a strong need for both improved and new information systems to support the E.O.P.

The Advisory Group identified a number of guidelines for the E.O.P., including the role to be played by an information systems head, the method of coordination to be used within the E.O.P., the need for an overall systems architecture and implementation plan, user responsibilities, the need for a security study, and the desirability of performing cost/benefit analysis for potential new applications.[4]

However, they pointed out that while these recommendations would produce a much better environment, more capacity, and the appropriate tools and techniques, the decisionmaking processes could only be improved to the extent that they are able to take advantage of these tools and techniques.

The Advisory Group did very little work on applications. It reviewed a list of potential applications and identified two that it thought should be given highest priority. Later, another group was formed to consider the functions and design of a local network and individual consultants were used to advise on specific projects.

What was Accomplished?

Much has been done to improve the use of information technology in the E.O.P.

Harden restructured printing, messenger, graphic, document preparation, financial management, personnel, procurement, and information services in O.A. to make them more responsive to users, and a Customer Services Unit was created to provide assistance to those using these services.

A White House Information Center was established to provide policy analysis research support. The Center uses a computer-based catalog to access materials generated by the Administration. A professional staff of researchers is available to assist policy analysts and speechwriters. In addition, the Center compiles and distributes briefing kits of background material on key issues.

The E.O.P. uses a variety of word processing facilities and has adopted or adapted basic support systems from other agencies to improve the productivity of staff activities, keep track of activities, and manage the voluminous paper workload.

The major application systems that have been built include the Vote Analysis System to help advisors track congressional action; a financial management system to improve the internal cost data available to E.O.P. managers, automating the budget system input; and the Domestic Information Display System (D.I.D.S.) to display census data on a more timely basis.[5] In addition, a number of tracking and status reporting systems have been built for varoius E.O.P. units, and use was made as well of a Treasury Department personnel and payroll system. Of these systems, the Vote Analysis System and the Budget Input/Output System are mainline to the policy process. The Vote Analysis System permits profiles to be created of congressional action on subjects of interest to Presidential advisors. These profiles are used by the White House and O.M.B. Congressional liaison staff in tracking the voting records of Congressmen and in marshalling support for Presidential initiatives.

Prior to the automated budget systems (before 1968), each agency was responsible for providing necessary budget data to O.M.B. and verifying its accuracy. As the form of budget input became more standard, agency expertise in the mechanics of budget preparation gradually deteriorated, remaining only in O.M.B. The purpose of the Budget Input/Output System is to decentralize much of the responsibility for budget preparation and to involve the agencies fully in the process, thus improving the timeliness and quality of the product. It also is reported that budget processing proceeds more quickly and reliably than it did three years ago. One might speculate that this quicker budget processing cycle was a factor in President Carter's ability to submit a second so-called 'balanced' budget for 1981.

Considerable progress has been made in upgrading the information systems facilities and development staff. In the past three years, the machine capacity of the E.O.P. has doubled and the information systems development staff has increased by 50 percent. The staff quality also has been upgraded and there is less reliance upon technical staff borrowed from other government agencies. Managers with strong qualifications have been brought in to head the two operational groups, the Facilities Management Division and the Information Systems Division. Competitive procurements have been held for the facilities management contract and for new hardware to be used for office automation. In the final year of the Carter Administration, another procurement was underway to upgrade the data processing equipment and to construct a local E.O.P. network.

How well, then, has the objective of improving the sources of information available in the E.O.P. for decisionmaking been met? Has this interest in information systems resulted in changes to the information available for decisionmaking, the process of decisionmaking, or the results of decisionmaking? How well have the implied objectives of upgraded facilities and staff been achieved? Has the presence of the new systems resulted in making the President or his key assistants less dependent on the agencies or the Washington establishment?

There have been two major areas of improvement. First, there are many more basic support systems running successfully and, second, significant improvements in equipment capacity, staff quality, and application system enhancement have been made. These changes were valuable prerequisites to the more ambitious information systems goals of the Carter Administration. They made for more efficient operation of staff activities and provided top aides with more time to consider policy issues.

With respect to changing the decision process, however, progress was slow. The budget process was improved and the new Vote Analysis System was installed, but we do not see major *new* information sources and there was no indication that the President was any less dependent upon the Washington bureaucracy. To the extent that decisionmaking changed at the White House, it is more likely to have occurred as a result of new advisors rather than as a result of changes in the use of information systems. There was little evidence in 1980 that the policy staffs were making more direct use of computer systems or external data bases than they did early in 1977.

The Elusive Goals

In spite of the obvious and conventional improvements, progress toward the important goals of freeing Presidential decisionmaking from establishment dependency and improving decisionmaking has not been affected directly by information systems. This is not surprising. The same results have failed to materialize in the senior management activities of other large organizations, whether industrial or governmental.

Let us examine in more detail what Richard Harden, the President's Special Assistant for Information Management, tried to do. One concept advanced by Harden soon after taking over O.A. was that a system of terminals would improve the flow of information within the E.O.P. and provide easier access to files and computers. [6]

While it is true that a network of terminals (with appropriate protocol translation) could make data files and computers more accessible to users, it is questionable whether or not this network, in turn, would make *information* for policy analysis or decisionmaking more accessible. Most of the data for policy analysis are gathered from many diverse sources (few of which, in practice, are machine readable) and the information content is the interpretation made by the participants in the policy formulation process. In a sense, information is part of the process; it is an interaction among the participants, rather than an entity itself.

Furthermore, there is an assumption that has not been sustantiated. The assumption that *more* information (or even better information, if that could be defined) leads to better decisions is open to question. Many observers agree that either the data necessary does not exist (or will take too long to obtain), or that executives (or, in this case, policy analysts) have too much information and that their problem is one of selection, and of judicious use of analytic skills and interpretations, rather than a need for more or new data.[7]

Policy analysis is a specific, demanding activity requiring many years of training. By the time a policy analyst (in either the public or private sector) reaches a top post, he or she has developed data sources, contacts, and analytic and interpretive skills. The key elements are the richness of the set of action alternatives considered and the accuracy with which the consequences of action alternatives are forecast. These skills *cannot* easily be replaced or augmented by a computer system. This is not to say that computer technology may not be a component of the analysis and interpretation process, only that it is *not* a principal component. If the analyst does not know what the data mean, then the application of statistical procedures generally will lead to false conclusions. If the analysis is not satisfactory, then the analysts should be changed rather than attempting to find a technological remedy.

If we look at policy decision activities in industry, we find that they use highly summarized data. Analysts do not present raw or even edited data to executives except for monitoring events. As soon as there is unusual variation in the data, elaborate human screening activities (analysis) are applied to look beyond the data, determine causes, and suggest alternative reactions. Such activities, filtering and interpreting the data at various levels in an organization, resist formalization. They change and adapt continuously to the changing environment. In most organizations, they are taken for granted.

The pressure in the White House is so intense that no policy analyst working there has an opportunity to learn these skills on the job. In this demanding environment it is even difficult to get a person to read a short memo. No wonder then that there has been little effort devoted by the analysts to developing formal aids to support the process.

Now, let us look at the other possible use of a network in the E.O.P.: to provide an electronic mail or message service. As far as discussions on critical policy issues are concerned, most communications, particularly on intermediate levels, take place orally in pairs or in groups. Under these conditions it is questionable if linking White House staff members together with a computer based message system[8] would improve their ability to communicate with each other, or if they want a record of such discussions. Therefore, we would expect an electronic message system to be helpful only indirectly, to the extent it could improve the existing physical mail system.

Another new technical tool that Harden pursued was the Executive Work Station. Presumably, a work station similar to the one designed by Citibank[9] would be used to interconnect White House executives. Reportedly Harden was personally experimenting with a Xerox prototype system built around the Alto work station, an Ethernet type distribution system, and a laser based, multifont Xerographic printer.[10] While this is clearly advanced office automation equipment, there were no announced application plans that showed who might use production versions of such equipment, for what purpose, or how much it might cost. Harden's objective was to improve the productivity of an executive, rather than doing advanced text editing type applications.[11] Yet, by all reports, the Altos were only being used for text editing.

Furthermore, it is not apparent what improving executive productivity means in this context or how it might be measured. In both government and industry, this is still an open question. Use of word processing can and often does provide clerical cost reductions or productivity gains by the substitution of machine costs for labor. On the other hand, gains in productivity or effectiveness or staff functions usually occur indirectly as a result of office automation, and in most reported cases, a considerable investment has been required before there is a substantial payoff.[12]

A fundamental question then arises, is the White House an appropriate agency to lead what is basically a research and development activity? More specifically: is the environment in the E.O.P. sufficiently fertile to make any research seem worthwhile; and does the E.O.P. have the appropriate resources and leadership to carry out effective research and development?

Given the day-to-day pressures on policy analysts in the

E.O.P. and, except for President Carter and Richard Harden, the lack of interest in technical help—even perhaps some resistance to it—the environment seems inhospitable. Given that current resources are pressured constantly to respond to urgent requests, it seems unlikely that there will be much time to experiment and reflect on activities unless an independent group is set up to do so. Putting both of these factors together, it is surprising that experiments have been considered, let alone attempted.

What can be Done

If one wants to improve policy analysis performance in the E.O.P., then the policy analysis process itself, rather than particular tools, should be the subject of investigation. Considering the nature of the E.O.P. environment, improving policy analysis performance probably means improving the people who do policy analysis. Upgrading the quality of the basic research tools used by these analysts may be helpful (such as the improvements that have taken place in the E.O.P. libraries) and changes in the process of policymaking may remedy specific problems (such as providing feedback about those aspects of the process that are deficient). But, significant improvements in content and quality will only come from the people who produce the analyses, their leaders, and their working relationships.

It is no accident that the great board rooms of industry contain little more than a table and chairs. The symbols of technology are significant by their absence. At this level, the most important skills are political, and the operative mechanisms are persuasion, bargaining, and negotiation. If detailed information is needed, there are assistants and specialists close at hand to provide it. This is not an environment conducive to the use of interactive computer systems. The risk of misinterpretation is too great. At the executive level, the need is for more thoughtful deliberation, discussion, and argument rather than for cathode ray tube displays, large data bases, English-like query languages, and networks. This is not to say that at the operational or control levels of the agencies, these systems are not important. Clearly they are. But different functions take place at the Presidential level and the utility of the *direct* use of these systems is still questionable.

Consider a simple but specific example, the decision to admit the Shah of Iran to this country for medical treatment in October, 1979.[13] A key issue appears to be whether or not the State Department obtained a second opinion on the Shah's condition prior to approving entry. It is hard to imagine how a computer based system would have helped in this case. There is no data base that would help a person, without a medical background, to determine the Shah's condition. There was no need to convene a group of medical consultants using a computer based message system; the telephone would be better since it permits a two way dialogue. It is unlikely that there is a role for computer based application systems in such situations.

There are usually some executive activities within any organization that do lend themselves to the development of a computer based decision support system.[14] Such activities are characterized by *repetitive decisions* where the *values* for the parameters on which the decision will be based can be determined in advance, and the parameters can be related in an *analytic* manner. One example of such a system within the E.O.P. is the interactive analysis system developed by S.T.R. to assist trade negotiators: others are the budget systems, which were mentioned earlier. Such activities usually are automated for cost and labor reduction reasons and the decision support activities became natural extensions or spin-offs created by applications that tap the data bases that have been created. As specific needs become apparent, we would expect a steady but slow increase in such systems to continue to develop in the E.O.P., but not to be the major tools used in most policy decisions.

Conclusion

Better use of information systems technology can be useful in the E.O.P. There is much opportunity to improve many basic processes and much has been done in this regard by the Carter Administration. The particular attempt to improve decision-making has had some success, but progress is inevitably slow.

Not only is this process basically difficult, but the climate of pressure and urgency in the E.O.P. is not hospitable to such research, and it is projects with immediate payoff that gain acceptance.

How then should the E.O.P. seek further improvements? The general approach should be continued with particular emphasis in four areas. First, it is important to provide a more stable development environment. There has been an abundance of ideas, frequent staff changes, and pressure from the E.O.P. environment. This can be improved by better management, setting a clear direction, adopting a short-term plan that identifies a consistent set of goals, providing strong support to the development staff by internal E.O.P. management, and ensuring that projects are of short duration with well defined outputs.

Second, the E.O.P. should stop managing its own research activities. To the extent that the E.O.P. wants to sponsor research projects, they should be performed by agencies with the proper resources and management skills.

Third, continue to build the E.O.P. information systems staff and facilities. In particular, the E.O.P. should obtain and become familiar with development tools for building application systems quickly, build the support systems needed for internal facilities and project management, and make prospective investments in facilities such as a local network, that simplify future application development and have long lead times to acquire, develop, and install.

Fourth, continually seek out new application opportunities that will make a difference in the way the E.O.P. performs. The most successful systems have been those where a well-defined need existed, such as the lack of information on congressional voting records that prompted the vote analysis system, and which needed no advanced technology.

In general, keep doing what is being done, work for stability and consistent internal managerial direction, concentrate on development of applications, and contract out research. This means adopting a managerial rather than a marketing perspective.

CHAPTER THREE

Executive Privilege:
A Political Theory Masquerading
as Law

ARTHUR S. MILLER

I.

Any study of American constitutional law should begin with distinguishing between the *formal* and the *living* fundamental laws. Oft-times the law in books bespeaks one thing, even in purportedly absolute terms, but what governmental officers do in fact is quite another. As Woodrow Wilson observed in 1885, in language still not heeded by the professoriate: "The Constitution in operation is manifestly a very different thing from the Constitution of the books."[1] So it is — both generally and specifically. The "doctrine" of Executive privilege is a classic example. Not mentioned in the Constitution, the convention of 1787, statute,[2] or procedural rules of court, the privilege, nonetheless, exists as an exemplar of the living Constitution. It is no more a doctrine than is the concept of separation of powers; rather than a definite rule of conduct, to the extent that it exists, it is a political accommodation.

That may well explain the paucity of cases decided by Federal courts concerning the privilege. They began with *Aaron Burr's Case* (the precedential value of which is nil)[3] and run through *Reynolds* v. *United States*[4] to the two cases involving President Nixon — *Nixon-I* being the 1974 decision commanding surrender of the tapes by which he "bugged" his White House office[5] and *Nixon-II* being the 1977 decision by which the former Chief Executive could not keep "his" Presidential papers secret.[6] Few others exist, and none in the Supreme Court, save an odd 1979 decision, *Federal Open Market Committee* v. *Merrill*, decided, however, on statutory rather than constitutional grounds. Another Nixon case — by the Senate's Watergate Committee — was decided in favor of the President by a court of appeals in *Senate Select Committee* v. *Nixon* of

1974.[7] That gaggle of judicial decisions add up to so little that it may fairly be said that, as with international law, more gibberish has been written about the privilege, based on fewer formal statements of doctrine, than almost any other area of constitutional law. Save in high level abstraction — at a level that is next to meaningless — there is no law of Executive privilege in the sense of positive law. As such, it illustrates once again that Americans have a government of men, not of laws — although the pretense is otherwise. And it helps to explain why the term Executive privilege has no precise meaning at this time.

It is only when one scrutinizes the living law — the actual practices of government officials in all branches — that one can construct the beginnings of a theory of that part of the Executive's secrecy syndrome that travels under the banner of Executive privilege. (In law, the word "privilege" is one of multiple meanings: as used here, it fits into a category of situations which are called evidentiary privileges — attorney-client, doctor-patient, etc. — and to the extent that it reaches the plane of constitutional law it is similar to the privilege against self-incrimination.) The practice of Presidents (and other executives) keeping some matters from both Congress and the public runs back to George Washington. He first tested the waters in 1792 when Congress asked for papers concerning the Army's defeat by Indians; Washington capitulated at that time, but reluctantly.[8] A few years later he refused to give the House information about the Jay Treaty (although he did inform the Senate). His 1796 success was the first (known) use of what is now (but not then) called Executive privilege.

Data do not exist on how many times, in what types of situations, and with what results the "doctrine" has been invoked by Washington's successors.[9] Enough, however, is known that it is an integral segment of that bundle of rights and powers that constitute the corpus of actual Presidential authority. And that is so even though it is not known, save in impressionistic form, how the privilege compares with other techniques by which executive officers refuse, neglect, or delay to give information desired by Congress or the courts. In this, be it said, they seem to have pliant allies in most judges and most Members of Congress, who are usually quite ready to kowtow when the President cries privilege.

Those data, when available, would go far to make up a body of living law that would reify Max Weber's astute observation: "Every bureaucracy seeks to increase the superiority of the professionally informed by keeping their knowledge and intentions secret."[10] Secrecy, and thus the aggrandizement of actual power, is accomplished by the President through a number of techniques, only one of which is Executive privilege. Although it has received the greatest — almost sole — attention from commentators, the privilege is one of the least used means of evasion of congressional (or judicial) requests for data. In the "information society," information (and expertise) is power. Despite the Freedom of Information Act (5 U.S.C. 552) and various demands for openness in government, the organizations of a corporate society attain and retain power by hoarding information. Those organizations are both public and private (or, as with weapons manufacturers, a combination of both), and they are legislative and judicial as well as executive.

In this brief overview, I should like to proffer a few comments on the theory and practice of Executive privilege. This is a mere adumbration, not a full-blown analysis. Raoul Berger, a Fellow in American Legal History at Harvard University, has contended, with characteristic hyperbole, that the privilege is "a constitutional myth" — a piece of intelligence that would have amused, perhaps bemused, almost every President and every scholar who has studied the question. Berger's assertion was made just before the unanimous decision of the Supreme Court in *Nixon-I*.[11] Executive privilege, however defined, is emphatically *not* a myth. It is an indubitable part of the living American Constitution.

II.

What, then, may be said about the privilege that has not been said *ad nauseam* before? I am not so temerarious as to suggest that the following propositions, which taken together may serve to show the present status of the "doctrine," have any flashing new insights. If this commentary has any useful purpose, it is to set out a way of thinking about Executive privilege in the context of the secrecy syndrome of government. The propositions are listed in no particular order.

1. Increased employment of the privilege coincides in time with aggrandizement of power in the Executive Branch — a constitutional development that, despite the travail of Jimmy Carter, shows no signs of abating. As the United States has become deeply immersed in world affairs and as the President and the bureaucracy have been delegated large chunks of actual governing power — or have assumed it without delegation — a penchant for secrecy, always present, has flowered. The term "Executive privilege" is a latter-day neologism, dating only from the 1950s. It put a convenient label on a long-established practice of doing the public's business in private.

Every political action tends to have a reaction, not necessarily in accordance with Newtonian principles; and it was not long after assertions of the "privilege" by Executive officers that a counter-movement began to open the corridors of government to greater scrutiny. The success of the counterattack has been, and likely will continue to be, minimal. Despite the willingness of some judges to comply with the Freedom of Information Act, and thus to force the bureaucracy to crack its doors of secrecy, and despite the forays of some "investigative" reporters into the bowels of the bureaucracy there to uncover a few derelictions, it may be said with some confidence that the very complexity of government, the staggering amount of information, and the ingenuity of bureaucrats either to hide or destroy evidence will protect government from any thorough-going or comprehensive revelation of the innermost secrets of the organizations of our corporate society. That is particularly true for the private bureaucracies (corporations, unions, foundations, etc.) and for the courts (despite *The Brethren*)[12] and Congress; but it is also true for that congeries of agencies, bureaus, departments, commissions, and offices that make up the Executive Branch.

2. The doctrine of Executive privilege is not a doctrine at all, in the sense of positive law. However labelled, it is not, despite Chief Justice Burger's opinion in *Nixon-I*, a logical derivation from the constitutional text. An instrument of politics, it is invoked only as a last resort — after all tactics of evasion have been exhausted. Only by an intellectually indefensible fiction can it be said to be rooted in the Constitution, as Burger maintained. (Whether that was Burger's language may be doubted; if Woodward and Armstrong are correct, the opinion was a colle-

gial effort — a fact that may go far toward putting some of the professoriate — they who peruse and parse Court opinions as if they truly reflected what the judges thought — on welfare.)[13]

The Court made up the law in *Nixon-I*, just as they have in other diverse decisions rendered since 1789. That makes nonsense out of Chief Justice Marshall's oft-quoted assertion in 1824 that judicial power "is never exercised for the purpose of giving effect to the will of the judge; always for the purpose of giving effect to the will of the legislature; or, in other words, to the will of the law."[14] The "law" did not exist until that July day in 1974 when the decision was announced, which lends credence to Professor Ray Forrester's call for "truth in judging" — by which he meant that it should be openly acknowledged that judges are legislators (and Constitution-amenders).[15] Forrester's plea is not likely to be followed, simply because there is a wellnigh infinite capacity of the human mind for self delusion; and there is a cadre of specialists (lawyers and others) with a vested interest in the orthodoxy (as stated by Marshall). Those specialists are the greatest barrier to change in methods and institutions honored only by time; the man in the street is much more willing to accept change.

Americans, however, seem to want to believe that theirs is a government of laws, not of men. They believe in the myth that a set of known external standards called law may be drawn upon when any government official is alleged to have strayed beyond the pale of constitutional propriety. Not that Executive privilege differs from other constitutional decisions. Quite the contrary: any Supreme Court decision on the merits is law-creative, as Justice Byron White candidly acknowledged while dissenting in *Miranda* v. *Arizona*.[16] Law is made, not found; and insofar as the Court makes law, we have a government of lawyers, not of men.

The point is relevant to prediction of future results in Executive privilege cases. When (and if) made, they will be based on political accommodation rather than on interdictory principles of law. The Supreme Court is a political organ, pure and simple, speaking in the language of law but uttering juristic theories of politics. Whether a President or executive officer will succeed when invoking some type of Executive privilege will turn on considerations of high policy at the time a controversy arises. (Whether Congress can enact standards of greater specificity in the "doctrine" is discussed below.)

3. Richard Nixon found it politically necessary to surrender recordings made in the Oval Office. He did so only reluctantly, not being able to face a unanimous Court backed by a House of Representatives on the verge of voting out articles of impeachment. To some, *Nixon-I* was a victory for the Rule of Law; but if so, it was only minor as compared with the major gain the Presidency won. Richard Nixon lost but the office prevailed. A presumptive privilege for Presidential confidentiality was found lurking somewhere in the murky depths of Article II by the American "legiscourt." The Justices, as usual, did not inform us how they reached that conclusion. It should thus be called an "immaculate conception" of a legal concept — *Presidential* privilege, however, not that of the entire Executive Branch (as Attorney General Richard Kleindienst once asserted).

If one may infer a general principle from one particular, then *Nixon-I* established the "rule" that there is a quantum of data that Presidents need not disclose, however immeasurable that amount may be. Furthermore, the Court managed to do other things that merit separate attention: (a) it asserted, drawing on *Marbury's Case*,[17] that it is "emphatically the province and function of the judicial department to say what the law is," and thereby nailed another wall to the edifice of judicial supremacy in constitutional interpretation; and (b) the writ of the Supreme Court, for the first time in American history, ran against the President *qua* President.

Worthy of note also is the fact that the court in *Nixon-I* capitulated to arguments of "inherent" Presidential power. That is by no means novel; the practice runs at least as far back as the *Prize Cases*,[18] which upheld President Lincoln's exercise of the prerogative. Since the beginnings of the Republic, arguments over executive power have been waged. Only on rare occasions, as in the *Steel Seizure Case* of 1952,[19] has the Court not agreed with what the President wanted. Lincoln in the *Prize Cases*, and the Court in *In re Neagle*,[20] *In re Debs*,[21] *Midwest Oil*,[22] and *Myers* v. *United States*[23] are all testimony of judicial deference to Presidential will. I do not suggest that the Court is an arm of the Executive. Far from it. But I do say that the Justices are cowardly lions at best when it comes to eyeball-to-eyeball confrontations with Chief Executives. Other than in such exceptions as the *Steel* decision, *Humphrey's Case*[24] (on removal of a Federal Trade Commissioner contrary to statute), and perhaps the *Pentagon Papers Case*,[25] what the President wants the President gets when the Court enters the fray. Nixon's surrender paradoxically aggrandized the office's power and constitutional stature. Nothing in *Nixon-II* dilutes that conclusion. The Presidential Recordings and Materials Preservation Act (88 Stat. 1695) was essentially a one-shot statute, aimed only at the disgraced Richard Nixon, and is not likely to have lasting significance.[26]

Nixon v. *Administrator of General Services* (*Nixon-II*) is noteworthy mainly for an abortive attempt of the ex-President to control disposition of "his" documents. Congress stepped in and created a category of one — Richard Nixon — to which the Act applied. That, opined Justice Brennan, made Nixon a "legitimate class of one" — a remarkable conclusion that could, but will not, add a new dimension to equal protection and class-action law. The case would be confined to a legitimate class of oblivion were it not for the fact that the decision seems to signify, but does not flatly say so, that Congress has the upper hand in the disposition of Presidential papers. Perhaps the most that should be concluded is that when a President resigns in the fact of certain impeachment, "his" papers come under the control of Congress. Since only one Chief Executive has departed the White House by that route, one should not read much into the decision, particularly since the Court was badly splintered.

Two other comments are apposite. First, Executive privilege is akin to the "state secrets" privilege; as such, it may be invoked for the benefit of the Nation, not the individual. It is not something behind which a President's peccadilloes or other derelictions can be hidden. Second, it is difficult to see why, despite long-standing practice otherwise, papers accumulated by all government officers in the course of their duties are not, by definition, the property of the United States Government.[27] If that is accepted, then it is clearly Congress's prerogative under Article IV to dispose of them.

4. "Human experience teaches," Chief Justice Burger asserted in *Nixon-I*, "that those who expect public dissemination of their remarks may well temper candor with a concern for appearances and for their own interests to the detriment of the decisionmaking process."[28] That is the ultimate argument for secrecy, which, in Professor Carl J. Friedrich's view, serves a useful purpose. Says Friedrich in *The Pathology of Politics*: "secrecy is eminently functional in many governmental operations."[29] He cites jury deliberations among other examples and then goes on to dispute Woodrow Wilson's flight of hyperbole in *Congressional Government* that "there is not any legitimate privacy about matters of government. Government must, if it is to be pure and correct in its processes, be absolutely public in everything that affects it." (It is worth noting that Wilson as President a generation later saw matters differently.)

Whether Burger was correct about "human experience" may well be doubted. He cited no authority for the statement, apparently believing it to be self evident. But is it? Who knows? When the contrary has not been tried in government — in any branch — can it be definitively said that the teaching of human experience is so clear? Hardly. Surely there are other reasons, even if Burger were correct, for tempering candor than the possibility, even probability, that disclosure will subsequently occur. For example, Irving Janis, in his insightful *Victims of Groupthink*, has related psychological factors why advisors to Presidents tend to say what they think the President wants to hear.[30] Americans do not have, although they probably need, an *advocatur diaboli* in their governmental structure. Furthermore, there is more to fear from deliberate "leaks" from the White House, issued in efforts to manipulate public opinion, or from executive officers "stroking" members of the press and co-opting them (thus getting a favorable press), than there is in eventual disclosure. No one other than a Special Prosecutor, operating in a unique situation, has ever been able to crack the secrecy syndrome of the Oval Office. That means, finally, that no one would have the requisite stature — in legal jargon, "standing" — to hale the President into Court and force disclosure of what Burger termed "the decisionmaking process." The writ of the Supreme Court did run against a sitting President, but, as will be shown below, that is a principle that should not be carried very far. Senator Barry Goldwater's suit against President Carter on abrogation of the Taiwan treaties failed in 1979 on the grounds that it involved a "political question" and was not justiciable.[31] The Justices have numerous techniques for avoiding ruling on a case, and will likely find one of them should some other litigant try to penetrate the Oval Office.

Moreover, as the Grand Inquisitor and Charles de Gaulle, among others, have maintained, mystery—i.e., secrecy—may be necessary for prestige and power. As an organ of government with a legitimate political function to perform, the Supreme Court is not at all likely to dilute Presidential power in any substantial way. Professor J. A. G. Griffith has persuasively argued in *The Politics of the Judiciary* that the function of judges is to stabilize the existing order and to resist attempts markedly to change it.[32] Only when the political order is in turmoil, as in the 1952 *Steel* case, or perhaps in *extremis*, as in 1974, will the Justices enter the battle. During times of crisis, such as World War II, they have in the past come perilously close, as Professor Alpheus Mason put it, to becoming part of the "executive juggernaut."[33]

5. Whether documents are kept is basically a matter of Presidential provenience. No internal memo written and circulated within the White House need be retained. Presidents like to keep records, as the several Presidential libraries attest, but that seems to be more a matter of ego than of need. And certainly Nixon was under no compulsion to "bug" his office, or to keep the recordings (his promise to the Senate's Watergate Committee not to destroy them may have obligated him morally, but surely did not legally bind him; had he destroyed them, he would have suffered a major political loss). Records, furthermore, are kept for multiple purposes. After all, some continuity in government is desirable. And situations do arise when it is necessary to refer to records of what was done in the past.

The latter point has some dangers. By no means should one believe that any documentation, no matter how massive, can reveal the full account of what occurred at a given time and place. Successors in office know only what their predecessors wanted them to know. Records are simply not kept of some decisions. Nixon and his types aside, how likely is it that anything adverse to a President will appear in "his" documents? With paper shredders readily available, anything that reflects on a Chief Executive or his office will almost certainly find its way to the incinerator. In final analysis, it is impossible for historians to reconstruct, often long after the event, what actually took place in the past. Each generation writes its own history.

6. The President as President is amenable to judicial process. He is not above the law. In *Nixon-I*, the Supreme Court's writ ran against a sitting Chief Executive for the first time in history. Although it was not the first time a Federal court had held a President subject to a court order—in January 1974 the Court of Appeals in the District of Columbia did so on a personnel question in *National Treasury Employees Union* v. *Nixon*[34]—the Court put an effective quietus on the notion, bruited since *Mississippi* v. *Johnson*,[35] that something akin to a royal prerogative attaches to the Presidency.

For present purposes, the meaning is clear: it is the judiciary, and of it, the Supreme Court, that claims to have the last word on assertions of privilege. One may ask how the Court can enforce a ruling against the President; and, indeed, there is no way that coercion can be judicially applied. Under no circumstances would a recalcitrant President be held in contempt and transmitted to durance vile to purge his contumacy. Reliance is placed upon "our constitutional tradition [that] rightly relies," avers Archibald Cox, "upon the moral and political force of law."[36] Cox, however, assumes the answer by calling a Court decree "law." Were a Chief Executive to defy a court—as, for example, President Lincoln did after *Ex parte Merryman*[37] was decided—there is little that judges can do. (Chief Justice Taney's order in *Merryman*, on habeas corpus, remained unenforced—vivid testimony to judicial impotence.) Nixon capitulated because the political order—the imminence of impeachment—forced him to do so. He could not withstand the political force of a unanimous Supreme Court decision. (Only by equating morality with obedience to law, however promulgated, can *Nixon-I* be said to have a moral force, as Cox maintains.) The Supreme Court prevails when the *zeitgeist* is favorable to its rulings.

The larger meaning of *Nixon-I* is that it has paved the way for a number of lawsuits to be filed against the President *qua* President. Senator Barry Goldwater's 1979 action on President Carter's abrogation of the Taiwan treaties is only one example among a growing number. Congress—more precisely, individual members thereof—has begun to use the courts in efforts to bend the Executive to its will. This makes for more work for courts in areas clearly unsuited to general judicial action—exactly what the Court held in the *Goldwater* suit. When the political branches cannot agree, too much is asked of the Supreme Court to umpire those disputes. Questions of separation of powers are questions of political theory and cannot be answered by reference to the constitutional text. It will not do to say, with Archibald Cox, that the moral and political force of law will prevail, when he not only assumes that the decision is law, but also fails to acknowledge the obvious: that if it is law, it is newly created for the purpose of that very lawsuit. That means that Chief Justice Marshall's assertion in *Marbury's Case*, that it is "emphatically the province and duty of the judicial department to say what the law is," a statement repeated by Burger in *Nixon-I*, is a partial truth only. It is the "province" of the other branches to say what the law is, even to the extent of making decisions that are of constitutional dimension. The Supreme Court, furthermore, has no way of enforcing its decrees against either the President or Congress. The uneasy balance of the three departments does not permit "government by judiciary."

An appreciation of their impotence may be one of the reasons why judges, speaking generally, are reluctant to intrude into the thorny thickets of Executive privilege; or when they do, why they tend—as in the *Reynolds* case—to uphold the claims of the Executive. In final analysis, *Nixon-I* is a sport, an aberration noteworthy less for bringing Nixon to heel than for writing a notion of Presidential confidentiality into one of the silences of the Constitution. To the extent that the Presidential interest in confidentiality "relates to the effective discharge of a President's powers, it is constitutionally based," said Chief Justice Burger in a notable example of trying to create law out of the whole cloth. President Nixon's actions, furthermore, had the result of permitting the Court, in theory, to be the final arbiter of claims of privilege by his successors.

7. *Nixon-I* raises more questions than it answers. How much confidentiality does the President have? In what circumstances? What are those powers Burger mentioned when he called the privilege "constitutionally based"? Are they solely those of Article II? Do they include powers delegated by Congress? And, finally, what of the constitutional power of Congress to demand Presidential papers?

8. The latter question is the only one that has received judicial scrutiny. In *Senate Select Committee on Presidential Campaign Activities* v. *Nixon*, the Court of Appeals for the District of Columbia concluded that the Senate Watergate Committee's subpoena against Nixon would not be enforced, mainly because, on balance, the judges determined that the Committee had no need for the Nixon tapes. No appeal was taken to the Supreme Court.

The decision is far from definitive. By the time the court ruled, the House of Representatives was well down the road toward impeachment. Nixon's culpability was obvious to all save the willfully blind. Furthermore, one Senator on the Committee had blithely announced on nationwide television that the Committee really did not need the recordings, thus making it easy for the judges to rule against the Committee. It had not shown, said the court, that the desired data were "demonstrably critical to the responsible fulfillment of the Committee's functions" — a bit of judicial hocus-pocus that says judges are capable of telling Congress what data it needs and how it can act responsibly. That reasoning, if that it be, is as full of holes as a block of Swiss cheese.

What the Supreme Court will hold when and if another case involving a congressional subpoena of a sitting President reaches it is difficult to predict. Quite possibly, the Justices will flee into the swamp of political questions and tell the two branches to settle their own differences. *Nixon-I*, after all, involved allegations of criminality. The Supreme Court made only passing reference to state secrets or national security information. One need not be a clairvoyant to be able to predict that an argument of national security will probably prevail against even a congressional subpoena. That would not be true for a subordinate executive officer, unless that person is able to get the President to invoke the privilege in his own name. But for the subordinates, there are several other ways of evasion, most of which have been efficacious in the past.

9. Those other ways have been called a form of Executive privilege but, at this time, the term has become sufficiently precise to say that they do not fit within its ambit. One listing of other techniques includes the following: (a) invocation of Executive privilege by a subordinate. At times, a pusillanimous congressional committee or administrative law judge will allow the bureaucrat to prevail, thus lending some credence to Richard Kleindienst's assertion that the privilege extended throughout the Executive Branch. (b) At times White House officials claim that certain internal documents are insulated from congressional scrutiny by the separation of powers concept. (c) Finally, on numerous occasions executive officers have refused to testify or produce documents, citing various reasons not one of which is Executive privilege.

In none of the other ways has the question been litigated. An appropriate label is "congressional cowardice," or at least a marked reluctance to pursue lines of inquiry to their ultimate, the reasons for which may go beyond pusillanimity to a tacit recognition that pushing too far would deeply immerse Congress in the details of government. That, speaking generally, is precisely what the membership does *not* want. Should, however, Congress work up its courage and hale the executive officer into court, it is difficult to see why it should not prevail. (Not even a special statute giving jurisdiction to Federal courts is needed, as in the Senate Watergate's Committee's abortive lawsuit; initially the Committee was told that it did not show the requisite jurisdictional amount (that the controversy involved at least $10,000) for Federal court consideration, an obvious error by the learned Judge John Sirica.) The spirit of the Constitution, and perhaps the letter (see below), suggests that Congress should be able to win. Surely it involved a justiciable question (no one should be judge and jury in his own cause), although judges may want to retreat into the "political question" shelter. Assuming a court willing to participate, one may forecast with confidence that subordinate executive officers would be forced to comply with judicial decrees. That is so, even though it is probable that no high-level officer will be summoned before a court. The President, in all likelihood, would step in and invoke "his" privilege, which would then give judges another opportunity to make more law concerning the need for secrecy.

Ultimately, to be sure, Congress need not rely on the courts. If the judiciary proves to be too timid, Congress can punish contumacious witnesses itself. Since *Anderson* v. *Dunn*,[38] it has been recognized that either House can punish a person for contempt of its authority—a principle that got later approval in *McGrain* v. *Daugherty*[39] and *Marshall* v. *Goroon*.[40] *Jurney* v. *MacCracken*[41] was a direct holding to that effect. Recalcitrant witnesses may be imprisoned, but under *Anderson*, not beyond adjournment of the body that ordered it. Again, however, the possibility of such congressional action is remote at best.

No attempt has ever been made by the President to enjoin a congressional committee from inquiring into Executive actions. *Gravel* v. *United States*,[42] however, held a Senator and his aide immune under the Speech and Debate Clause of Article I from questioning by a grand jury concerning their investigations preparatory to a subcommittee hearing, except insofar as those acts were criminal or related to third-party crime. Although *Gravel* narrowed the Speech and Debate immunity, it merely is an admonition to Members of Congress to stick to their "legislative" duties, and thus is no precedent at all for halting an investigation. That conclusion draws ample support from *Eastland* v. *United States Servicemen's Fund*,[43] in which the Supreme Court held that Federal courts cannot bar an ongoing congressional investigation. True, that involved a private litigant, not the Executive Branch; but there is nothing in the amorphous contours of the separation of powers "doctrine" that would suggest a contrary result.

It is of some interest to iterate that judicial action is, speaking generally, a one-way street. Members of Congress can, as individuals and as Members (and, presumable therefore, Congress itself), bring suit and, not only get the courts to accept jurisdiction, they can prevail. There is little Supreme Court precedent on the matter, other that Senator Goldwater's suit dismissed because it was a political question, or *Kennedy* v. *Sampson*[44] (a court of appeals ruling on the validity of a pocket veto) and *Na-*

der v. *Bork*[45] (a district court's decision on the improper discharge of Special Prosecutor Archibald Cox; Nader was dismissed for lack of standing, but co-plaintiffs, Members of Congress, were not). Of course the Senate Watergate Committee lost, as has been said, in its litigation on Executive privilege, but that decision emphatically does not mean that in a subsequent suit, particularly if it were to be better prepared and argued by counsel for Congress, the court would hold against Congress, even for a sitting President.

9. That leads to the question of whether Congress could, by statute, enter the field and impose definite limits on the exercise of the privilege by either the President or his subordinates. As for the latter, since all of the bureaucracy, except the President and Vice-President, are creatures of Congress, surely Congress can condition its powers to make failure to testify or produce documents a punishable offense. The question is more difficult for the Chief Executive, not only for himself but when he seeks to cast his mantle of constitutionally protected immunity over subordinate officers.

Such a statute was once proposed by Senator Sam Ervin, but it remained in committee. The Mutual Security Act of 1959 (73 Stat. 246) had a provision that records were to be available to Congress; but no court test was ever made. President Eisenhower, furthermore, expressed his discontent over the proviso, even though he signed the bill into law. Whether congress can enact a valid statute controlling the use of Executive privilege remains an unanswered constitutional question. The arguments pro and con are reduced to the President maintaining that the term "the executive power" in Article II has some undefined content that insulates not only the President, but his subordinates, from Congress (once Congress has delegated power to the other end of the avenue); and Congress asserting that Article I's elastic clause (see below) is express constitutional warrant for such a statute. These arguments have been posed in testimony before Congress and also may be found in litigation, not yet definitive, over the validity of the congressional veto and the provision in the Impoundment Control Act of 1974 (88 Stat. 332) giving the Comptroller General authority to challenge failures to spend appropriated funds.

In final analysis the decision, when and if made by the Supreme Court, would seem to turn on what effect the Justices would give the plain meaning of Article I, Section 8, Clause 18 (the elastic clause): "The Congress shall have power . . . to make all laws which shall be necessary and proper for carrying into execution the foregoing powers [in Article I, Section 8] and *all other powers vested by this Constitution in the government of the United States, or in any department or officer* thereof." (Emphasis added.) Does that clause have a horizontal effect? We have known since *McCulloch's Case*[46] that it has a vertical dimension (Congress has implied as well as express powers). Its horizontal effect is unknown, although a few Supreme Court decisions point in the direction of validating congressional power. For example, Congress can control the jurisdiction of the Federal courts, and can create legislative courts to help carry out legislative functions. In the wake of the Teapot Dome scandal, Congress, by Joint Resolution, directed the President to bring suit to cancel certain oil leases allegedly obtained by fraud. Furthermore, if the War Powers Resolution of 1973 (87 Stat. 555) is valid, it must be based either on an implication from the power to declare war or the horizontal application of the elastic clause, or both.

Whether that bit of judicial and legislative history would be sufficient to uphold a statute is problematical. Professor Charles Black apparently thinks that it does: "The powers of Congress," he said in 1974, "are adequate to the control of every national interest of any importance, including all of those which the President might, by piling inference on inference, be thought to be entrusted."[47] Would, however, the language in *Nixon-I* about a quantum of Presidential confidentiality override the plain language of the elastic clause? That answer will likely come not from the courts but from the play of political processes. (It should also be remembered that the Court in *United States* v. *Richardson*[48] in effect ignored the plain language of Article I, section 9, clause 7, about the need of a public accounting of receipts and expenditures (a taxpayer was denied standing to require public accounting of CIA funds).)

10. Finally, Executive privilege protects the communication, not the communicator. It is thus akin to the common-law

privileges of doctor-patient, lawyer-client, etc., and to the constitutional privilege against self-incrimination. It differs from the "informer's" privilege and the nascent "newsman's" privilege to protect his sources (the communicator). See, however *Branzburg* v. *Hayes*,[49] holding to the contrary.

III.

A final question remains: Is the use of Executive privilege desirable in a nation that calls itself a democracy? Does it serve a useful *public* purpose? However advantageous it may be for Presidents, it must be shown to have a larger function — the protection of that nebulous concept called "the public (or national) interest." Answers to those questions will require much more study and analysis than has been forthcoming. Legal and other scholars have mainly contented themselves with parsing judicial opinions. They have not inquired into the sociology and psychology of decisionmaking. Chief Justice Burger's confident *ipse dixit* about "human experience" is of the same stripe as his assertion in the *Pentagon Papers Case* about an inherent power of courts to enforce secrecy. (He now has, with publication of *The Brethren*, a perfect opportunity to test that observation.)

How open should government be? The question applies to all three branches, not merely to the Executive. Ideally, perhaps there should be no disagreement with the Supreme Court's statement in *Watkins* v. *United States*.[50]

"The public is, of course, entitled to be informed about the workings of its government." In their brief submitted to the court of appeals in *Nixon* v. *Sirica*, the contrary argument came from Nixon's lawyers in 1973: "The right of presidential confidentiality is not a mystical prerogative. It is, rather, the raw essence of the presidential process, the institutionalized recognition of the crucial role played by human personality in the negotiation, *manipulation*, and disposition of human affairs." (Emphasis added.)

One can believe that governmental openness is desirable (functional) and still assert that some secrecy is needed. If that be so, then the problem is one of drawing lines through the application of appropriate criteria. Those criteria do not presently exist. Suggested above is that Congress could take the initiative for the employment of Executive privilege. We should not expect that to be done. Perhaps, because of a tacit recognition that this is the age of executive government (throughout the world) or perhaps because of innate pusillanimity, neither Congress nor the courts have displayed any willingness to challenge the President's secrecy syndrome. Executive privilege is now, and will remain, a political maneuver, an instrument of policy, and a means by which those with knowledge will remain in control of the levers of power in government. In sum, the President is privileged when he can get away with it politically. Presidents, from Washington in 1796, to the present, have been doing so.

CHAPTER FOUR

The President and National Security Information*

MORTON H. HALPERIN

The year 1974 marked a fundamental turning point in the history of the President's power, under the Constitution, to withhold information relating to national defense and foreign relations from Congress, the public, and the courts.

Prior to that time, the President appears to have had unfettered power to decide what information should be released outside the Executive Branch. The Supreme Court had held in *United States* v. *Reynolds* that it was the court's duty to determine whether the state secrets privilege had been properly evoked.[1] Nevertheless, the Court indicated that the assertions of the Executive Branch as to injury would be given very substantial weight and there are no cases on record in which the Executive Branch was ordered to disclose national security information in civil litigation. In criminal cases, the situation was and remains clear—the Government may not withhold information relating to national security which is otherwise relevant and admissible and still continue with the trial. But it is the Government that retains the choice—it may either release the information and have the trial go forward or it may drop the prosecution.[2]

The enactment of the Freedom of Information Act in 1966 (80 Stat. 250), while bringing about a revolution in many aspects of control of Executive Branch information, had almost no impact on national defense and foreign relations. Congress, in enacting the statute, paid almost no attention to foreign relations or national defense and took the position, as was stated in the House report on the legislation, that "citizens both in and out of Government can agree to restrictions on categories of in-

* The author wishes to thank New Republic Books for permission to quote from *Top Secret: National Security and the Right to Know.*

formation which the President has determined must be kept secret to protect the national defense or to advance foreign policy such as matters classified pursuant to Executive Order 10501."[3] For the first time, Congress linked access to information by the public under the Freedom of Information Act to the Executive Branch classification system established under a succession of Presidential orders and concerned primarily with the appropriate storage and dissemination of information rather than with the standards and procedures for classifying that information.

In interpreting the meaning of this first exemption to the Freedom of Information Act, the Supreme Court, in *EPA* v. *Mink*, held that Congress had built into the first exemption "no means to question any Executive decision to stamp a document 'secret' however cynical, myopic, or even corrupt that decision might have been."[4] Thus, it held that the Government need only show that the information was in a document that had been stamped "Confidential" or higher by some Executive Branch official and the entire file in which that document rested was exempt from review or disclosure under the Freedom of Information Act.

However, what was acceptable in 1966 when Congress passed the Act, and even perhaps in 1973, when the *Mink* decision came down, was no longer acceptable a year later. In the intervening period, Congress had held a number of hearings on the Freedom of Information Act.[5] The release of the Pentagon Papers, the growing disenchantment with the Vietnam war, and the Watergate debacle all created pressure for congressional enactment of an amendment to the Freedom of Information Act (88 Stat. 1561) to require for national security information the same kind of court review applied to other files which the Government sought to keep secret.

In debating this issue, Congress did not take up the invitation stated in the *Mink* decision to establish its own standard for the release of classified information; rather, it continued to rely on the Executive order on classification issued by the President. Congress provided that the courts would make their own determinations as to whether or not information was properly classified under the order. In doing so, the courts would be free to inspect the documents secretly while at the same time they would be obliged to give significant weight to the expert opinions of Executive Branch officials stated in affidavits submitted to the court both on an adversary basis and secretly.

President Ford, coming into office shortly after both Houses had passed separate F.O.I. Act amendments, wrote a letter to the conferees considering the proposals, threatening a veto and alleging that review of classification decisions by the courts, to determine if they were properly made, was unconstitutional. After both Houses of Congress agreed to the conference report and enacted the bill, the President did, in fact, veto it, but the veto was overridden and the Act came into effect in 1975.

The Government sought in the courts to win the battle that it had failed to win in Congress, arguing that the courts should simply determine if a decision of the Executive Branch was "reasonable" and if the document and the information appear to fall within the category of properly classified information. After some skirmishing, the D.C. Court of Appeals appears to have definitively established that national security information is now to be treated as all other information, with the courts free to make secret inspections of the document and to make their own *in camera* determination of whether information is to be released. The sole differences are that the court is to give significant weight to Government affidavits and it is to permit *in camera* inspection of documents and the submission of affidavits on an *ex parte* basis after a full public hearing.[6]

Thus, when President Carter issued a new Executive order in 1978 he, in effect, amended the Freedom of Information Act as it relates to national defense and national security information.[7]

To withhold records, the Government must now meet the new standard for "Confidential" which requires that information, if released, would do "identifiable" damage to the national security. Information also must be within one of seven specified categories to be so protected and there must be no reasonable doubt as to whether it is properly classified. None of these changes is very substantial and they are not likely to effect, in any significant way, either the judicial interpretation of the Freedom of Information Act or the willingness of courts to order the release of national defense or foreign relations information. However, one addition to the Executive order could make a significant difference. It requires that, in declassification decisions, the public value of the information, as well as the possible injury to national security, be taken into account. The remainder of this commentary is devoted to a discussion of the so-called balancing test and its possible implications.[8]

Balancing Needs

Perhaps the most important provision in the new Executive order on classification is the provision in section 3 which requires in certain circumstances the application of a "balancing test" in determining whether classified information can be released.[9]

It is presumed that information which continues to meet the classification requirements in Section 1-3 requires continued protection. In some cases, however, the need to protect such information may be outweighed by the public interest in disclosure of the information, and in these cases the information should be declassified. When such questions arise, they shall be referred to the agency head, a senior agency official with responsibility for processing Freedom of Information Act requests or Mandatory Review requests under this Order, an official with Top Secret classification authority, or the Archivist of the United States in the case of material covered in Section 3-503. That official will determine whether the public interest in disclosure outweighs the damage to national security that might reasonably be expected from disclosure.[10]

Since, under the terms of the Freedom of Information Act, national security information can only be withheld if it meets the substantive and procedural criteria of the Executive order, this change in the procedures and criteria of the order constitutes, in effect, an amendment to the Freedom of Information Act.[11]

A number of questions are raised by this provision and its application under the Freedom of Information Act, including the following:

1. Under what factual circumstances affecting the information requested should the balancing test be applied?

2. Procedurally, how does the issue "arise"? Who decides

whether the issue has, in fact, been raised? Can someone in the public requesting documents raise the issue?

3. Is the decision to balance or not to balance subject to review by the courts under the Freedom of Information Act?

4. Can the court review a decision by the Executive Branch that the balancing test does not require release of the information and if so, under what standards?

Before turning to these questions, let us consider a brief "legislative history" of the balancing test as it now appears in the Executive order.

Development of the Balancing Test

As far as I am aware, the first reference to the possibility of a balancing test on classification came in a book which I authored with Daniel Hoffman, *Top Secret*.[12] In that book we proposed a number of changes in the classification system, including a proposal for requiring the automatic release of certain categories of information.[13] We describe the need for the balancing test as follows:

. . . For a few narrow categories of information, mostly technical, public disclosure does not appear useful for policy debate. It could, however, be expected to give substantial assistance to potential adversaries. Such information, though it should be available to Congress on a secret basis, is entitled to a heavy presumption against public disclosure. Specifically, we refer to (a) weapons systems: details of advanced system design and operational characteristics; (b) details of plans for military operations; (c) details of ongoing diplomatic negotiations; and (d) intelligence methods: codes, technology, and identity of spies.

Information not in these clear-cut categories should be made public unless a reasoned judgment is made that the probable costs to national security clearly outweigh the value of the information for public debate; and that judgment should be subject to independent review.

. . . These efforts to specify categories of information that must be released and those that should be kept secret do not pretend to cover entirely the field of national security information. Much information will fall, properly so, into a middle category requiring case-by-case judgment. In such cases, the balancing of the value of disclosure to the public, as against the possible harm to the defense or foreign policy of the United States, is left initially to the classifying official. Weighing these factors should proceed on the principle that release is required unless one can reasonably judge that the probable costs to national security clearly outweigh the value of the information for public debate.

. . . To justify the existence of a middle category should not require extended discussion. While we have argued at length against the system of unlimited official discretion, we do not believe that such discretion can or should be entirely eliminated. The legal designation of mandatory disclosure and presumptive secrecy categories is an appropriate way of dealing with a few specific kinds of information. Those are cases where the balance between the values of secrecy and disclosure can meaningfully be determined in advance, without reference to particular circumstances. However, the attempt to assign all national security information to one or the other of these categories would be extremely unrealistic and counterproductive. In most cases, a rational decision will require a sensitive weighing of the requirements of national security and of public debate in the particular situation. The initial decision must be left to responsible officials of the executive branch. Yet careful provision for the guidance of those officials is obviously essential.

In the past the executive branch has not been accustomed to taking responsibility for the interest in public debate. That interest has not been central to the political environment in which the national security bureaucracy operates; nor has it been emphasized by the formal rules that apply to secrecy decisions. The executive order on classification does not instruct officials to balance the need for publicity against the need for secrecy; rather, their task is simply to determine whether secrecy would serve the broadly defined national security interest. In practice, it appears that public debate has been regarded as inherently prejudicial to the national security, and that documents have consciously been classified, under color of law, for the express purpose of preventing public debate. . . .[14]

Congress has expressed its support for a balancing test provision in creating the Senate and House Intelligence Committees. The procedures for congressional disclosure of information, contained in the resolutions establishing those committees, provide that if the President objects to the release of information which the committee wishes to make public, he must certify that the injury which would result from release outweighs the public value of the information. That provision reads as follows:

(2) The committee may disclose publicly such information after the expiration of a five-day period following the day on which notice of such vote is transmitted to the President, unless, prior to the expiration of such five-day period, the President notifies the committee that he objects to the disclosure of such information, provides his reasons therefor, and certifies that the threat to the national interest of the United States posed by such disclosure is vital and outweighs any public interest in the disclosure.[15]

The process of revising the Executive order on classification began with the issuance, by President Carter, of a Presidential Review Memorandum calling for a revision to substantially reduce the amount of secrecy because of the public's right to know.[16]

In the deliberations following the issuance of the P.R.M., the proposal for a balancing test was introduced but apparently not accepted at the working level.[17] Subsequently, at a meeting of the Cabinet-level committee which considered the new draft Executive order — the Security Coordinating Committee — a decision, in principle, was made to add some kind of a balancing test to require that the public value of the information be taken into account in a decision as to whether or not information could be released. However, the draft Executive order, which subsequently was released for comment, did not contain a clear provision calling for a balancing test.[18]

In response to the release of the Executive order for comment, a group of public interest organizations joined in a letter urging a number of changes in the Executive order, including the addition of a provision calling for a balancing test. That portion of the letter reads as follows:

. . . 3. require that in all cases officials always weigh the value and importance of the information to the public (or a member of the public) against the possible risks of disclosure; . . .

. . . 4. *Balance the Public's Right to Know.* The public's right to know will often outweigh any "significant damage" to national security that might occur if information is disclosed. If we interpret the draft Order's statement of intent correctly, it is the position of the Administration that in such cases the information must be disclosed. To implement this policy a balancing test should be applied by those authorized to classify documents.

We strongly urge such a test. We recommend that a third section (3) be added to Section 2 (a) to provide the following:

(3) the damage to national security posed by the disclosure of the information is of such gravity that it outweighs any public interest in the disclosure.

We note that this test has been adopted by both the House and Senate Intelligence Committees to guide their decisions to make public classified information.[19]

Subsequently, a decision was made to include a balancing test. However, it was to be limited to declassification review and only to some circumstances. The new Executive order itself left open what those circumstances would be and how the issue of a balancing test would arise.

In the statement by President Carter accompanying the release of the Executive order, no specific reference was made to the balancing provision, although the statement did emphasize that "the public is entitled to know as much as possible about the government's activities" and that "the government classifies too much information, classifies it too highly and for too long. These practices violate the public right to know. . . ."[20]

The implementing directive issued by the new Information Security Oversight Office, created by the order, did not provide any further guidance as to the meaning of the balancing test provision, stating only that in making the test the agency should respect the desire of foreign governments to continue to protect information obtained from them or from foreign sources.[21]

Subsequent inquiries from agencies as to the meaning of the balancing test led to a letter from the President's Assistant for National Security Affairs, Dr. Zbigniew Brzezinski, to Dr. James Rhoads who was then the Chairman of the Interagency Classification Review Committee. That letter reads as follows:

This is in response to your letter of November 28, in which you request my views on the implementation of the balancing test in section 3–303 of Executive Order 12065.

The purpose of the balancing test provision is to permit the declassification of properly classified information in those exceptional cases where the public interest in protection of such information is outweighed by the public interest in its disclosure. The Order recognizes that cases meeting the criterion of section 3-303 will be rare, and that information considered for declassification that continues to meet the classification requirements of section 1-3 despite the passage of time must, in most cases, remain classified.

This provision is not intended to modify the substantive criteria or procedures for classification; rather, it reflects this Administration's policy that properly classified information nevertheless may be classified under some circumstances. It is for these reasons that the provision was included in section 3-3 on declassification policy rather than in section 1, which details the relevant classification criteria.

The Order does not establish a particular procedure to be followed in those exceptional cases where section 3-303 might apply. Instead, it provides that when questions arise, a senior agency official will make the determination whether the public interest in disclosure outweighs the damage to the national security, and, hence, to the public interest, that might reasonably be expected to result from disclosure. Each agency should establish its own procedures to ensure that individuals making declassification decisions identify those cases that should be referred to senior agency officials designated to make the discretionary determinations under section 3-303.[22]

As of this writing, the only agency that has published specific regulations implementing the balancing test is the Central Intelligence Agency. Those regulations state the following:

c. In some cases the public interest may warrant declassification of information notwithstanding the national security damage reasonably expected to result from its disclosure, although continued protection from such disclosure of properly classified information is normally not only consistent with the public interest but required thereby. The need to balance such conflicting interests thus exists only when the public interest in disclosure appears so compelling as to outweigh the national security interest in continued protection. For example, it might be in the public interest to disclose classified information during a trial to ensure that a criminal is brought to justice or that the rights of a defendent are protected; such information might also be disclosed if the failure to do so could endanger the public health, safety, or welfare. However, general assertions of public interest raised by one person purporting to act on the public's behalf will not automatically result in further review under this provision, and weighing the public interest need not be conducted merely because a requester demands it.

d. When it appears that the public interest in disclosure of an item of information being reviewed for declassification may outweigh any continuing need for its protection, the case shall be referred for decision:

(1) To an official having Top Secret classification authority who shall refer it to the appropriate Deputy Director or Head of Independent Office with appropriate recommendations.

(2) The Deputy Director or Head of Independent Office concerned, in coordination with OGC, as appropriate, shall refer the matter and their recommendations to the DDCI for a determination as to whether the public interest in disclosure of the information in question outweighs any damage to national security that might reasonably be expected from such disclosure.[23]

In court cases in which the issue of a balancing test has been raised, the Justice Department, on behalf of the CIA, has taken the position that the decision whether or not to balance rests within the exclusive jurisdiction of the agencies and that the agency need not balance unless one of the specific categories cited in its regulations in fact applies.[24]

The Meaning of the Balancing Test

The first issue raised by the balancing test is the factual circumstances under which the balancing test should come into play. In approaching that problem, it is important to begin with the fact that neither the Freedom of Information Act nor the Executive order on classification requires that any information be withheld. The Freedom of Information Act allows withholding under certain conditions and the Executive order establishes criteria for situations when information can be withheld and must be stored so as not to be disclosed in an unauthorized manner.

In fact, senior officials of the government in practice constantly make decisions to disclose information which fit the criteria for classification in that its release could reasonably be expected to cause damage to the national security. They do so because of the belief that public debate on the issue involved will more likely support their position if the information is made public.[25]

Thus, the purpose of the provision in the new Executive order must be to require the balancing test to be conducted in those "rare" situations in which there is strong public value attached to the information. The kind of situations designated in the CIA directive quoted above do not appear to be those contemplated by the provisions of the Executive order. For example, in a situation in which failure to release information could reasonably be expected to place a person's life in jeopardy, information obviously would be released even if its release could reasonably be expected to cause some damage to the national security. The balancing test provision was not required for that purpose.

The kind of situations in which a balancing test would appear to be in order are ones in which there is strong public interest and congressional debate on an issue and in which the information being withheld would play an important role in determining the outcome of the public debate. For example, information which related to the ability of the United States to verify the SALT agreement or to Soviet compliance with the provisions of SALT I would appear to fit the categories in which a balancing would be required under the Executive order. To take another example, if there was information in the possession of the Government which cast a different light on the Middle East peace agreement than that presented to the public, that information would also require balancing before it was withheld.

A decision to balance does not mean that the information must be declassified, but simply that the public's right to the information must be taken into account along with the injury to national security which might result from release before a decision was made not to declassify the information.

The second question relating to the balancing test is how the issued is to be raised. The Executive order is ambiguous, suggesting simply what should happen when the issue does arise. The Justice Department, thus far, has taken the position in litigation that the decision whether or not to balance is an administrative decision to be taken by the Government on its own initiative and not subject to judicial review.

Obviously the Government is always free to consider the public value of the information and to release information which has previously been classified. In response to a request under the Freedom of Information Act, it is also free to release information which is properly classified and, hence, which could be withheld under the first exemption. Indeed, the Attorney General's memorandum directing Government agencies to take account of the public interest would appear to require that, in all cases, the public value of the information be considered before a decision is made under the Freedom of Information Act to withhold documents.[26]

The spirit and intent of the balancing provision of the Executive order would appear to require that balancing be engaged in by a senior official whenever a person requesting a document under the Freedom of Information Act makes a reasoned presentation of evidence which suggests that there is strong public interest in the release of the information. This evidence might consist of a discussion of public interest in the topic of the request and the importance of the information sought for shaping an opinion of the issue currently being debated in the public arena. Upon the presentation of such evidence, the Executive Branch ought to be required to engage in balancing since a decision to balance is not a decision to release, but simply a decision to take account of the public value of the information and to test that against the injury to national security which would result from release of the information.

A third question is whether or not the decision to balance or not to balance is subject to judicial review. Since it is well-settled that, in order to withhold information under the first exemption of the Freedom of Information Act, the Government must comply with the procedures as well as the substantive criteria of the Executive order and that the court can and will determine for itself whether the procedures have been followed, there does not appear to be any question that there can be judicial review of a determination that a balance is not required.[27] The court determining whether or not a balance was in order will have to make its own judgement about the meaning and intent of the paragraph in the Executive order in light of the kind of "legislative history" presented here.

Finally, there is the question of whether the court can engage in its own balancing. Given that the court must make a *de novo* determination of whether information is properly withheld under the first exemption,[28] the court will, once it determines that balancing is appropriate, need to make its own determination. This will mean that the court will need to consider evidence not only about the injury to national security which might result from the release of the information, but also about the public value of the information.

The Government seems determined to prevent the courts from engaging in its own balancing by arguing that the decision to balance and the balance itself is not subject to judicial review. However, the Freedom of Information Act seems to require such judicial review and the Executive order does not appear to have been written with any intent upon the part of the President to seek to avoid it.

CHAPTER FIVE

The Evolution and Value of Presidential Libraries*

LARRY BERMAN

I am sure the historians will protest, but I think historians cannot complain if evidence for history is not perpetuated which shouldn't have been created in the first place.

Philip Buchen
Counsel to President Ford[1]

The primary function of the (Presidential) libraries is to preserve the valuable historical papers of the President and his associates and to make them available for research purposes. . . As long as valuable historical materials are being created, and as long as this country looks to the past for guidance for the future and feels that history is important, it seems to me that it is incumbent on us to preserve those materials which truly do have research value.

James Rhoads
former archivist of the United States
National Archives and Record Service[2]

The recent evolution of Presidential libraries is best understood within the context of several historically controversial questions. The first involves public vs. private ownership of Presidential papers. Moreover, only seven of our thirty-nine Presidents even have libraries, (with an eighth scheduled for 1981 opening)[3] and none of these Presidents was legally bound to deposit his papers in such a library. This question of ownership was only recently resolved by the Presidential Records Act of 1978 (92 Stat. 2523), effective January 1, 1981, under which "The United States shall reserve and retain complete ownership, possession, and control of Presidential records."[4] The Presidential Records Act ended a long and unfortunate tradition which resulted in the deliberate or accidental destruction of valuable historical materials. The second question for in-

* The author wishes to thank Lisa Sumner for her research assistance in support of this essay.

quiry concerns the circumstances which led President Roosevelt in 1938 to propose "for the first time in this country what might be called a source material collection relating to a specific period in history."[5] Third, how successfully has the decentralized Presidential library system evolved as a research laboratory for historians and political scientists? Fourth, what types of questions might students of the Presidency investigate while utilizing this valuable primary source information? Finally, is there a future for Presidential libraries as we now know them?

Where Have All the Papers Gone?

First, the question of ownership. When George Washington retired to Mount Vernon in 1797, he had no Presidential library in which to deposit his papers. Washington soon decided to take all personal and official papers with him, establishing the precedent that a President's papers are personal and not public property (Washington did leave his successor, John Adams, some official documents relating to pending administrative and policy matters).[6] At the time, Washington's decision was probably a wise one. Philadelphia, the nation's capital, provided no adequate storage facilities, whereas Mount Vernon guaranteed a relatively safe and supervised environment. Washington even contemplated building some type of facility on his estate to safeguard the documents, but the former President's death in 1799 preempted such plans. In his will, Washington provided that his nephew, Associate Supreme Court Justice Bushrod Washington, should receive "all the papers in my possession, which related to my civil and military administration of the affairs of this country . . . (and) also, such of my private papers as are worth preserving."[7] Unfortunately, Bushrod Washington utilized little discretion ("hazardous generosity"[8] as one observer put it) in limiting access to his uncle's papers. Lester Cappon noted that the young Washington's "open-handed attitude in fulfilling requests for manuscript souvineers compromised the archival integrity of the papers."[9] For example, Supreme Court Justice John Marshall was allowed to utilize the original papers while writing his *Life of George Washington* (1804–1807).[10] When Jared Sparks, editor of the *North American Review* later requested permission to visit Mount Vernon in order to prepare *The Writings of George Washington*,[11] Washington's nephew not only provided three weeks hospitality, but allowed the Boston editor to take eight boxes of Washington's personal papers back to Massachusetts—six boxes shipped from Alexandria to Boston, and two of the most important carried personally by Sparks over land—where they remained in Sparks possession for the next ten years. "Thus," J. Frank Cook wrote, "more of the public's heritage ended up in private hands."[12] Following Bushrod Washington's death in 1829, nephew and heir George Corbin Washington sold the President's official records to the Government in 1834 for $25,000 and fifteen years later completed the transaction by selling Washington's private papers to Congress for $20,000.

Today, largely due to the efforts of the State Department, the Library of Congress, and congressional appropriations, 95% of George Washington's papers are housed in the Library of Congress. Nevertheless, Washington's decision to claim his papers as personal property, and later to bequeath this material to his heirs, created insurmountable obstacles in assembling and preserving historical records. At one time, for example, the papers of Thomas Jefferson were located in the Library of Congress, the Massachusetts Historical Society, the Historical Society of Pennsylvania, the Buffalo Historical Society, the American Philosophical Society, the Missouri Historical Society, the Pierpont Morgan Library, the Yale University Library, and the Virginia State Library.[13] One hundred separate purchases were needed to buy the scattered papers of Andrew Jackson. Moreover, at least the preceding examples are one's in which the historical record remained relatively intact. Such was not the case for several of our Presidents. William Henry Harrison's papers were burned accidently when fire destroyed the Harrison homestead at North Bend, Ohio. President John Tyler's papers also were destroyed by fire during the burning of Richmond in 1865. President Fillmore's son directed the executor's of his will "at the earliest practicable moment . . . (to) burn or otherwise effectively destroy all correspondence or letters to or from my father, mother, sister or me."[14] Fortunately, these instructions were never carried out and the personal papers later were discovered in the attic of a home in Buffalo, New York, and today are part of the Buffalo Historical Society collection. President Franklin Pierce and Ulysses S. Grant willfully destroyed parts of their personal papers, and Mrs. Warren Harding admitted destroying virtually all of the President's private correspondence. President Lincoln's son, Robert, was caught by Mary Butler in the very process of destroying his fathers' Civil War correspondence. Even President Truman, while personally presiding over the construction of the Harry S Truman Library, excluded his most important papers until the completion of his memoirs. The President's daughter, Margaret Truman, utilized such hitherto unavailable records while writing her own memoirs of life with father.[15]

Moreover, the history of Presidential papers has most often depended on the whims of Presidents or their heirs. This is well illustrated by President Grover Cleveland's 1886 response to a Senate request for an executive file: "I regard the papers and documents withheld and addressed to me or intended for my personal use and action purely unofficial and private, not infrequently confidential, and having reference to the performance of a duty exclusively mine. . . . I suppose if I desired to take them into my custody I might do so with entire propriety, and if I saw fit to destroy them no one could complain"[16] (The 1974 Nixon-Sampson agreement, discussed later, echoed these sentiments).

The Evolution of Presidential Libraries

Today, the papers of Presidents Washington through Coolidge are located in the Manuscript Division of the Library of Congress. This occurred under the active leadership of Herbert Putnam, Librarian of Congress (1899–1939), under whose direction custody of all Presidential papers was transferred from the State Department's Bureau of Rolls and Library to the Library of Congress (the National Archives was not established until 1934). "It is remarkable," Lester Cappon noted, "that of the twenty-nine Presidents before Herbert Hoover, the corpus of papers of each that is extant has been preserved in a research library, four-fifths of them are in the Library of Congress."[17] While such arrangements were certainly satisfactory, it soon became evident to President Roosevelt that the sheer mass of documentation from his Presidency would overwhelm the existing archival resources. Therefore, on December 12, 1938, President Roosevelt sent a "personal and confidential" memorandum to a distinguished group of fifteen historians inviting them to the White House in order to discuss plans for the disposition of Roosevelt's Presidential papers.[18]

Roosevelt was both a serious student of history and pragmatic enough to realize that if historians were to utilize his official papers, some degree of advance organizational planning would be required. During the luncheon, Roosevelt told his guests that he wanted to establish a permanent structure to house and protect the records of his Presidency.[19] At a press conference following the luncheon, Roosevelt disclosed publicly the concept of a Presidential library, "one of the most important and promising developments in all archival history."[20] The Franklin D. Roosevelt Library soon was established as part of the National Archives by a joint resolution of Congress in 1939 (53 Stat. 1062) and later became the first of the Presidential libraries authorized by the 1955 Presidential Libraries Act (69 Stat. 695). On July 4, 1940, Roosevelt deeded sixteen acres of his family's estate in Hyde Park, New York, for the planned library and museum.[21] Within several months, a small group of supporters quietly solicited private funds for construction of the facilities. The museum opened to visitors on June 30, 1941, and research activities started on May 1, 1946.[22]

While Roosevelt was singularly responsible for the precedent setting decision to build a library for his Presidential materials, the President did not differ from George Washington on the question of ownership. These were Roosevelt's papers — given as a gift to the United States. H.G. Jones, writing in his seminal work, *Records of a Nation*, observed that "Roosevelt made his most significant departure . . . by recognizing the paramount right of the public and by subordinating this claim to public custody, support, and management under the direction of civil servants governed by professional standards. This . . . fell short of the natural and logical goal. But it was a long, unprecedented step forward that no president thenceforth would be likely to disregard."[23]

There remained however, a need to institutionalize the process of building and maintaining libraries for the future. Presidents Truman and Eisenhower both followed FDR's procedures and, in 1955, the Presidential Libraries Act provided the legal basis for accepting Presidential papers and maintaining Presidential libraries.[24] The legislation covered only the acceptance of papers and maintenance of facilities, not ownership (to the extent that *anyone* other than the President had a legitimate claim to the papers). The 1955 legislation never addressed the problem of what a President *must* do with his papers. "Because of this omission, the entire system is a house of cards whose existence is dependent on the goodwill of individual presidents."[25] The 1955 Act brought all libraries into the National Archives system and guaranteed professional care for Presidential materials. The libraries would be built with private, not public, dollars and *allowed* the President to leave (voluntarily) his documents with the Archivist of the United States, setting whatever restrictions deemed appropriate. The President really got the best of this deal: the National Archives and National Park Service would maintain the library, museum, and grounds; and professionally trained archivists would care for his papers. During testimony for the 1955 legislation, Dr. Wayne Grover, Archivist of the United States, estimated that the cost of such operations would be about $150,000 annually per library. The cost today is roughly $500,000.[26] (Another important debate during the 1955 session involved the question of centralized or decentralized libraries—perhaps the major issue of today).

The question of ownership reached a head immediately following the Nixon Administration and centered around the disposition of Watergate materials. As J. Frank Cook observed, "what was an unsatisfactory arrangement in George Washington's day (had) . . . become a threat to the very function of a democratic government."[27] In September, 1974, former President Nixon and Arthur Sampson, Administrator of General Services, signed an agreement which allowed Nixon legal title and literary property rights to all papers and files from his administration.[28] "Sampson, neither a historian nor an archivist, administers the National Archives as a subordinate agency. By the terms of this agreement Nixon could begin to destroy the tape recordings on or after September 1, 1979, so that all of them would be destroyed by September 1, 1984, or following the death of the former President, whichever occurred first."[29] In a time of general public suspicion of executive secrecy, the Nixon-Sampson agreement gave Nixon possession of 42 million documents and materials relating to his Presidency—including the infamous tapes. "The United States gained from the agreement only the restricted use of the material for a few years and the promise of eventual donation of those portions of the papers so designated by Nixon. Nixon, rather than the National Archives, would determine the historical record to be preserved of the administration of the 37th President of the United States."[30]

Most political observers are well aware of the controversy surrounding the Nixon-Sampson agreement. While this negotiated settlement had all the tones of another cover-up, it also served to raise public awareness on the issue of "ownership"—facilitated, in part, by the media's seizing on the issue.

The controversy subsided with the passage of the Presidential Recordings and Materials Preservation Act of 1974 (88 Stat. 1695), signed by President Ford on November 11, 1974.[31] The legislation nullified the Nixon-Sampson agreement;[32] required former President Nixon to assure complete access of the public to documents from his Presidency; and established the National Study Commission on Records and Documents of Federal Officials to explore the question of control, ownership, disposition and preservation of historical materials. Following several delays, the Commission submitted its report on March 31, 1977. Lester Cappon summarized this report in writing that "the commission recommended that all documentary materials made or received by public officials in discharge of their official duties should be recognized as the property of the United States; and that officials be given the prerogative to control access to the materials for up to fifteen years after the end of their federal service."[33] Based upon those recommendations, President Carter signed the Presidential Records Act of 1978, effective January 20, 1981. The law finally settled the legal question of ownership—the public, not the President, had legal right of access and ownership of all official Presidential records. The law left great leeway, however, in deciding just what constituted personal rather than official documentation.[34]

The Value of Presidential Libraries

Researchers will notice a great deal of variation in the six federally administered (and one nearly completed) Presidential libraries. All are United States Government agencies, authorized by the Presidential Libraries Act of 1955 and administered by the National Archives and Records Service of the General Services Administration (constructed with private contributions from friends and admirers of the former Presidents). According to the General Services Administration, Presidential libraries "serve as depositories for the papers and other materials of each president, and of those who were associated with him during his administration; and to present museum exhibits which will illustrate for the American public important aspects of the careers and the times of our most recent Presidents."[35] The variation exists primarily in the nature of their holdings and in the availability of materials. In a recent analysis of the accessibility of Presidential papers, Lovely found few restrictions for the Roosevelt (less than 0.1%), Truman (3%), Eisenhower (10%) and Hoover (2%) Libraries; whereas the Kennedy (60% closed for a variety of reasons, including courtesy storage) and Johnson (67% closed or unprocessed) Libraries contained large amounts of unreviewed materials—reflecting to a large extent the newness of the library.[36]

For too long, Presidential libraries have been the domain of historians and not of political scientists. One of the greatest ironies of the post-behavioral period would be to "give" the libraries to historians because such primary source materials are not the "quantitative" data needed by political scientists. Moreover, the lack of original empirical research on the Presidency has already resulted in a situation where, according to Professor Hugh Heclo, there is "remarkably little substantiated information on how the modern office of the President actually works."[37] As a result, much of the Presidency literature has been limited to broad, undocumented assertions, relying on memoir, case study, or journalistic reporting, and not on primary source evidence from official records centers. As Steven Puro cogently observed, "documentary evidence of presidential actions has only rarely impinged on political scientists' hypotheses, propositions or theories about the presidency. . . . The information in Presidential libraries can be used to document institutional relationships—i.e., regular or routine interactions —between the President, office of the Presidency and governmental and non-governmental actors."[38] How can these materials be utilized? Take, for example, Presidential campaigns: the holdings of the Johnson Library have been especially useful for gaining a finer appreciation and understanding of the Presidential campaign process—details on campaign organization, advance planning, delegate selection, grass roots organizing, fund-raising, the relationship between the Democratic National Committee (DNC) and the White House, campaign scheduling and the state-by-state polls. Most of this material is located in the White House Central Files (Aides and Subject). This empirically rich data base supplements the 1964 election literature and provides a hitherto unavailable perspective on campaign organization. The Johnson Library recently sponsored a volume of essays on sources for the study of the Johnson Administration, edited by Professor Robert Divine of the University of Texas.[39] Listed below are the contributors to the study, which is intended to illustrate the *types* of domestic and foreign policy topics available for research at the library: George Herring, The Vietnam War; Walter LaFeber, Latin American Policy; Steven Lawson, Civil Rights; Marc Gelfand, The War on Poverty; Hugh Davis Graham, Youth and Violence, Task Forces; David Culbert, Johnson and the Media; Larry Berman, Campaigns and the White House Staff.

Before visiting a Presidential library, it is well to write in advance about your research interest, requesting a list of the library's holdings (recently opened materials are listed in *Prologue*, a quarterly publication of the National Archives). Resources within the library are usually classified into four types: manuscripts (Presidential papers, aide files, etc), microfilm, audio-visual materials, and oral history interviews. The libraries offer detailed finding guides which assist researchers in locating materials. More important, researchers will discover that their best resource is often the resident archivists. These professionals have no vested interest in protecting a President; they possess the "best" perspective on available materials and they are prepared to work with you on mapping out a research strategy.[40]

All of these resources may sound too good to be true, and, indeed, may be. The most frustrating aspects of archival research are the unevenness of records, the staff time required in reviewing or declassifying materials, and the problem of verification. Oral histories can be self serving and a vivid illustration of the bureaucratic adage, "where you stand, depends upon where you sit." Written memoranda "to the file" may misrepresent the influence of an advisor or contradict other documentation. Moreover, how can we measure the impact of unanswered memos? The President may receive twenty memos from advisor A and only one from advisor B; advisor A may be listed on the daily appointment log ten times; advisor B only once. But advisor B is meeting privately with the President each evening and either kept or destroyed all records. Only an "imperfect" solution is suggested: always triangulate the data (almost like a reporter checking source against source) by comparing oral histories, official documentation, personal interviews, texts, memoirs, or media reports.

There are two ways of utilizing archival data from Presidential libraries. First, there is the great temptation to spend hours and hours looking through Presidential papers for that one "sensational" memo an archivist overlooked. Few of these can be found. There are, however, many "less-than sensational" but significant memos which "set the historical record straight." Additionally, because archivists have no vested interest in protecting "their" President, documents often are released which (to the untrained mind) seem embarrassing, but have nothing to do with national security. Listed below are a few examples of these interesting, highly quotable, memorable, but less than analytically useful materials from the Johnson Library.

(1) One of the most often quoted Johnson stories is how the President, unable to reach Budget Director Kermit Gordon on the phone because he had gone to a concert, called Gordon the next morning and asked, "Well, playboy, did you have a good time last night?" Gordon wrote to Bill Moyers:

> If you are keeping score on the press stories portraying the President as a man who constantly abuses his staff, you might want to have (this memo) for the record . . .

The incident never occurred. Moreover, in all the time I worked for President Johnson, I suffered but a single mild rebuke—much milder than the circumstances would have justified.[41]

(2) John Steinbeck writing to Jack Valenti with advice for the President:

What I suggest is a napalm grenade, packed in a heavy plastic sphere almost the exact size and weight of a baseball. The detonator could be a very low power—just enough to break the plastic shell and ignite the inflammable. If the napalm is packed under the pressure, it will spread itself when the case breaks. The detonator (a contact cap) should be carried separately and inserted or screwed in just before throwing. This would allow a man to carry a sack full of balls without danger to himself. Now we probably have developed some fine riflemen, sharp shooters, etc., but there isn't an American boy over 13 who can't peg a baseball from infield to home plate with accuracy. And a grown man with sandlot experience can do much better. It is the natural weapon for the Americans.[42]

(3) President Johnson receives an "important" memo (illustrating why some need a chief-of-staff):

Mr. Bryant came by to say that he is sending Yuki out to Walter Reed to be dipped and treated for the fleas he got in Texas. Mr. Bryant has tried everything he has, and Yuki is still scratching. He will stay at Walter Reed's until 1:30 p.m. Friday.[43]

(4) Robert Kintner, Cabinet Secretary and Special Assistant to the President, describing Rowland Evans to President Johnson:

I know the reasons why *not* to see him; he is pugnacious; quite unfriendly; extremely talkative in private conversation; has been giving the President, and certain members of the President's staff, an unfair beating.[44]

(5) Harry McPherson writes to LBJ about Robert Kennedy's credibility gap:

You may have thought you were the only national political leader who had a credibility problem.

The following quotation from Bill Shannon's book "The Heir Apparent—Robert Kennedy and the Struggle for Power" (a favorable book about Senator Kennedy) suggests that this is not so.

". . . in order to minimize the carpetbagger issue, Kennedy was not adverse to molding the truth about his upbringing into a more convenient shape."

" 'I lived in New York for twenty years, I grew up here. I went to school here. I held my first job here,' he told audiences over and over again in the opening weeks of his campaign. In inspired moments, he sometimes added, 'I was born here.'"

"Kennedy was, of course, born in Brookline, Massachusetts."

What's worse—a great-grandfather who did not fight at the Alamo, or a Senatorial candidate who wasn't born where he said he was?[45]

(6) On the more personal aspects of life, Bill Moyers instructs MJDR that:

LBJ wants the toilet bowl in his john moved right back against the wall. He can't sit on it now.[46]

It is hoped that readers take the above material in the spirit intended. More significant is utilizing documentation for improving historical understanding of the everyday functioning and operation of the Presidency. Professor Hugh Heclo identifies this as "in-depth, systematic research on what people connected with the presidency have actually done, and how well their arrangements have managed to deal with the substantive problems of government."[47] Moreover, political scientists especially should utilize primary source documentation to analyze the everyday operations of the Presidency. Such in-depth empirical analysis may help future Chief Executives adopt operational strategies for improving their own Presidencies.

The Future of Presidential Libraries

Presidential libraries today are under a great deal of scrutiny and the very future of decentralized libraries is in doubt. Critics maintain that the original Presidential library legislation was intended to establish only a small library system, built with private funds, and maintained at moderate cost to taxpayers. Moreover, just as surely as death follows life, libraries and museums now follow Presidents. When will it all end? In June, 1979, *U.S. News & World Report* reported, that whereas most of the money was raised from private donations, the taxpayers would pay 1.6 million dollars to start up the new Gerald R. Ford Presidential museum and library.[48] During congressional budget hearings, several Senators questioned Archivist James Rhoads about the cost of maintaining such libraries. Senator Chiles noted that "every time we change administrations, we have another library. We are seeing the cost of over $3 million a year for maintaining the records of former Presidents for researchers. I am just wondering at what stage it gets to where we can't afford former Presidents. If we look at what it is now costing, we are seeing that it doesn't end at the death of the President. It is a building thing."[49] Chiles went on to suggest that researchers be charged to use the libraries. It is significant that the Ford Library, located on the Ann Arbor campus of the University of Michigan, will be relatively modest in appearance and size (compared to the Johnson Library). Also, this is the first time that a museum (located in Ford's hometown of Grand Rapids) and the library will operate from separate locations.

Granted the costs of individual Presidential libraries, they nonetheless offer distinct advantages which should not be lost. The much discussed centralization of future Presidential materials in Washington, D.C. would hinder declassification and review procedures, as well as remove archivists as experts on a particular presidency. A centralized location would certainly be followed by an overall budget cut in resources and staff. This would be detrimental to serious scholarly work. Moreover, as former Archivist James Rhoads expressed it, "There are no bodies of papers in modern America that have more value, more research potential, that are a greater documentary treasure to this country than the Presidential papers."[50]

CHAPTER SIX

The Future of Presidential Papers

ALEXANDRA K. WIGDOR and DAVID WIGDOR

The Presidential Records Act of 1978 (92 Stat. 2523) is an elegant records schedule which defines with considerable precision the papers that a President must yield to the Government, those that he is at liberty to keep, and the procedures for making the documentary legacy available to the public. In essence, all of a President's papers relating to his term of office, with very limited exceptions, will become public records, subject to his control for 15 years. As records of the Federal Government, the President's papers are to be placed in the custody of the National Archives and Records Service and housed in a Presidential library or other appropriate Federal archival facility.

Although the main outlines of the process seem clear, they relate solely to the administrative mechanisms for securing whatever documentary legacy remains. The statute mandates an inclusive schedule from which very few materials are exempt. When one speculates about the character of the materials that scholars will examine, however, the future of Presidential papers is more ambiguous. While there are likely to be gains in the formal completeness of whatever records are produced, it seems equally certain that there will be corresponding losses in intimacy. These losses will be especially sad ones, for a modern President's papers are most valuable for the subtle illumination that they cast on the shadows of the policymaking process. One can find the structure of events in many sources, but the research value of personal papers is in the nuance they provide those who seek to recapture and interpret the dynamics of public life. The Presidential Records Act simply treats what were once considered personal papers as government records, and it is likely that the former will now begin to resemble the latter.

In declaring a President's papers to be public property, the Presidential Records Act reversed long-standing patterns of law and custom. Statutes and regulations combined with administrative practice and scholarly judgment to suggest that a public official could have personal files related to his public responsibilities that were not subject to official control. The *Code of Federal Regulations* acknowledges a category of "papers that need not be made a matter of record," and the Office of Management and Budget, in implementing the Privacy Act (88 Stat. 1896), makes a distinction between "agency records" and "those records which, although in the physical possession of agency employees and used by them in performing official functions, were not considered 'agency records.' "[1] There was, furthermore, the practical consideration, as the then Archivist of the United States, James B. Rhoads, observed several years ago, that "to declare these confidential files of an elected official public property would both diminish his political freedom and also lessen the likelihood that the most sensitive materials bearing on his conduct in office would be retained." If an official had no control over memoranda, private correspondence, and similar materials that had traditionally been regarded as personal, Rhoads continued, "he might not create or retain such documentation from the outset."[2]

Because a President is the most central figure in American government, his personal papers are critical for understanding the development of public policy. Although most recent students have condemned the practice of considering everything that came to rest in the White House to be part of the President's personal papers, no proponent of the Presidential Records Act wanted to alter the research value of these materials. It is especially ironic, however, that the impact of the statute on the character of Presidential papers was virtually ignored, and the issue received little systematic attention at any point beyond an occasional incantation about the chilling effects of access or the thawing effects of time. Very early in the course of debate, Arthur M. Schlesinger, Jr. cautioned that instant access to sensitive communications would create a chilling effect upon internal debate, a situation that would diminish the value of a documentary record for both government operations and subsequent scholarship.[3] This fruitful insight, however, inspired no serious discussion; most contending parties merely paused to consider the problem in haste as they passed on to issues they regarded as more central.

There was certainly ample opportunity to examine any matter of importance during the lengthy inquiry into the disposition of the papers of public officials. The Presidential Records Act concluded a legislative process that had begun almost four years earlier with the Presidential Recordings and Materials Preservation Act of 1974 (88 Stat. 1695), a statute designed to assure the preservation and availability of the Nixon papers. A matter that formerly had concerned an occasional historian or curator now received the attention of several congressional committees and a Presidential commission, and, through the largess of two foundations, independent examinations issued forth from conferences at Arden House and New Harmony.[4] With all this remarkable outpouring, however, there was little regard for the character of the documentary legacy that would emerge. Different groups brought different interests to the shaping of the Presidential Records Act, but the principal items on the collective agenda were concerns about the accountability of public officials, access to research materials, and custodianship of the record. In the end, most interested parties appeared to agree that it was better to ensure total Government control over and uniform access to surviving materials than to speculate about the quality of what survived.

The effort to secure a more responsible government was the most compelling theme in the process that led to the Presidential Records Act, and it was the element that brought the disposition of Presidential papers to a larger public. The immediate stimulus for change was the Watergate scandal, a rubric under which many thoughtful Americans included the Nixon-Sampson agreement. This was an arrangement that ex-President Nixon concluded in September, 1974, with Arthur Sampson, the Administrator of General Services, and it provided for the wholesale destruction of critically important historical materials. Congress immediately acted to cancel the arrangement and it created (88 Stat. 1698) the National Study Commission on Records and Documents of Federal Officials, a blue-ribbon panel popularly known as the Public Documents Commission, which was charged with examining the general problem.

Although many critics of the Nixon-Sampson agreement regarded it as yet another example of how Richard Nixon had corrupted government, others considered it to be endemic in the "Imperial Presidency," a condition of constitutional development given dramatic emphasis by this act of a former President, less than one month after his resignation. Critics of the Nixon Administration and the "Imperial Presidency" also were joined by critics of government in general, of whom perhaps the most vocal were those who insisted that American government was too secretive and that a more open government would be more honest and effective. Others feared that to acknowledge any private interest in public service led to profiteering. Walter Lippmann, no stranger to the sale of opinions, had earlier condemned the commercial publication of Franklin Roosevelt's messages, speeches, and press conferences, and more recent observers have been disturbed by cavalier tax deductions for gifts of papers created through public service.[5] All of these critics were concerned principally with responsible government, and they sought to make public officials more accountable through procedures that permitted greater access to both their personal papers and to official government records.

Congressman Allen Ertel, who played a leading role in framing the Presidential Records Act, was one of the principal spokesman for this position, and he urged that a President's personal papers be defined as narrowly as possible. Although some advocates of change had considered the political papers of a President to be private in character, Congressman Ertel insisted, during the hearings on the legislation, that materials relating to a President's party leadership and political activities were part of the national patrimony and should be regarded as public property. His colleague, Theodore Weiss, however, was disturbed by language in the Ertel bill that he thought would have the opposite effect. Congressman Ertel's reassurance that political papers would not escape the statutory net led to an exchange that should be read in full, both for its importance in understanding the Presidential Records Act and for what it reveals about legislative draftsmanship.

MR. WEISS.   Perhaps I am misreading. Please refer to page 5 of the bill.

MR. ERTEL.   Whose bill?

MR. WEISS.   Your bill.

Start on page 4. It says, "Definitions." As used under this title, you use the terms "personal papers." Then you go to (C). As I read it, all materials relating to the private associations or activities of individuals referred to in paragraph 1, which includes the President in his own private capacity as candidate, and activities of the President or his services and activities as the leader of his political party—

MR. ERTEL. You left out a very crucial part—the words, "which have no effect upon, do not relate to, and do not derive from the exercise of the official duties, services, and activities of the President or his services and activities as leader of his political party." That is an exception to what personal papers are.

MR. WEISS. I would suggest that that section be redrawn. It seems to me to say exactly the opposite of what you are saying.

MR. ERTEL. I guess there should not be a comma there. We talked about that when we went over the bill. We had two opinions—one that there should be a comma and one that there should not.

MR. WEISS. Maybe it needs a footnote. [Laughter.]

MR. ERTEL. What this is intended to do, and I think it does so, and careful examination will show that it does lay public claim to the records of the President's activities as leader of his political party.[6]

Congressman Ertel, like other critics whose interests focused upon accountability in government, felt that responsible government would best be served by transforming the President's heretofore personal papers into public records, providing for their disposition in the most predictable manner possible, and drastically narrowing the scope of those materials over which the President had ultimate control. The utility of an individual's papers as sources for historical research was, for this group of critics, an ancillary problem at best.

Representatives of the scholarly community were, of course, more concerned about the problems of historical research than those critics whose attentions were focused upon the problems of responsible government. Both groups, however, were concerned principally with access to existing materials rather than with the impact of new procedures upon the character of future materials. Most of the scholars who took an active role in the deliberations that led to the Presidential Records Act were historians of American politics and foreign policy of the post-World

War II era, and they were naturally most sensitive to restrictions that are placed upon documents already in the custody of archives and libraries. Very few students of post-war politics are troubled about collections of personal papers that have not yet come to rest in some repository, but they frequently complain that major appointment files in the Truman and Eisenhower papers are closed. Because historical sources yield their insights in fragments, scholars must examine the widest range of evidence to grasp the meaning of the historical process.

The question of access predictably dominated the recommendations of scholars, but some advanced the claims of scholarship in rather curious terms. In criticizing current restrictions on the Henry Kissinger papers, the executive director of the American Historical Association complained that "Dr. Kissinger is going to have a leg up on other diplomatic historians. He has access to a vast amount of material in that area. We think it is unfair."[7] Although this suggests that a public official's experience is less important than the record of that experience, it nevertheless demonstrates the centrality of the access question for scholars. The point was underscored with refreshing candor by Richard Kirkendall, a leading authority on the Truman Administration, who rendered the following judgment about a President's political papers: "I am not so much concerned whether those materials be called private property or public property as I am concerned with their preservation and with access to them."[8] Thus, scholars who participated in the debate over Presidential papers joined with political critics of the status quo to advocate reforms that would redress past deficiencies, but they did so with little regard to future costs.

There were some scholars who argued that there would be no costs, and they insisted that modern government could not function without creating a documentary trail. Many of those judgments were based upon the records of agencies like the Atomic Energy Commission, but the commissioners and staff undoubtedly thought that their internal communications would be more tightly controlled much longer than has proven to be the case. It is ironic to find proponents of the Presidential Records Act arguing that procedures to alter the behavior of public officials by making government more open will not, at the same time, have an effect upon the way they control their confidences. It is particularly curious to find Arthur Link, the distinguished biographer of Woodrow Wilson, insisting upon the inevitability in government of a documentary legacy that is uniformly useful, when his most intriguing recent interpretation of Wilson's personality is based upon confidential material which he is not at present able to disclose or describe. And this is about a President who has been dead for over fifty years![9] Obviously, public records created to facilitate the administration of government do not alone suffice for all purposes. Perhaps the greatest of the many ironies that characterized this recent debate, however, was the position taken by the three historians who served on the Public Documents Commission, all perceptive students of American politics who previously had argued that a President should have broad powers, and who now insisted that a President could exercise only limited control over his own papers.

There was a third drama unfolding in the wings as the National Archives and Records Service, the principal custodian of public records and contemporary Presidential papers, developed its position, and the difficulty of its task was increased by the dual character of its mission. As the depository of public records, it received materials from Executive agencies and departments through force of statute, but its system of Presidential libraries depended upon the donation of personal papers by a President and his associates. Although an occasional criticism of this dual function emerged,[10] few considered it to be a divided function; different organizational elements of the agency simply were dealing with different types of material. To the Archives were to go materials that Anthony Lewis has recently characterized as "part of the ongoing business of Government;"[11] to the Presidential libraries were to go the White House files as well as personal papers that had not been required for the dispatch of public business.

In accordance with established law, policy, and institutional arrangements, the National Archives, in November, 1972, invited government officials to donate their personal papers to a proposed Nixon Library, and it defined personal papers to include correspondence "that is not intended to be a part of the official records of the office. The correspondence may be with friends, family members, professional or business associates, or other administration officials. It may relate to purely personal interests or to national and State affairs, Government appointments, political campaigns, or other topics." In addition, personal papers also included "[w]orking drafts and notes, used and unused; [j]ournals, diaries, scrapbooks, and press clippings."[12]

Four years later, in an abrupt reversal of policy, the Archivist issued a bulletin in November, 1976, that apparently prohibited the removal of materials by Federal officials that the 1972 guidelines invited them to donate to the proposed Nixon Library. Personal papers now were defined narrowly as "material pertaining solely to an individual's private affairs. In other words, correspondence designated as 'personal,' 'confidential,' or 'private,' etc., but relevant to the conduct of public business, is nonetheless an official record."[13] No public explanation attended this change in policy, but it certainly was consistent with the demands that emerged from the other groups arguing for changes — advocates of responsible government and representatives of the scholarly community. The Archives, in short, had abandoned its earlier concern with the quality of the documentary record and argued simply that everything produced within government was ultimately to be in its custody. Like the political critics and the scholars, the Archives decided to ignore questions about the nature of the legacy it would preserve.

The legacy of the Presidential Records Act will be the preservation of more documents as public records of the nation, but in archives as in architecture, more can often be less. As Presidential papers are transformed into public records in character as well as in name, historians will be left with the mechanical, formalistic, and frequently lifeless documentation that inevitably accompanies an administrative process, particularly when documents containing private thoughts and personal counsel must serve a public information function as well. Such a pattern complements many features of contemporary society that make it convenient for people in both public and private life to avoid committing their private thoughts to paper; the continuing revolution in communication and transportation conspires with changing modes of discourse to encourage more direct, face-to-face (or at least voice-to-voice) exchanges without the impedimenta of paper. This is certainly true of small-group decisionmaking and, although Cabinet-level secretaries and the White House staff have expanded dramatically, more and more decisions, as Dean Rusk has said of his own experience, are being made by smaller groups of people, and made orally rather than in writing.[14] The new statute thus complements many familiar, and for historians not altogether happy, social trends.

The Presidential Records Act will certainly alter and probably impoverish the historical record, but the loss to history would be a small cost if the statute served to augment responsible government. Unfortunately, a contrary result is equally likely, for the critics of government who successfully urged adoption of the statute (and seek to apply its standards throughout Government) are creating a situation in which the Federal Government is to be the single custodian of its past. The only record will be an official one, and no private papers of a public officeholder will exist to lend a measure of diversity and balance.

Public records are extremely important for historians, but their principal role in illuminating the development of public policy is in what they reveal about institutional dynamics and demographic patterns. Personal papers are more fruitful for recapturing the human dimension of political leadership, for they give public officials an outlet for expressing private judgments and questions. "Private papers," remarks the English historian A. J. P. Taylor, "ought to be the great security against official secrecy," and he notes that Winston Churchill as Prime Minister frequently used a "private letter so as to be safe from the censorship of the Cabinet office."[15] Like the secretariat in the Cabinet office, the Presidential Records Act celebrates fixed procedures, automatic mechanisms, and the formalized precision of a tight administrative process. These are important values, but perhaps we should be grateful Winston Churchill recognized that they were not universal values.

The recent debate over the personal papers of Presidents and Federal officials is not a new one, for statesmen in the early years of the Republic explored the question. There is a fascinating 1792 exchange between George Washington and Gouverneur Morris, a diplomatic agent in London and Paris, about the role of private communications in the new Government. Morris wrote from London that he frequently included information in his letters to Washington that he was reluctant to share with others, even with colleagues in the State Department. He was troubled by this, because, he acknowledged, "it is I presume expected that the public Servants will correspond fully and *freely* with the Office of foreign Affairs. It might therefore be deemed improper not to say *all*, in my Letters to that Office. I wish therefore you would give me your candid Opinion on the Subject." Washington replied that there could "be but few things of a public nature" that should not be reported to the State Department, for the Secretary would need to be fully informed in order to be fully effective. He cautioned, however, that there were other considerations.

> But there may, in the course of events, be other matters, more remote in their consequence — of the utmost importance to be known, that not more than one intermediate person would be entrusted with; *here*, necessity as well as propriety will mark the line — Cases, *not altogether* under the controul of necessity, may also arise, to render it advisable to do this, and your own good judgment will be the best director in these.

And to make his point unmistakably clear, Washington enclosed a private letter that he instructed Morris to deliver to Lafayette.[16]

We need not frame all questions as the Founding Fathers did, but their salutary realism is frequently instructive, and nowhere more so than on questions like these, for they realized that the obligations and proprieties of public service in a democracy need not violate the dictates of common sense. We would do well to ponder this as the Presidential Records Act goes into effect.

CHAPTER SEVEN

The Refracting Lens:
The President as He Appears Through the Media*

MARTHA JOYNT KUMAR and
MICHAEL BARUCH GROSSMAN

News organizations provide the mechanism through which influential members of the Washington community, as well as important constituencies throughout the nation, take their assessment of the President. News about White House influences the actions of organized interests both within and without government. Congressmen, bureaucrats and lobbyists get their cues on whether to grant or withhold support for the President based on perceptions gleaned from the media. National concerns, as well as the immediate objectives of these important political actors, are at stake. White House news has a major impact on the unmobilized segments of the public.

This reality, refracted through the lens of the news media, is for most people their only glimpse of what is going on at the White House. It provides them with a basis to judge the person who occupies the Oval Office and suggests the activities that may be needed to secure an individual or a general interest. What the media present has important consequences for the public as well as the President, and for political institutions as well as the individuals and groups on the national stage.

Until the mid-1960s, White House assistants used the media with considerable success to portray a favorable image of Presidential leadership. Officials often played on reporters' respect for the Office of the President to disguise their man's warts while promoting his image and his issues. Most journalists regarded these activities as part of a harmless game that did not produce significant distortions of reality. Similarly, White

* Abridged from *Portraying the President*, to be published by Johns Hopkins University Press, all rights reserved; this research was supported by the Ford Foundation and The Towson State University Faculty Research Committee.

House aides seldom stayed angry at news organizations for stories they considered unfair, although Presidents' deep-seated resentment against unfavorable coverage goes back to the beginning of the Republic.

White House-media relations seemed to change between 1965 and 1974. Especially in the last months before President Nixon resigned, conflict grew between the White House and large segments of the Washington journalism community. Reporters who previously exhibited a high tolerance for White House smoke screens suggested that the President and his chief advisers told lies and withheld information about important events. During the Vietnam war and the Watergate crisis, large groups within news organizations and a substantial portion of their audiences began to suspect that what the White House presented as reality on one day might turn out to be inoperative on the next. Many observers still look back on this period as a decade of deception.

The spillover from this era of conflict continues to affect the relationship. Although most officials responsible for Vietnam policy and Watergate have departed, many reporters remain suspicious of both public White House pronouncements and informal background explanations they are offered. Yet, what is striking about the post-crisis era was the reemergence by the middle of the 1970s of most elements of traditional White House-media relations. What goes on today involves a continuing relationship with a high degree of predictability, a stable process of exchanges marked more by cooperation than conflict, and recurring patterns of behavior as the relationship passes through similar phases in each administration during which the interests of officials and journalists merge or divide.

The continuing, stable, and predictable aspects of the relationship are based on permanent and underlying trends that have shaped both sides throughout the period of the modern Presidency. For the White House, the main forces affecting its activities are themselves the products of the extensive institutionalization that has taken place in the Office of the President. Presidents and their chief assistants have created an enormous apparatus for political communications consisting of press aides, speechwriters, public liaison officials, directors of communications, and many others to influence both what appears in the media and the reaction of the audience. Although reorganizations of these offices may occur, each new administration finds that traditional functions and routines exist that the staff are expected to perform. Similarly, the Chief Executive's publics expect him to play the same roles as his predecessors as the nation's chief communicator. They expect him to define the nature of national problems and then to propose solutions.

The same type of forces affect the media. Journalists cover and present information about the President for news enterprises that are themselves bureaucratic organizations making decisions and conducting operations according to established routines. What they define as news about the White House depends on the limits determined by the form of media in which the story appears, the nature and structure of the particular news organizations, the expectations of editors and producers as to who is in the audience, and the accommodations individual reporters have made with the ethos of their profession.

Even some of the enduring changes brought about by Vietnam and Watergate are exaggerations of trends that have always been part of the ebb and flow of the relationship. For example, Presidents and their advisers are tempted to manipulate the media because it is easy to do, especially at the beginning of a term or in the midst of an international crisis when news is defined as whatever the President says and does. At the same time, the discovery that they have been manipulated leads reporters and editors to become cynical about all White House activities. In the case of Vietnam and Watergate, this price was paid by subsequent Presidents as well as those who were responsible for the policies at the time. Because both the Johnson and Nixon Administrations succeeded for long periods in their efforts to manipulate both the press and public opinion, many contemporary journalists pursued a more antagonistic style of reporting White House developments than was common prior to 1965. Both Presidents Ford and Carter were hampered in their efforts to reap the traditional benefits that ordinarily accrued to the nation's chief communicator.

Although post Vietnam and Watergate reporters expressed doubts about the credibility of the White House in print or on television, the techniques and routines of reporting about the President remain basically the same. Reporters find numerous ways to inform their audience that they do not regard the White House as a reliable source. Elite journalists, such as syndicated columnists, frequently suggest to their readers that what the President has said — or what his staff claims for him — is *prima facie* implausible. Although major newspapers, such as *The New York Times* and *Washington Post,* reflected their concern about relying on traditional sources of information by increasing institutional coverage of the White House, in much of the media the new antagonism has been expressed in personal terms.

In particular, television has been a major arena for the expression of this conflict, both because White House officials believe it is so important to their cause and because its emphasis on the public activities of the President made it susceptible to manipulation. Television reporters have not chosen to confront the White House directly by changing the manner in which they cover and report the news — the networks' presentation of the Presidency has not changed much in the past decade. What does occur is that reporters present news about the White House along with an item that casts doubt on the credibility of what has been said or the authenticity of the person who said it. They indicate to their viewers that a cynical approach is a realistic approach when analyzing the motives of the President and his advisers.

There is one overriding implication of these long term trends bearing on what the White House can expect to get out of its relations with the media: the President must understand that the way he communicates to his publics effects popular perception of him and his policies. Just as power tends to adhere to those Presidents who sense what it is made of, favorable publicity comes to those Presidents who have a sense for dramatizing and personalizing issues and policies. Jimmy Carter misunderstood this aspect of Presidential roles and thought he had a choice of whether or not to be a communicator. He did not have such a choice and did not understand the consequences of not meeting the expectations of those both in Washington and throughout the nation who wanted him to explain himself with force and precision. The fact that he did not perform this role resulted in adverse judgments of his performance as a leader.

In a similar vein, a President woos trouble if he does not understand the appropriate use of White House communications facilities. Chief Executives and their staffs have found that the enormous growth of resources available to the White House makes the domination of information received by the public a temptation. This should be resisted, however sweet its immediate fruits, because manipulation ultimately detracts from the President's effectiveness in political communications. The real value of a well-run and effectively organized publicity apparatus is that it enables the President to overcome advantages possessed by Congress, the bureaucracy, and interest groups, all of whom have better channels to communicate with their own group members or with particular segments of the public than does the President. On the whole, White House aides understand the value of using their resources in this manner, although many dream of finding a magic formula that would create a more supportive press. Beginning with the term of Dwight D. Eisenhower, each successive administration's publicity operations have shown some improvement over its predecessor once the President sorted out problems with staff assignments and internal White House power conflicts. An administration's failures in political communications seldom have been failures in management. It is not surprising that most Presidents have preferred to cite poor management or media hostility as the explanation for their poor reception by the public rather than any problems with their performance or with the content of their messages.

The central impact of permanent underlying forces on the media is that news organizations have become actors of considerable significance in the American political system. They plan a number of important public roles including influencing the selection and removal of those who hold office, determining the public perception of the importance of many issues and interpreting the significance of a leader's activities. Nonetheless, news organizations are neither traditional political actors nor are they a fourth branch of government. They do not have clearly defined objectives, as do interest groups, and they do not seek power in the sense of winning and holding office, as do most of the politicians. With the exception of a relatively few matters about which their owners and managers care a lot, or about which a few columnists, editors, and elite reporters do have opinions, most media organizations do not seek to determine electoral or policy outcomes.

What might be said of them is that they strive to become the arbiters of the political system. They legitimize and delegitimize individuals, points of view on issues, and even institutions such as the Presidency itself. Collectively and individually, news enterprises act as if they set the ethical norms for candidates and the criteria by which policies shall be evaluated. In sum, these organizations attempt to establish the criteria of rectitude for political operations in the United States. It is no wonder that the other actors, including the President, resent them.

The Presidency and Political Communications

Critical analyses of the media's coverage of the Presidency have focused on two contradictory elements: first, on the problems created by the press for the duly elected head of the Executive Branch; second, on the continued domination by the White House of what and how reporters cover the news.[1] To some extent, the type of criticism reflects the partisan or policy positions of whoever is making it at a particular point in time, as indicated in the following critical comment attacking the White House for withholding information.

> The concept of a return to secrecy in peacetime demonstrates a profound misunderstanding of the role of a free press as opposed to that of a controlled press. The plea for secrecy could become a cloak for error, misjudgements, and other failings of government.[2]

When Richard Nixon made those remarks in 1961 after the failure of the American backed invasion of Cuba at the Bay of Pigs, he was concerned about a coverup of the affair by the Kennedy Administration. Obviously, his perspective had changed considerably by 1972 when his White House staff prepared an official secrets act that would have made the publication of national defense material about the "military capability of the United States or an Associate Nation" a criminal action.[3]

Other observers, including most of those interviewed for this study, made similar comments. They suggested that reporters are both too overbearing and too compliant in their relations with White House spokesmen and sources. In spite of the apparent contradiction, both criticisms are relevant. Although White House officials have retained the powers that led them to their traditional position of advantage over the media, many organizational changes and alterations of the rules of reporting have worked in favor of the press. The enlargement and institutionalization of the White House publicity apparatus provides the President with mechanisms to influence, and at times control, what news organizations present to the public. At the same time, the increased ability and willingness of news organizations to present an independent and critical version of White House activity to the public is one of the most important recent changes involving the status of the media in national political life.

Perspective for the 1980s

Because each President in the modern era has brought different styles, ideals, and tactics to political communications, political observers have tended to emphasize the unfixed, unpredictable, and idiosyncratic elements of White House relations with the news media. We suggest that this always was incorrect. Defining White House-news media relations in terms of what may have been dramatic events when they occurred involves an exclusive concern with the President's personal relations with a small number of people on his staff and with news organizations. A narrow focus, even when placed on important relations, distorts the larger reality.

A more complete portrait of the relationship includes a picture of a highly stratified White House in which the President is the central and most exposed figure and representatives of the bureaucracies of news organizations of whom reporters are the most visible. While the White House is concerned with the President's problems of sending communications to his various publics and constituencies, the representatives of news organizations are fulfilling institutional goals of keeping the public focus on what they consider to be the newsworthy activities of the President.

In the 1980s, it will become even more likely that the institutional setting provides a stage that limits the behavior of an administration toward news organizations. Each new incumbent will discover that his relations with the media are limited by structural constraints just as they are with Congress, segments of the bureaucracy such as the defense and foreign policy establishments, and bureaucratized lobbies such as those representing labor and business. A President often must do what is expected of him. Although different personal styles provide some opportunities for varied approaches, each new President will discover that he has far less leeway to reshape his relations with news organizations than he anticipated when he ran for the office. Even if he exercises his option to change the format for his contacts with the small group of reporters and media executives who follow him full time, he must fulfill some of their expectations or pay a price. If, for example, he does not present himself to them on some regular basis, reporters will treat other informants as the authentic sources for accounts of his administration. Accounts by these informants will lack the authority of his own words. Because they may provide varying accounts of his activities, the resulting story may lend credibility to a picture in which he appears to be uncertain of his role or incompetent in command.

In the decades of the 1980s we can expect the continuing evolution of several major aspects of the contemporary relationship. Presidents will need the media even more than in previous times; news organizations will continue to move away from cooperation — but not too far; the working relationship between the media and the White House will be part of the story about the President; coverage by the media will continue to be more favorable than unfavorable, although the ratio will decline; and, finally, the publicity operations conducted by and for a Chief Executive will be an index to his concept of the Presidency.

The continuing need for the media. During the 1980s, Presidents will continue to depend on news organizations as the basic vehicle through which messages are sent. The relationship between the White House and the news media is vital for a President because of the decline of the layers of institutions that once were part of networks transmitting news, information, and orders from the President to appropriate audiences throughout the country. As recently as the Eisenhower Administration, Congress, the bureaucracy and interest groups could send their leaders to the White House and then communicate a message from or about the President to an attentive constituency. All of these institutions have been decentralized and their leadership is neither in the same position of command nor as respected as it once was, with the possible exception of lobbies for major corporations that appear better organized and more effective than at any time in the past. All other indications point to continuing fragmentation in the 1980s. Congressional leaders have neither the same sense of their membership nor authority over them as was the case in 1960. The bureaucracy continues to grow less susceptible to central control. Most interest groups represent special concerns and single issue constituencies rather than broad economic and social segments of society.

Both the White House and the leadership of these groups will increase their dependence on the media. Presidents will continue to be frustrated by what they cannot or will not accomplish through the exercise of their powers of command. The public appears to be the only group capable of helping them overcome their frustrations. News organizations provide a President with a route to the public, including the constituencies of all those leaders in Washington who either can not or will not cooperate with them. The stakes for the President will grow in proportion to the degree with which information within Washington and among opinion-makers throughout the country now funnels through the media. Therefore, it is likely that White House publicity operations will continue to grow in order to permit coordination between direct political communications operations such as public liaison and congressional liaison. Press operations will be the central channel.

The increasing independence of the media. If there ever was a golden age of partnership between the White House and the news media it occurred during the eight years of the Eisenhower Administration. Undoubtedly part of the explanation for the overwhelmingly favorable coverage that Eisenhower received was that the President's superb sense of publicity emphasized his almost heroic stature. In addition, the intelligent management of White House media relations by Press Secretary James Hagerty reinforced the proclivities of news organizations to provide time and space for the administration's message and image. Many reporters shared the admiration of most citizens for the wartime leader turned political head, while the top layer of senior editors and publishers found that Eisenhower's policies coincidently reflected their views. As they had since Roosevelt's day, the media turned to the White House to supply focus and drama to political news. The close working relationship journalists and officials established during World War II continued during the Cold War of the 1950s. News organizations accepted what they were told by the Government, even after the administration was less than candid in its cover-up for ten days after a U-2 surveillance plane was shot down on May Day, 1960 over Soviet territory. Eisenhower restored credibility when he personally assumed responsibility for the U-2 mission in a May 11 press conference.[4]

The decline in the partnership that began after Eisenhower left office scarcely was noticeable during the Kennedy Administration because the amount of coverage increased. The new President received publicity from a vastly expanded Washington press corps that arrived at about the time of his inauguration. Although Kennedy complained that news organizations provided less support for him than Eisenhower, he admitted that at crucial episodes, such as the Bay of Pigs invasion, he later wished they had been less cooperative. Lyndon Johnson, however, suffered no such ambivalent feelings. He was dismayed after his first months in office when he found that news organizations pursued their separate goals in spite of his courting and cajoling. Later, the demand that both he and Richard Nixon made, that news organizations remain loyal during tension over Vietnam, ultimately backfired. During the weeks prior to President Nixon's resignation, the partnership was dissolved.

Although important elements of the partnership were restored under Ford and Carter, cooperation continued to de-

cline at approximately its pre-1965 rate. The growing independence of news organizations can be attributed to the size and
stability of the major enterprises; to the talents, sophistication
and sheer numbers of journalists who compete to turn up information about blameworthy and, therefore, newsworthy White
House activities; and the underlying consensus among the media's elite that the failure to resolve national problems should be
laid at the White House door. Thus, the direction that news organizations have cut for themselves lessens the likelihood of pro-
longed periods of partnership during the next decade.

Presidents and their advisers worry about how to reverse this
trend, but the usefulness of their concern is questionable, especially because they can do little to change it. The fact that news
organizations follow the beat of their own drums ought to be, at
most, a matter of discomfort rather than a subject for dismay.
Past performance indicates that news organizations will communicate the essential message and image of a President whose
mastery of the arts of political communications includes an
ability to formulate and articulate a coherent description of his
intention. The pre-Watergate Nixon Administration was able
to achieve most communications objectives even though most
news organizations always kept their critical distance. Of course
major developments distract the media from efforts by any
White House persuaders, as Nixon and others discovered.

White House-media relations as part of the story. On almost
no subject have members of the White House staff applied more
energy and gained more expert knowledge than they have to
learning about the needs and routines of news organizations.
There are few people who work as White House aides in the
area of political communications who do not understand that
the needs of news organizations must be serviced, that reporters
should get answers to their questions, and that honesty is the
best policy—or at least that outright lying is usually disastrous.
In a book about his experiences as Press Secretary to President
Ford, Ronald Nessen described an incident soon after his appointment when he was tempted to mislead his former colleagues in the press. His associates on the White House staff not
only were startled at his suggestion, but also incredulous at his
assumption that he would not get caught.[5] They undoubtedly

knew that a story about a Nessen lie would become a lead item in what major news organizations, especially television, would present to the public.

Because news organizations have become major participants in the processes of White House politics, conflicts between the media and the White House have become an important part of the story about a Presidency. In addition, as White House publicity operations were institutionalized, they became personalized and thus a subject for the attention of reporters who wanted to portray the activities of the President's assistants. As these activities became the central focus of White House political communications, they became an item discussed among media people in their forums, in the books and journals on the press that began to appear in the late 1950s, and, slowly, as part of the daily stories. This evolving interest was resisted by important segments of the journalistic community, however, because of this conviction that the internal operations and problems of the press were not a legitimate news story.

White House-media relations became a major story because of three important developments during the 60s and 70s. First, the issues of news management and the President's credibility that were raised during Vietnam affected support for the war; second, the Nixon Administration's war against the media legitimized the story of all but the most reluctant members of the media's old guard; and finally, the emergence of individual reporters as heroes during Watergate accelerated the public's acceptance of individual reporters as being part of the story. The trends stemming from these developments continued during the remaining years of the 1970s and seem likely to be part of the picture during the 80s. Presidents can expect to see articles about the relations between the White House and reporters in the extensive feature sections of newspapers and magazines, broadcast talk shows, and in specialized publications such as journalism reviews.

Continuing favorable stories about the President. In spite of the trends in the relationship emphasizing its adversary elements, a large number of stories about any President will continue to be positive and favorable. At the beginning of a Presidential term, both news organizations and their audience can be expected to exhibit a keen interest in the nation's new royal family and its plans for reigning and ruling. Although these stories become less important when the controversies of the day dominate the news, they continue to be features on the inside pages. In addition, personal stories are featured by family, home, women's, and "people" magazines throughout a term. These stories invariably are favorable, although officials sometimes view them as negative because they mention family problems such as divorce, drink, or scrapes with the law by members of the younger generation. Stories about Presidents' brothers, especially younger brothers, seem to be the one exception to this pattern of positive impact.

Presidents have a number of opportunities to recapture enough positive stories to maintain their favorable impact on their Washington and national audiences. When a President seizes the initiative and appears to take strong measures to resolve or respond to a crisis, news organizations ordinarily line up behind him. At the onset of the Iran and Afghanistan crises during the last months of 1979, major news organizations permitted the President to have almost unlimited access to their columns and broadcasts. Although some nationally syndicated writers demurred, the overall impact was to relegitimize the Carter Presidency at a time when it seemed near collapse.

Publicity operations as an index to a Presidency. Near the beginning of the 20th Century, Woodrow Wilson suggested that a President's relations with his Cabinet provided an index to his concept of the Presidency.[6] During the last decades, the way in which the Chief Executive conducted publicity operations and his relations with news organizations provided the best guide to his understanding of how he expects to fulfill the central role of communicator. The way in which he conducts publicity operations provides an indication of the degree to which he sees himself as an explainer of policy and actions. A President's publicity campaigns thus reflect important aspects of his Presidency. A fragmented sense of publicity and communications is a product of a fragmented Presidency. A President who centralizes publicity in the White House usually centralizes power there. The control that a few White House aides exercise over interviews given throughout the Executive Branch shows how far the

Chief Executive has moved from his promises of an open Presidency. Since publicity operations are of such critical importance, it will be useful to look at some of the perceptions and misperceptions shared by recent Presidents about their relations with the media.

Perceptions and Misperceptions

Those who work at the White House believe the President's reputation in the Washington community and his public prestige throughout the nation are the key determinants of his influence. Richard Neustadt, who introduced this notion of the basis of Presidential power to the public, described the Washington community as an entity that based its judgements on impressions received through multiple conduits of information, including the news media.[7] The contemporary White House looks to its relations with the media as the most important factor determining its reputation and prestige. Officials have a good sense of several important elements of the relationship. Unlike reporters, who often minimize their institutional, although not their personal, roles, White House officials consider news organizations to be important political actors. In both interviews and conversations, officials describe their relations with news organizations in analytical terms that would indicate that they think about these relations and discuss them among the staff.

There are a great many aspects of their relations with news organizations that Presidents and their advisers accurately perceive. They usually know who is important; their sense of the configuration among elite journalists is usually correct. While print media reporters complain about their zealous courting of the electronic media, officials know that, although television may not be the basic source of information for elites in Washington, it is essential for the vast majority of citizens, especially those with a low level of attention (not to be confused with interest) to national affairs.

Many reporters complain that the White House is neither responsive nor sensitive to their individual and organizational needs. This is not true. White House officials often understand the operations of news structures, such as television networks or newsweeklies, better than anyone other than the correspondents who work for the enterprise. With a few infrequent but notable exceptions, they provide all reasonable services required by correspondents. Some reporters, like all Presidents, have long memories of every real or imagined grievance. Like a President who can reel off incident after incident of press errors, distortions, or irresponsible reporting, these reporters cite a litany of Press Office goof-ups in the form of incomplete information or inaccurate statements. Such complaints, even if accurate, are misleading. Just as a President's activities, character, and style are accurately reflected by the press over the course of his term, the White House does provide most news organizations with the necessary access and information.

Yet, although White House assistants and even most President are knowledgeable about the technical aspects of media operations, they continue to misperceive several important features of their relationship with news organizations and their representatives. One set of misperceptions stems from their view that the Presidency is the central political institution on which the success of the Republic is hinged. From this they conclude that the press ought to be supportive. They believe, that at the very least, the media should transform the President's message to the people without amendments, analysis, or interpretations. Another set of misperceptions stems from the view that there is some sort of magic formula that will generate good publicity and favorable coverage. Their search for a publicity elixir stems from the view that the right combination of publicity factors will make news organizations supportive, or at least get them to be "accurate."

Thus, Presidents and their staffs try to hire alchemists to develop publicity because they confuse strategies for getting political communications across with the substance of the message they send out. Recent Presidents have searched for a publicity genius who would ensure that the message news organizations send out about them is positive. Lyndon Johnson thought that John Kennedy had that genius in Pierre Salinger. He expected his Press Secretaries to perform a kind of magic that had no relationship to what he did as President. Richard Nixon tried to be that genius himself since he could find no one with the required qualities. While he got tremendous mileage from the shrewd use of resources available to him, these tactics could not prevent the true character of his administration from coming through. Publicity cannot change the appearance of an administration for more than a short time. It cannot take someone or something and make it into what it is not. Publicity can be an aid in pulling together the message that an administration wants to communicate when that message is complicated and fragmented. It cannot invent a message; at best, it simply delivers it in the most effective way, at the right time, and to the correct audience.

Perhaps the most common practical application of these misperceptions may be seen in the attempts of the White House to make personal relations between the President and representatives of news organizations into a forum that can affect the way the President will be portrayed in the media. Because the President does maintain contacts with a small group of reporters, columnists, editors, bureau chiefs, anchorpersons, and media executives, most Presidents believe that their personal relations with journalists will be more productive of good publicity than they really can be. At times, the efforts of some Presidents in this regard have become ludicrous. Lyndon Johnson indicated to reporters that he would put in a good word for them with their "bosses" if they cooperated, not really an enticing offer to men who already were near the top of their profession. Most other Presidents shared Johnson's belief in the importance of personal relations. In a number of instances, they have tried to rid themselves of a particular journalist by telling his editor or bureau chief that they thought the reporter was hostile and unfair. In a number of instances, Presidents or their aides have suggested to news executives that their organizations would be better treated if the reporter were replaced.

Although such strident language and blatant threats rarely succeed, the more subtle techniques of not responding in a timely manner to a reporter's need for information and access has led to problems for correspondents. The fact that the White House seldom employs punishments does not mean that the portent that they might be imposed does not have an affect on some reporters. Most news organizations want reporters who are well regarded at the White House. Because organizations expect their representatives to spend a great deal of time and energy covering the public activities of the President, reporters need assistance from inside sources so that they will not be caught unaware of important developments and so that they may explain complex activity, such as monetary policy or defense strategy, beyond their professional familiarity. Such help is usually an important ingredient in a successful career for reporters assigned to the Chief Executive. Thus, White House pressures on reporters may succeed in altering the behavior of some and in getting others reassigned, although it would be difficult to prove that this was the direct cause in either case. A reporter who is the victim of a White House freeze-out may be regarded as too abrasive by his or her organization. Reporters are sensitive to this possibility. Few correspondents want to take the chance that they will be regarded as failures at what executives at news organizations regard as one of the most prestigious assignments in the media.

A more positive attempt by Presidents to exploit the benefits of their personal relations with journalists involves meetings in which they talk informally and off the record with reporters and executives of news organizations. Most Presidents and/or their advisers believe that if journalists meet with the President in the White House setting, they will gain and report a positive vision of the Chief Executive's capacities to deal with the nation's problems. Officials expect that reporters will be impressed by the setting as well as by the man. Correspondents may feel awed at their proximity to power. In fact, this technique does provide some short-run benefits. Many reporters do prepare favorable stories about the President that are displayed prominently by their news organizations. Especially after the initial period of cooperation during the first months of a new administration has been replaced by the competitive phase, White House officials attempt to build on these personal relations between reporters and the President. They hope that what results will enable them to recapture the dominance over the news they enjoyed earlier. However, since what news organizations are interested in at this time are stories about conflict within the administration or between the White House and opponents in Congress or the private sector, the salutary effects of these personal contacts with news organizations is short-lived. In contrast to what Presidents believe, the importance of personal relations is at the margin. The fact that reporters have been impressed by the President in a meeting or even feel indebted to him for the help he has offered does provide the White House with an additional benefit, but it will not distract reporters from what they are after.

What a President Needs to Know

In a political system in which fragments of power are held by many, a President needs to learn how to use the advantages and resources of his office if he is to pull together his position's potential to command and to persuade. Whether the office is inherently weak or inherently imperial, the notion that the President can gain a monopoly of power at the national level does not fit the experience of Chief Executives during the post-World War II period. His agenda is often set by others or by events. What he needs to know in order to influence the political process is how to distinguish the avenues of power from the dead ends. In the area of political communications, this means that the President and his staff must understand four essential points: first, that even though they may be outsiders who have just arrived in Washington, they do not start off with a clean slate; second, that political communications must be well-integrated in the White House, but that the appearance that an administration speaks with several voices reflects the unavoidable reality that they do speak with several voices; third, that there are fixed and malleable aspects to the President's relations with the news media that all who deal with publicity should learn to distinguish; and, finally that they all must understand the role of the President as a communicator so that they can adjust the mechanisms of communications to suit his personality and talents.

The election or succession of a new President is, in part, a transfer of power from one leader and his entourage to another and, in part, a transition from one group of officeholders to another. As a transfer, the changes that the new officeholders may bring about are limited only by the forces that impelled them into office and the groups that form the basis of their support. After a clear victory for a side, as in 1932 and 1936 — rather than for a person as in the two Eisenhower wins — the President mobilizes his supporters to bring about changes. Of course reading and understanding the nature of a winning coalition's demands and then translating them into policies is not always easy. After a close election, some Presidents have proceeded with considerable caution. Following the 1960 election, John Kennedy stated his goals, but was reluctant to try to mobilize the power of his office behind them for fear that his support would dissolve. On the other hand, after Richard Nixon won an almost equally close election in 1968, he mobilized his supporters into adversaries without concern that he was polarizing the opposition.

The Washington community regards an election as a transition. The permanent government expects the President and his staff to continue. Although its members want to please the new leadership they expect the new group to move slowly before routines are changed. At first, they are ready to make minimal adjustments to suit the style and personality of the new group. More dramatic changes must be made gradually after there is an opportunity to adjust. It is in this area that a new administration has an important lesson to learn. They do not start with a clean slate. As the new government, they are expected to perform continuing leadership roles as legislators, bureaucrats, and managers of the national security. As chief communicator, the President must touch base not only with his constituencies, but with those groups who will implement his ideas by changing them into words and images. In his relations with the media, a new President is supposed to resume the "open Presidency" that characterizes the beginning of each administration. News organizations expect he will provide them with at least the same level of accoutrements they already possess, that his staff will keep reporters informed of his smallest movements and the possibilities of major developments, and that officials will be available for both on the record and background meetings.

Most Presidents know that failure to satisfy these expectations may prompt retaliation. In fact, some administrations welcome such conflict. What they should understand is that the real consequences will not come as a result of retaliation—few news organizations really want to go toe to toe with the White House, or let their reporters do it for them. Instead, they stem from the efforts news organizations make to fulfill their institutional goals without help from the White House. If denied traditional avenues of access and information, they will seek them along paths that the White House would prefer were off limits to the press. Most administrations do not recognize this, especially during the early weeks of their term when everything seems to be going their way anyway. Later, when an administration finds things going less smoothly, the President may relent to try to establish the traditional pattern. Reporters may be invited in for "cocktails with Clawson." A President, like Carter, may bring in an adviser for communications to "Rafshoonize" the process. By that time, it is probably too late. The administration's image in the media has been sculpted in bronze.

A second point that an administration should know when it takes office involves the relations between its press operations and its other efforts to manage the President's political communications. News operations must be well-integrated into an apparatus consisting of several elements that are not obviously part of publicity operations. The central business is scheduling. The President and his aides must determine the best use of his time so they can maximize the impact of his meetings with key national leaders, smaller groups of influentials such as members of Congress below the leadership rank, larger influential groups such as the AFL-CIO or the Foreign Policy Association, and direct appearances before the public at press conferences and in addresses to the nation. Although almost everyone at the White House has become familiar with the importance of these operations—in this sense, at least, an American Presidental campaign prepares its participants for what is to come—they do not always see how these activities of the President must be coordinated with the institutionalized White House lobbying and liaison activities with political leaders, Congress, and interest groups. Also, it is not clear to them how these activities fit in with those of the White House press office in its dealings with the Washington press corps, or of the Office of Media Liaison in its relations with news organizations in their home locations throughout the country.

Yet they should recognize that, ultimately, almost everything of consequence gets into the press. From the White House point of view, many items "appear" at the most awkward time. Obviously, integrating publicity operations will not hide failures or minimize the damage from major political crises. Vietnam and Watergate did not become major political failures because of poor political communications emanating from the White House any more than they did because of hostile pictures or distortions presented to the public by news organizations. On the other hand, well-run political communications operations will make it more likely that the media will reflect rather than distort what the White House is doing. White House officials often emphasize the desirability of ensuring that all administration officials speak with one voice. They usually give up in despair at the impossibility of this task after a certain amount of internal bloodletting. If they recognize that it is the aim and direction of their activities that becomes the story, they might concentrate on establishing those priorities they want to reenforce through political communications. They would not waste so much time on the counterproductive activity of quieting dissident voices, or merely those of the people who speak out of turn.

A President and his staff must learn what is fixed and what is malleable in their relations with news organizations. In particular, since they invariably are looking for ways to redress the relationship in favor of the White House, they must learn that what cannot be changed is the determination of what constitutes news. What they need to understand are the ways in which news organizations are likely to present their activites. A President can squeeze more juice out of the orange when he tries to present his messages through activities that are likely to receive favorable coverage in the media.

Sudden shifts from favorable to unfavorable treatment by news organizations often can be foreseen. Clearly, many recent Presidents failed to learn this lesson. For example, when President Carter retreated to Camp David to plan a major response to the energy crisis during the summer of 1979, his disappearance from Washington to hold private discussions with national leaders caught the attention of the media and the public. For the first time in months, Carter had an audience eager to hear what his message would be. When, finally, he came down from the mountain to address the nation, he had succeeded in switching the public agenda to a subject of his choosing. When he continued the next day to speak vigorously on the same subject, he was portrayed as a man who was in charge. On the second day after his speech, he changed course and engaged in activities that elicited a predictably negative response from the media: first, he requested wholesale letters of resignation from his top advisers and Cabinet; second, he followed these requests with acceptances that immediately were regarded as dismissals. What happened next was that the dismissals, rather than Carter's renewed drive for an energy program, became the central story. Furthermore, news organizations portrayed the simultaneous removal of several influential Cabinet officials as unstable leadership.

What Carter had done was to drive from the front pages and evening news broadcasts the favorable stories about the renaissance of his administration that appeared immediately after his television address. Instead of stories about an administration taking charge of its own house, the media showed a frightened leadership unable to tolerate strong independent associates. Members of the White House staff complained bitterly that news organizations overdramatized the resignation story, and they were right. What they should have and did not recognize was how predictable it was that all this would happen.

An administration can set the stage on which its activities will be observed and reported. But even though a President may dominate the news agenda, he cannot distract news organizations from what they see as the central questions. Typically, a President thinks that the media deals with the lesser questions of politics while he tries to communicate the important issues of policy. Whether he or news organizations are right about what ought to be the news focus, he cannot change it. There is nothing that a President can do to steer reporters away from conflict, controversy, scandal, or interesting personality stories. Theres is no way to change the manner in which news organizations view these stories.

Finally, a President must understand that he is expected to

be the great national explainer. This means that his public must receive a continuous stream of messages through the media explaining what he wants to do or not do, with reasons for his actions and inactions. There has been a great deal of concern in the White House, particularly since the advent of live national television coverage, with the question of how much public exposure a President can receive without generating public antipathy. This is certainly not a small issue. The question of whether a President becomes less effective if he speaks too often on too many subjects is important. But the President has to communicate his message all the time in formats other than an address to the nation. He must address elite audiences of the scientific, technological, economic, religious, ethnic, and political communities. He must use the publicity resources of his office to make certain the message gets through the proper channels of news and the direct links of lobbying. In all of this, the President himself must be an active communicator. If he shies away from this role, his administration will have major problems on this basis alone. It is not merely a question of being a smooth salesman that is at stake. It is the whole process by which leadership is glued together.

The Media as an Actor in Presidential Politics

With the notable exception of the Eisenhower Administration, the media in the post World War II era have reflected an erosion of support for the institution of the Presidency and perhaps helped to shape the perception that less support is deserved. From the perspective of the White House, their role has shifted from that of cheerleaders to demonstrators. The changes that have taken place, however, are more the result of an evolutionary process affecting news organizations and the journalists who work for them than a fundamental shift in loyalties.

The growth of the organizational structures of the major news enterprises has made it possible for them to cover the President in ways that suited journalists' inclinations, but that had not previously been possible. The large financial resources commanded by the broadcasting industry permitted the networks to cover the Presidency with an immediacy and intensity that magnified the faults of the institution and of its occupant. News media organizations use their new technological and human resources to explore dimensions of Presidential activities that had not been covered in the past.

Influencing and Being Influenced

News from the White House alters Washington's political landscape. As actors in Presidential politics, news organizations force some decisions and prevent others that might have been taken in their absence. They influence what the President will do and what others in the Washington community will do in response.

But there are limits to the ability of news organizations to change the public's assessments. There is no evidence that journalists' efforts could reverse strong currents of opinion. If a President is well thought of or if he has a poor reputation, the media cannot do much to change it.

The relationships' balance of power, which is still favorable for the Presidency, prevents both sides from becoming full-time adversaries. It is true that the corps of journalists have shifted away from their easy alliance with and protection of the White House that characterized an earlier period. Many reporters focus on the problems of the Administration from a cynical or even antagonistic point of view. At the same time, reporters swing back to portraying favorable as well as unfavorable aspects of a President. Although his problems create the most intense audience interest, news organizations need his successes to reflect the continuing importance of the Presidency as the central political institution of the nation. Without a cycle of successes and failures, the media's coverage of him would have far less impact. Warts on an ugly person are of far less interest than the appearances of blemishes on someone who is expected to look beautiful.

Contemporary news organizations hire journalists with much better training and more impressive credentials than was the case in 1936 when Leo Rosten published his classic study of Washington correspondents.

125

An important reporting or editing position with one of the better news organizations today requires an individual to pass standards of employment at least as high as those of the best run corporations, law firms, or universities. In one important respect, however, little has changed. Although reporters have definite views about the rules of the game, they do not feel committments to political causes or policy outcomes. Some White House correspondents indicated that they did not vote in Presidential elections. While a few in this group explained their position as an effort to remain uninfluenced by their own desires during a political campaign, others suggested that they just did not care who won.

In few respects are what appears as the media's judgments a product of journalists' own judgments. The shape of stories that news organizations present to the public is molded by such factors as the views of the important and well-positioned sources who talk to reporters and editors, the trends of public opinion, and the group-think of the crowd of journalists concerned with the story. With rare exceptions, mostly among columnists and commentators, their views are not based on ideological or partisan positions. Personal vendettas, although more frequent, are restrained either by the news organization or by the widespread knowledge that what is appearing is in fact the outcome of a personal vendetta.

To a large extent, the way in which reporters frame their stories about the President reflects the opinions of influential members of the Washington community. For example, the evaluation made by many journalists that Jimmy Carter revealed himself to be a bumbler and incompetent may have been a congressional creation that was moved through the media to the public. Dennis Farney described the process by which this impression was created.

> Carter came in as an outsider, and frightened and perplexed members of Congress. . . . He came in as a tough bastard who was going to stop dams. Then he went to a supplicant's position. He started complementing Congress in the most unconvincing ways. So they talked to journalists and were judging him by the way of how other Presidents behaved. It dawned on members that this guy could be had.[8]

Because reporters' views were influenced by their friends on the Hill, they tended to pick out and emphasize Carter's words and deeds that showed him alternately as too demanding or too surrendering. They chose for their articles those items that showed Carter to be ill at ease in Washington, as well as those that showed that he was unable to mobilize support behind coherent programs either in the capital or among the people. If an event involved a change in a decision, the emphasis they placed on the change in their story suggested that the President displayed qualities of indecisiveness.

This picture of Carter represented the prevalent view in Washington. At times and on particular stories it was unfair. The story was not, however, a total fabrication. In general terms it reflected the reality that the outsider, Jimmy Carter, had a lot of on the job training to get through before he could gain control of his office. It reflected the reality that, in many important areas, Carter had difficulty in establishing his priorities, that he had difficulty in establishing priorities among policy areas, and that where he clearly had established certain policies as important priorities, he had not succeeded in learning his personal role in convincing others to follow his lead. But if the story was a reflection of the reality, it also contributed to the reality of the story. Carter's reputation, as shaped and hardened by the media, contributed to his difficulties in getting control of his office.

Just as news organizations mirror, form, and reenforce the opinions of influential individuals, they reflect and shape the public perception of the President as a leader. The trends in opinion that indicate the level of support for the President affect the way the media covers him. Stories tend to be supportive of a President for whom things are going well. They accelerate the decline of a man when he is perceived as not up to the job. Walt Rostow suggested that the press reflects inherent public ambivalence toward the Presidency.

> When the President leads and successfully rules the nation, there is in the press as in the people, the tendency to be supportive. When things aren't going well, the press both reflects and amplifies the problems of the nation as reflected in the problems of the President. . . . There is an instinct to do this because we had to create

this powerful figure [in 1788, and now want] to cut him down to size.[9]

Not only are journalists influenced by others in the Washington establishment and by the national consensus, their judgments about the President also are influenced by other journalists. When greater numbers of unfavorable stories about the President appear, news organizations will probably produce more stories viewed from an unfavorable perspective until the trend changes. During the summer of 1978, the percent of unfavorable stories about the Carter Presidency climbed to nearly 25 percent in the three forms of media examined in our larger study, *Portraying the President*, a trend that appeared common among most news organizations. Unfavorable stories produced a momentum for continuing unfavorable stories, as the following example illustrates.

The survey research company known as the Roper Organization sampled public sentiment on President Carter's proposed tax reforms in 1978. On July 27, Art Pine wrote a story in the *Washington Post* assessing the results in which he led with the statement that "a new nationwide tax survey brought more bad news for President Carter." The story went on to maintain that the important disagreements between the people and the President found by the survey "mark another blow for the Carter Administration." Ten days later, on August 6, 1978, another story on the survey appeared by Barry Sussman who conducts and writes about polls for the *Post*. Sussman indicated that economics correspondent Pine had been mistaken. "Surprise: Public Backs Carter on Taxes" read the headline on the second story which analyzed the same poll. "If public opinion is to be cited in the tax debate, it seems only fitting to point out what the public really does think," Sussman wrote. "And if polls that show Carter doing poorly are highly publicized, as they are, those that show him in a favorable light ought to be publicized as well."

Establishing the Criteria for Rectitude

One way to examine the role news organizations play in Presidential politics is to consider what might happen in the absence of their independent activities. The Vietnam war presents a revealing illustration. President Johnson wanted the media to portray stories about Vietnam that supported his version of the war. At first, a few stories indicated that their authors did not share the President's assumptions. Most of what appeared in the media pictured events as perceived by reporters and editors who did not disagree in any essential way with the official version. Eventually, however, news organizations ran a larger percentage of stories on developments in Vietnam based on a different perspective, stories that the White House thought were harmful and distorted. President Nixon wanted to keep news of American involvement in Cambodia away from the public, but the bombings and incursions were continuing subjects in the media that remained beyond the President's control. News stories neither stopped the incursion, however, nor does the evidence indicate that the media can be judged an anti-war group. In fact, Presidents Johnson and Nixon continued to receive a large share of favorable stories about their leadership during this period.

What the press did was focus on news issues involving the conduct of the war — subjects about which it was difficult to portray the leadership in a positive manner. In the end, the picture of the war's futility spread to the public and then to official Washington. When it was clear that he could no longer define the war for public opinion, President Johnson withdrew from politics. The war was covered, but not the way the President wanted. President Nixon was forced to accept a legislative restriction on a President's ability to move militarily in Southeast Asia or in "other Vietnams" throughout the world. This act by Congress was their response to the cross-pressures of White House demands that it continue to support its Vietnam policies and the wishes of a large segment of public opinion that was war weary. Congress yielded to the public. The role of the media was indirect but still of great importance. "The press, not Congress, told the truth on Vietnam," James Reston observed. "They made it part of the conscience of America."[10]

The news stories about both Johnson's and Nixon's conduct of the Vietnam war were framed by the judgments that some journalists made about Presidential behavior. These judgments became the basis on which a large segment of the public evaluated the two Presidents' conduct of the war. Reston may be correct that news organizations performed a service to the nation in the case of the Vietnam war. Viewed from other perspectives, however, there are many instances when this role is played for small stakes in a petty fashion. Rather than contributing to the evolution of a public conscience, news organizations act as the nation's nanny, bustling with demands for their own version of good conduct. Although no single view of the criteria for rectitude is shared among journalists, the selection of news stories by an organization is imbued with these values.

First, their view of what a President is supposed to do is reflected in the questions they ask and the stories they compose. A large percentage of both may be summed up in their query, is he up to the job? During the primaries and the campaign, a period with an opportunity for considerable access to the candidate, they ask him if he's up to winning and if he's qualified for the job. The questions will be somewhat different when asked by a character assessor such as Bill Moyers, a strategy evaluator such as David Broder, or the ordinary reporter who asks, "What makes you think you can carry Texas?" After a candidate is elected to office, elite journalists and columnists focus on their version of whether he is tough enough to make the hard decisions. The stories of other reporters frame his behavior in the context of their views of such qualities as decisiveness, ability to handle people, effectiveness with Congress, diplomacy, and sympathy with the people. Although their answers would be different because their viewpoints are different, they are all asking the same question: Is he the right kind of President?

Second, they are on the lookout for conflicts of interest and shady behavior. Some elite journalists, especially those with a strong commitment to substantive policy positions, are less concerned with these matters. Other editors and reporters, who may have a high tolerance for personal shenanigans, ignore some of the smaller stories in this area, especially when they involve someone who has been a good source. It may be that it is organizations rather than individual reporters who regard this issue as a personal morality play. It also may be that what is involved is the intense drama of seeing the ground turn to quicksand under the feet of someone who had been a strongly rooted public figure. Basically, however, these stories permit journal-ists to assert their values as to what are the proper rules of the game in Presidential politics or national political life. Their un-stated and perhaps unconscious premise is that they should be the judges.

Coping

Although some of the men and women who come to Wash-ington as reporters may dream of covering a story that will blow the lid off the Capital dome and let in the air of reform, most veteran journalists are uneasy with a role as participants in the political system. Their self-perception is that they cope with the routines of their beat. Although a few deny that they are actors and many suggest that their power is vastly overrated, almost all are aware that the public perception of them in Washington and the nation is quite different. There are a number of politi-cal roles that most journalists admit they play: they identify problems that the White House has to deal with; their interpre-tations, especially when accompanied by leaked information, can influence the decisions that are made; they stimulate inves-tigations; they contribute to a separate information channel in Washington that carries some important matters; they change timetables. Finally, their most direct political role involves their relationship with the White House.

News organizations identify problems that require specific governmental or political actions by the White House. Fre-quently, events become problems for the President because they were reported in the media. The unbuttoned remarks of a high official who had not realized that he was on the record cre-ates problems for the White House as does an encounter with a legal problem by a member of the staff. This latter situation can be particularly embarrassing because it may lead to the me-dia's reporting previous occasions when the same event had oc-curred but when the law had not been involved. Sometimes the questions reporters ask at the briefing identify problems the ad-ministration can expect to face. Most frequently, the press is an actor forcing a response from the White House because the matters raised in news stories would not have surfaced through bureaucratic channels. "The press could provide information that would lead to a policy decision," an aide to President Ford recalled. "I would say that two or three times a week there is a press account that leads him to ask a question."[11]

When stories appear in an influential medium interpreting an event in a manner unfavorable to the President, many White House officials respond with steps to defend the President's image. They are particularly alarmed when stories stress political complications because they fear that the prediction of problems may become a self-fulfilling prophecy. Thus, a story about a vote against a legislative proposal that is interpreted to mean that the President is in trouble in Congress may soften the President's support in Congress among his marginal followers there. They are especially concerned with obtaining a positive interpretation during a political campaign because they (and journalists) believe that an image of success created its reality. The most damaging kind of result occurs when a story interpreting a controversial decision is accompanied by leaked information. When that happens, as was the case during the Kennedy Administration's Skybolt missile crisis, officials have to react quickly to stave off embarrassment. "That story led to some rather hasty decisions," Walt Rostow recalled.[12]

News organizations also influence policy outcomes by stimulating investigations. Although the media has no legal power to investigate wrongdoing and cannot require that reporters be given information, press reports may create a demand for a government investigation. Once the investigation is underway, news organizations present reports that affect the reputations of those conducting the investigation and those who are the subject of its scrutiny. Sometimes government officials will leak information to the press that they hope will stimulate an investigation that the official could not get by going through channels.

What appears in the press can change the White House timetable, particularly on questions involving appointments or dismissals. In 1975, President Ford and his advisers decided to make Cabinet changes in a dramatic way in order to put his stamp on the administration he inherited from Richard Nixon. When the press released the story, it had the opposite effect. "It gave the public the appearance that it was a disorderly process," a Ford official explained. "It took several weeks to really get that behind us."[13]

In another political role, the media operates an internal network that provides information to Washington insiders. At one time they passed on personal information of importance about the health or personal activities of prominent political figures. The importance of this network declined during the 1970s because news organizations now publish hearsay information about people and activities that was previously off limits. Nevertheless, reporters are still cross-pollinators who provide as well as pick up information from their sources. Reporters may inform officials of what they believe to be the story about their counterparts in other organizations, although they are not ready for that story to appear in the media. Some officials want to befriend reporters so they can "cultivate their sources."

Finally, the relationship between news organizations and the White House is itself a form of political activity. Efforts by the White House to shape what appears in the media is a recognition by the President's assistants that it is a basic relationship affecting his reputation, policies, and the quality of support he receives from the public and influential interests in Washington. As has been indicated throughout this presentation, journalists are not innocent participants in this relationship, although they do chafe at both institutional and conscious manipulation by the White House. They do not like to be channeled, and of course, are outraged when they are deceived. Most of the time, however, they are partners, even when they are being used by the White House. "The real strength of government in the communications process comes from . . . its ability to trade on the hunger of the communications media for news about public affairs," Francis Rourke wrote in 1961.

> Critics of government information activity often draw a picture of newsmen as the willing victims of government propaganda. Often, however, newspapers themselves are so anxious to get the "inside story" from official sources on a current issue of domestic or international importance that they will become willing if not enthusiastic collaborators in the process by which government influences public opinion.[14]

White House Reporting: Adequate or Not?

For a brief period after the revelations of Watergate led to the resignation of Richard Nixon, polls showed a public appreciation for the role of news organizations in national politics. Several reporters who pursued the story, when the power of the President's office weighed heavily to squash it, became heroes. The media, which had been under public attack by the Nixon Administration, appeared to be a defender of traditional constitutional values against usurpers who did not think that the safeguards of the system applied to them. The lovefest was shortlived. Doubts about the media's role as the public's source for information and communications from the White House were reasserted as soon as the glamor of the Watergate achievement faded. Of course, much of the criticism of White House reporting can be attributed to the President's aides and supporters who claim that the unposed, unretouched picture the media presents is unfair. Brushing off their criticism as self-serving is also unfair.

White House critics complain that the media distort and misinterpret what happens and thus scramble the President's message en route to the public. They assert that news organizations fail the public because instead of providing full explanations of complicated policies, journalists deal with the politics of issues, assessing whether or not the adoption of a program means that the President is a winner or loser. The real losers, they suggest, are those who need to understand the policy.

Journalistic critics of White House reporting are not more generous. They suggest that elite journalists include both willing recipients of the White House glitter and others who make a career of attacking the President. They find the White House regulars to be alternately too abrasive and too obsequious in their relations with the President and his aides. They are often manipulated at the White House because it is so difficult for them to change their routines. Their emphasis on hard news events means that they are too closely tied down to the coverage of the ceremonies and major events that take place at the White House. Thus, their efforts to explain less visible and harder to define activities takes second place to the body watch of the

President. For these reasons, the White House press corps never "got" the Watergate story.

Clearly, the public has a major stake in whether White House reporting is adequate or not. The President's message, as filtered through and interpreted by the news media, often determines the role that the public will play in the shaping of policy. The President's conduct, as portrayed and evaluated by news organizations, affects the choices made by the electorate. Some serious critics of the process that provides White House information to the public have been particularly harsh in their evaluation of the role of the media. The gist of their argument may be summarized as follows:

News organizations make it difficult either to govern or oppose the government. The media's emphasis on the President's unresolved conflicts, unreached goals, inconsistencies, and personal peccadillos erodes the legitimacy he needs to command and the credibility he requires to persuade. They create major distractions that force his attention from the essential problems of the nation. According to this argument, his opponents are given an equally hard time when they become a large enough target to warrant the media's full attention. Should a critic or opposing candidate become prominent, the same media treatment the President gets makes it difficult for the public to evaluate the nature of the alternative they offer.

Behind these criticisms lie some assumptions about the relative positions of the two institutions in the constitutional system: the President is charged with the central role of governing; the media is given the opportunity to assess and criticize the government without fear of punishment. Since the President and the media represent the public in different ways, the media must be held to higher standards of accuracy while the President is judged by his effectiveness. Because the President is curtailed by the requirements of political life and the day-to-day process of government from engaging in an on-going pursuit of the public interest, that responsibility is placed on the media. What is expected of White House reporting requires a delicate balance. The media must portray the President clearly and honestly, alert the public when there are dangerous abuses of power, but not endanger the stability of the Presidency.

In assessing the adequacy of White House reporting, it is not difficult to compile a list of areas where the public is not well served. What the media define as news about the President is not always what is important. The organization and routines of reporting discourage the prominent display of important stories explaining the institutional structure of the Presidency. The public learns more about the style than the substance of developments because of the news values of reporters and because of the manner in which the White House presents the agenda of the President's activities. The President's message does not get through to the public when its complexities require constant reiteration because those who run news organizatons believe their audience does not want different versions of the same explanation.

In spite of the demythologizing of the Chief Executive during the 1970s, the mystique of the Presidency still overwhelms some reporters. White House aides encourage these tendencies by scheduling the President to play symbolic roles on stages that emphasize the charisma of office. A major result of this is overexposure. The heavy investment of both news organizations and the White House in exploring the drama of the Presidency leads to a heightened sense that the achievements are very great while the failures appear abysmal. A surfeit of information and pictures showing the President makes it difficult for the public to obtain a clear sense of the realities of a President's capabilities, his power, or powerlessness. Neither exaggeration helps the political system. The media tends to deal in superlatives, however, and thus there are often greater swings in the tone of the coverage of an administration than there are real swings in momentum.

A similar, shorter, but not less important list can be compiled describing the ways in which the public is well served by White House reporting. It is useful to remind ourselves first that news enterprises are private organizations. The public role in what is defined as news is filtered through editors and bureau chiefs who select the areas that are given extensive coverage by reporters. Reporters for mass audience news organizations gravitate toward personal and dramatic items. Those who work for elite publications or programs provide a more sophisticated analysis of White House policies presented from the perspective of both critics and supporters of the President. The public does get the story in the long run. If there are important delays, as there were in the general reporting on Watergate developments, there are also circumstances when news organizations bring an important story to an uninterested public. The energy crisis became a prominent story in the media after 1973, but public attention to the reality of the crisis did not occur until the skyrocketing prices and gas lines of 1979.

The media does provide the public with an important protection against abuses of power by the White House. If they hound suspects rather than pursue wrongdoers, this form of McCarthyism should not be passed over lightly. With few exceptions, however, the media has served as an important check on those in the White House who took it for granted that they could use their position for personal gain, to remain immune from the ordinary legal processes governing citizens and officials, or who abused their power in the pursuit of political goals for themselves or for the President.

Finally, what appears in the media does reflect who the President is and what he is doing. Although some stories may be unfair or inaccurate, and a large number present a fuzzy image, the picture that emerges reflects the tone and substance of the administration and the character of the President. In particular, the impact of large numbers of stories left an impression of the Presidents' leadership that seems accurate in retrospect. What emerged was a portrait of Johnson as an activist leader with a strong penchant for introducing new programs on which he could place his imprimatur, a wheeler-dealer who knew how to manipulate the political process, and a man given to using pressure tactics; Nixon as a strong partisan with a penchant for secrecy, little tolerance for his opponents, a vindictive streak, and as an opportunist who fronted his positions with conservative rhetoric; Ford as a good man who was not prepared for the job when he took office, who exercised both courage and common sense, but who frequently stumbled as he learned the ropes; Carter as a leader who did not establish his priorities, who tried to win the support of both sides in a dispute and often lost both, and of an intelligent man who did not understand the uses of power.

Most of the time the picture that was presented of each of

these Presidents was much more favorable. The built-in advantages possessed by Chief Executives enable them to keep the more critical appraisal in the background as they go about their activities. The fact that the unfavorable undertones become part of the public's assessment does not stop a President from pursuing governmental or electoral objectives. Polls indicate that the public's assessment of Nixon in 1972 was not far from the picture just described, but it reelected him by an overwhelming majority.

News organizations have *not* made it more difficult to govern. What has made the exercise of power more difficult for Presidents are the forces that gave to the media its present status — the diffusion of governmental authority and the breakdown of traditional lines of communications. The fact that those who govern seem dependent on news organizations is a symptom of the problem, not the problem.

Notes

NOTES FOR FOREWORD

1. R. Gordon Hoxie. *Command Decision and the Presidency*. New York: Reader's Digest Press, 1977, p. 280.
2. *Ibid.*, p. 261.
3. *The New York Times* (editorial), January 30, 1976.
4. American Academy of Political and Social Science. *Bicentennial Conference on the United States Constitution*, II. Philadelphia: University of Pennsylvania Press, 1980, p. 209.
5. John C. Fitzpatrick, editor. *The Writing of George Washington*. vol. 32. Washington, D.C.: U.S. Government Printing Office, 1939, pp. 63–64.
6. R. Gordon Hoxie. "The Not So Imperial Presidency," *Presidential Studies Quarterly*, Spring 1980, p. 202.
7. *The Bicentennial Conference on the Constitution*, II, p. 216.
8. *Ibid.*, I, p. 239.
9. Hoxie. *Command Decision*, p. 343.
10. Dwight D. Eisenhower. *Waging Peace*. Garden City, New York: Doubleday & Company, 1965, p. 548.
11. *Ibid.*
12. *Ibid.*, p. 549.
13. Dwight D. Eisenhower. *Public Papers of the President, 1960–61*. Washington, D.C.: U.S. Government Printing Office, 1961, pp. 403–404.
14. *Ibid.*, pp. 439–440.
15. Herbert S. Parmet, *Eisenhower and the American Crusade*. New York: Macmillan Company, 1972, p. 557.
16. Hoxie, *Command Decision*, p. 258.
17. Bryce N. Harlow in keynoting the Fourth Annual Leadership Conference, Center for the Study of the Presidency, October 21, 1973. See *Center House Bulletin*, Winter, 1974, p. 5.
18. Hoxie, "The Not So Imperial Presidency," p. 203.
19. *U.S. News & World Report*, August 17, 1981, p. 41.
20. James Bryce, *American Commonwealth*. Vol. II. London: Macmillan & Co., 1889, p. 718.

CHAPTER ONE NOTES

1. See Louis W. Koenig. *The Presidency and the Crisis: Powers of the Office From the Invasion of Poland to Pearl Harbor*. New

York: King's Crown Press, 1944; James G. Randall. *Constitutional Problems Under Lincoln*. Revised edition. Urbana: University of Illinois Press, 1951; Robert S. Rankin and Winfred Dallmayr. *Freedom and Emergency Powers in the Cold War*. New York: Appleton-Century-Crofts, 1964; Bennett M. Rich. *The Presidents and Civil Disorder*. Washington: The Brookings Institution, 1941; Clinton Rossiter. *Constitutional Dictatorship*. New York: Harcourt, Brace and World, 1963; J. Malcolm Smith and Cornelius P. Cotter. *Powers of the President During Crisis*. Washington: Public Affairs Press, 1960; U. S. Congress. Senate. Special Committee on National Emergencies and Delegated Emergency Powers. *A Brief History of Emergency Powers in the United States: A Working Paper* by Harold C. Relyea. Committee print, 93rd Congress, 2d session. Washington: U. S. Govt. Print. Off., 1974.
2. From an account appearing in Cincinnati *Daily Commercial*, February 13, 1861; also see Roy P. Basler, ed. *The Collected Works of Abraham Lincoln*. Vol. IV. New Brunswick: Rutgers University Press, 1953, p. 197.
3. For an elaboration of these considerations see Harold C. Relyea. "The Provision of Government Information: the Federal Freedom of Information Act Experience," *Canadian Public Administration*, v. 20, Summer, 1977, pp. 320–324.
4. Letter to W. T. Barry, August 4, 1822, in Gaillard P. Hunt, ed. *The Writings of James Madison*. Vol. IX. New York and London: G. P. Putnam's Sons, 1910, p. 103.
5. While the focus here is upon the Presidency, it should not be forgotten that other institutions of national government were enamored of secrecy. On November 9, 1775, the Continental Congress resolved:

. . . that every member of this Congress considers himself under the ties of virtue, honour, and love of his country, not to divulge, directly or indirectly, any matter or thing agitated or debated in Congress, before the same shall have been determined, without leave of the Congress; not any matter or thing determined in Congress, which a majority of the Congress shall order to be kept secret. And that if any member shall violate this agreement, he shall be expelled this Congress, and deemed an enemy of the liberties of America, and liable to be treated as such.

(*Secret Journals*)

When the Constitutional Convention began in Philadelphia in 1787, rules quickly were adopted for its proceedings to be conducted in secrecy. It was not until 1820 that these restrictions were removed and provision subsequently was made that same year for the publication of the records of the Convention as well as certain portions of the journal of the Continental Congress which were still secret (see 3 Stat. 609).

While the Senate was delayed by the absence of a quorum for almost two months before it could begin its official proceedings on the last day of April, 1789, it was not until December, 1795, that the chamber opened its doors to the public.

6. See S. I. Bushnell. "Crown Privilege," *The Canadian Bar Review*, v. 51, December, 1973, pp. 551-583; Mauro Cappelletti and C. J. Golden, Jr. "Crown Privilege and Executive Privilege: A British Response to an American Controversy," *Stanford Law Review*, v. 25, June, 1973, pp. 836-845; Peter E. J. Wells. "Crown Privilege," *Quenn's Law Journal*, v. 3, Winter, 1976, pp. 126-151.

7. See Arthur S. Miller. "Executive Privilege: A Political Theory Masquerading as Law," appearing in this symposium; the term "Executive privilege" apparently first appeared in a court opinion in *Kaiser Aluminum and Chemical Corp.* v. *United States*, 157 F. Supp. 939 (Ct. Claims 1958), but it is likely that the press had used the term prior to this date.

8. Telford Taylor. *Grand Inquest*. New York: Simon and Schuster, 1955, p. 18.

9. See, generally, *Ibid.*, pp. 17-29.

10. Alvin M. Josephy, Jr. *On the Hill: A History of the American Congress*. New York: Simon and Schuster, 1979, pp. 80-81.

11. Stephen Horn. *The Cabinet and Congress*. New York: Columbia University Press, 1960, pp. 22-25.

12. Andrew A. Lipscomb, ed. *The Writings of Thomas Jefferson*. Vol. I. Washington: The Thomas Jefferson Memorial Association, 1903, p. 303.

13. *Ibid.*, pp. 303-305; with regard to the power of a parliament to make inquiries, a British tradition followed by Congress, see Raoul Berger. *Executive Privilege: A Constitutional Myth*. Cambridge: Harvard University Press, 1974, pp. 15-31.

14. See, generally, Wilfred E. Binkley. *President and Congress*. New York: Alfred A. Knopf, 1947, pp. 42-44.

15. While the nature of the desired response is not totally clear, it appears that testimony was sought; see correspondence in *Congressional Record*, v. 17, March 12, 1886, p. 2332, and *Ibid.*, March 22, 1886, p. 2618; also see H. J. Eckenrode. *Rutherford B. Hayes: Statesman of Reunion*. New York: Dodd, Meade and

Company, 1930, pp. 272-275; on the general circumstances surrounding this inquiry see Binkley, *op. cit.*, pp. 155-161.

16. Of relevance here is President Eisenhower's May 17, 1954 letter to Secretary of Defense Charles Wilson which, with an accompanying legal memorandum, initially appeared in U.S. Congress. Senate. Committee on Government Operations. Special Subcommittee on Investigations. *Special Senate Investigation on Charges and Countercharges Involving: Secretary of the Army Robert T. Stevens, John G. Adams, H. Struve Hensel and Senator Joe McCarthy, Roy M. Cohn, and Francis P. Carr.* Hearings, 83rd Congress, 2d session. Washington: U.S. Govt. Print. Off., 1954, p. 1169ff.

The Eisenhower Administration produced two lengthy studies on the exercise of Executive privilege. The first of these was based largely upon a study originally published by Herman Wolkinson, a Justice Department research attorney, in 1949. It also appeared in differing versions of varying length and detail. The most complete text of both studies was published by the Senate Committee on the Judiciary in 1958: see "Is a Congressional Committee Entitled To Demand and Receive Information and Papers from the President and the Heads of Departments Which They Deem Confidential, in the Public Interest?" and "Memorandum Reviewing Inquiries by the Legislative Branch During the Period 1948-1953 Concerning the Decision-making Process and Documents of the Executive Branch" in U.S. Congress. Senate. Committee on the Judiciary. *The Power of the President to Withhold Information from the Congress: Memorandums of the Attorney General.* Committee print, 85th Congress, 2d session. Washington: U.S. Govt. Print. Off., 1958, produced in two parts with the items in question appearing at pp. 1-73 and pp. 87-165 respectively. Also see Herman Wolkinson. "Demands of Congressional Committees for Executive Papers," *Federal Bar Journal*, v. 10, April, 1949, pp. 103-150; July, 1949, pp. 223-259; October, 1949, pp. 319-350.

Also see Robert Kramer and Herman Marcuse. "Executive Privilege — A Study of the Period 1953-1960," *George Washington Law Review*, v. 29, April, 1961, pp. 623-717; June, 1961, pp. 827-916. Rebuttal to all of these studies may be found in Raoul Berger. "Executive Privilege v. Congressional Inquiry," *U.C.L.A. Law Review*, v. 12, May, 1965, pp. 1044-1120; August, 1965, pp. 1287-1364 and _____. *Executive Privilege: A Constitutional Myth*. Cambridge: Harvard University Press, 1974.

17. All of the letters of agreement may be found in U.S. Congress. Senate. Committee on the Judiciary. *Executive Privilege: The Withholding of Information by the Executive.* Hearings, 92nd Congress, 1st session. Washington: U.S. Govt. Print. Off., 1971, pp. 33–37.

18. Letters were sent to both President Ford and President Carter during their initial year in office by the chairman of the House Subcommittee on Government Information and Individual Rights asking them to express their policy on the exercise of Executive privilege. No response to these letters has been received by the Subcommittee.

19. U.S. Congress. Senate. Committee on Government Operations. [and] Committee on the Judiciary. *Executive Privilege, Secrecy in Government, Freedom of Information.* Vol. I. Hearings, 93rd Congress, 1st session. Washington: U.S. Govt. Print. Off., 1973, p. 30.

20. *Ibid.*, p. 39.

21. *Ibid.*, p. 40; see, generally, *Ibid.*, pp. 30–52.

22. For a full appreciation of the significance of these and related considerations bearing upon the outcome of the Court's decision, see Bob Woodward and Scott Armstrong. *The Brethren: Inside the Supreme Court.* New York: Simon and Schuster, 1979, pp. 287–347; also see Howard Ball. *No Pledge of Privacy: The Watergate Tapes Litigation.* Port Washington: Kennikat Press, 1977.

23. *United States* v. *Nixon*, 418 U.S. 683, 706 (1974).

24. See *United States* v. *Reynolds*, 345 U.S. 1 (1952).

25. *Nixon* v. *Administrator of General Services*, 433 U.S. 425, 446 (1977).

26. *Ibid.*, p. 448; also see *Ibid.*, pp. 448–450.

27. *Ibid.*, p. 444.

28. See *Federal Open Market Committee of the Federal Reserve System* v. *Merrill*, S.C. No. 77–1387, June 28, 1979, p. 19 (slip opinion).

29. There is no intent here to suggest that Congress, in spite of the constitutional problems involved, should not also consider a statutory response establishing such procedural responsibilities.

30. *United States* v. *Nixon*, 418 U.S. 683, 706 (1974).

31. See James G. Randall. *Constitutional Problems Under Lincoln.* Revised Edition. Urbana: University of Illinois Press, 1951, chapters 3, 4, 7, and 19.

32. See Dallas Irvine. "The Origin of Defense-Information Markings in the Army and former War Department." Washington: Na-

tional Archives and Records Service, General Services Administration, 1964; under revision, 1972 [typescript], p. 3. All references from revision typescript; military orders, regulations, and directives referred to may be found in the annexes of this study.

33. *Ibid.*, p. 4.
34. *Ibid.*, p. 26.
35. See *Ibid.*, pp. 26–27.
36. *Ibid.*, pp. 28–29.
37. *Ibid.*, pp. 31–32; for a concise overview of the legislative development and prosecutorial problems associated with the Federal espionage laws see Harold Edgar and Benno C. Schmidt, Jr. "The Espionage Statutes and Publication of Defense Information," *Columbia Law Review*, v. 73, May, 1973, pp. 929–1087.
38. Irvine, *op. cit.*, p. 34.
39. *Ibid.*, pp. 48–49.
40. Both the Atomic Energy Act and the National Security Act subsequently were amended but their official secrets authority have remained and presently are codified at 42 U.S.C. 2161–2166 and 50 U.S.C. 403(d) and 403g respectively.
41. U.S. Congress. House. Committee on Government Operations. *Executive Classification of Information—Security Classification Problems Involving Exemption (b) (1) of the Freedom of Information Act (5 U.S.C. 552).* Washington: U.S. Govt. Print. Off., 1973. (93rd Congress, 1st session. House. Report No. 93–221), p. 8.
42. *Ibid.*, pp. 8–9.
43. See U.S. Congress. House. Committee on Government Operations. *Safeguarding Official Information in the Interests of the Defense of the United States.* Washington: U.S. Govt. Print. Off., 1962. (87th Congress, 2d session. House. Report No. 2456), pp. 29–31.
44. *Ibid.*, pp. 31–32.
45. See *Ibid.*, pp. 33–35.
46. See H. Rept. 93–221, pp. 9–11; amendments to E.O. 10501 included:

Memorandum of November 5, 1953, specifying 28 agencies without original classification authority and 17 agencies in which classification authority is limited to the head of the agency.

E.O. 10816 of May 7, 1959, which clarified certain declassification matters deriving from a hiatus which resulted when E.O. 10501 replaced E.O. 10290; allowed access to classified information to trustworthy persons engaged in private historical research projects, provided access was "clearly consistent with the interests of national defense; and permitted the transmission of "confidential" records within the United States by certified and first-class mail.

Memorandum of May 7, 1959, adding 2 agencies to the 28 entities previously designated as having no authority to classify information.

Memorandum of March 9, 1960, providing that agencies created after the date of the issuance of E.O. 10501 shall not have authority to classify unless specifically authorized to do so; and listing 8 new agencies so authorized to classify.

E.O. 10901 of January 9, 1961, which listed by name those agencies granted authority to classify information, including 32 entities with blanket authority to originate classified material with the head of the agency having discretion to delegate this authority to subordinates, and 13 entities with blanket authority to originate classified materials with the head of the agency having no discretion to delegate this authority.

E.O. 10964 of September 20, 1961, which created an automatic declassification and security downgrading system.

E.O. 10985 of January 12, 1962, which removed the authority to classify records from certain agencies and granted it to others.

47. H. Rept. 93-221, p. 11.
48. See U.S. Congress. House. Committee on Government Operations. *U.S. Government Information Policies and Practices—Security Classification Problems Involving Subsection (b) (1) of the Freedom of Information Act*. Hearings, 92nd Congress, 2d session. Washington: U.S. Govt. Print. Off., 1972, pp. 2926-2937.
49. *Ibid.*, p. 2532.
50. See *Ibid.*, pp. 2888-2889; also produced in *Congressional Record*, v. 118, May 15, 1972, pp. 17340-17341.
51. See *Ibid.*, pp. 2933-2934.
52. H. Rept. 93-221, p. 31.
53. *Ibid.*
54. "National security" is one of the most elusive policy referents in Federal law, yet few would deny that it provides one of the broadest grants of administrative discretion available to the President. The term appears about 390 times in the 1970 edition of the United States Code, with additional inclusions in the uncodified statutes. Of these 390 entries, a little more than 100 pertain to government institutions such as the National Security Agency or National Security Council; another two score are section head-

ings or cross-references; and another two score refer to the National Security Act. However, slightly more the 240 of the remaining citations are descriptions of a policy condition granting the President extensive discretionary power — e.g. "for reasons of national security," "for purposes of national security," "in the interest of national security," or "detrimental to the national security."

While the precise origins of the national security concept are uncertain, its adaptive value was well appreciated by 1949 when Sidney W. Souers, then Executive Secretary of the National Security Council, called it "a point of view rather than a distinct area of governmental responsibility." (*American Political Science Review*, v. 43, June, 1949, p. 535.) At times, it seemingly may be distinguished from other policy states or conditions of close similarity. In this regard, the Code variously pairs national security and "defense of the United States," "public peace or safety," "military requirements," "the public interest," "financial policies of the United States," and "economy of the United States." Other groupings include "health and safety and national security," "economy, efficiency, or national security," or "health or safety of the United States or its national security or welfare."

At best, "national security" is a phrase of convenience for lawmakers throughout the Federal Government, yet rarely is it defined or meaningfully explained. At worst, it is a term with little precise denotation, but subject to broad interpretation by Executive Branch officials. It has been the justification for the Nation's clandestine operations overseas, for broad claims of official secrecy, for domestic surveillance and for Government electronic eavesdropping everywhere in the world. Indeed, the danger underlying "national security" is that it could become the justification for excusing actions contrary to the law.

55. H. Rept. 93-221, p. 31.
56. *Ibid.*, pp. 58-59; for a detailed section-by-section analysis of E.O. 11652 see U.S. Congress. House. Committee on Government Operations. *U.S. Government Information Policies and Practices—Security Classification Problems Involving Subsection (b) (1) of the Freedom of Information Act, op. cit.*, pp. 2849-2883.
57. H. Rept. 93-221, pp. 102-103.
58. *Ibid.*, p. 104.
59. See U.S. Congress. House. Committee on Standards of Official Conduct. *Report on Investigation Pursuant to H. Res. 1042 Concerning Unauthorized Publication of the Report of the Select*

Committee on Intelligence. Washington: U.S. Govt. Print. Off., 1976. (94th Congress, 2d session. House. Report No. 94-1754), pp. 43-44.

60. See *The Presidential Campaign 1976*. Vol. I (Jimmy Carter). Washington: U.S. Govt. Print. Off., 1978, pp. 4, 226, 494; the commitments in question were made by candidate Carter in his formal announcement for the Presidency in a speech before the National Press Club, Washington, D.C. (December 12, 1974), his platform proposals to the platform committee of the Democratic Party meeting in New York (June 16, 1976), and an address to the American Bar Association in Atlanta, Georgia (August 11, 1976).

61. One of the drafts of the order appears in U.S. Congress. Senate. Committee on the Judiciary. *Freedom of Information*. Hearings, 95th Congress, 1st session. Washington: U.S. Govt. Print. Off., 1978, pp. 458-467; a critique of the draft which was offered by a coalition of civil liberties organizations appears in *Ibid.*, pp. 469-472; another critique, offered by the chairman of the House Subcommittee on Government Information and Individual Rights, appears U.S. Congress. House. Committee on Government Operations. *Security Classification Exemption to the Freedom of Information Act*. Hearings, 95th Congress, 1st session. Washington: U.S. Govt. Print. Off., 1979, pp. 95-103 and in *Congressional Record*, v. 123, October 13, 1977, pp. H10983-H10985; the order was published in *Federal Register*, v. 43, July 3, 1978, pp. 28949-28962.

62. The order was signed on June 28 but was not officially released to the press until the following day; see *The New York Times*, June 28, 1978.

63. See Washington *Post*, July 12, 1978.

64. See "Critique of the Proposed Executive Order on Security Classification" in U.S. Congress. House. Committee on Government Operations. *Security Classification Exemption to the Freedom of Information Act, op. cit.*, p. 95.

65. *Ibid.*, pp. 96-97.

66. *Ibid.*, p. 97.

67. *Ibid.*, pp. 98-99.

68. *Ibid.*, p. 99.

69. *Ibid.*, p. 100.

70. *Ibid.*, p. 101.

71. U.S. General Accounting Office. Report to the Congress of the United States by the Comptroller General. *Continuing Problems In DOD's Classification of National Security Information*. Wash-

ington: U.S. Govt. Print. Off., October 26, 1979. (LCD 80-16), pp. i–ii; also see *Ibid.*, pp. 5–11.
72. *Ibid.*, p. ii; also see *Ibid.*, pp. 12–24.
73. See *Snepp* v. *United States*, S.C. No. 78-1871 (with No. 79-265), February 19, 1980.
74. See *United States* v. *Progressive*, 467 F. Supp. 990 (1979); appeal vacated after material in question subsequently appeared in other publications; criminal prosecutions in these matters are under consideration within the Justice Department at present.
75. *Weekly Compilation of Presidential Documents*, v. 16, January 28, 1980, p. 198.
76. Testifying recently before the legislation subcommittee of the House Permanent Select Committee on Intelligence, Deputy Attorney General Robert L. Keuch voiced the reservations of his department regarding legislation to prohibit the identification of intelligence agents, warning that such a bill would have a "chilling effect" on freedom of speech. While he stopped short of judging the measure unconstitutional, other law experts have indicated it clashes with First Amendment guarantees. See Washington *Post*, January 31, 1980.
77. See U.S. Congress. House. Committee on Government Operations. *Availability of Information from Federal Departments and Agencies*. (17 Parts). Hearings, 84th-86th Congresses. Washington: U.S. Govt. Print. Off., 1956-1959.
78. See U.S. Congress. Senate. Committee on the Judiciary. *Freedom of Information*. Hearings, 88th Congress, 1st session. Washington: U.S. Govt. Print. Off., 1964; _____. *Administrative Procedure Act*. Hearings, 88th Congress, 2d session. Washington: U.S. Govt. Print. Off., 1964; _____. *Administrative Procedure Act*. Hearings, 89th Congress, 1st session. Washington: U.S. Govt. Print. Off., 1965; and _____. *Clarifying and Protecting the Right of the Public to Information and for Other Purposes*. Washington: U.S. Govt. Print. Off., 1965. (89th Congress, 1st session. Senate. Report No. 813.)

Also see U.S. Congress. House. Committee on Government Operations. *Federal Public Records Law*. Hearings, 89th Congress, 1st session. Washington: U.S. Govt. Print. Off., 1965; and _____. *Clarifying and Protecting the Right of the Public to Information*. Washington: U.S. Govt. Print. Off., 1966. (89th Congress, 2d session. House. Report No. 1497).

In addition, a general legislative history may be found in U.S. Congress. Senate. Committee on the Judiciary. *Freedom of Information Act Source Book: Legislative Materials, Cases, Arti-*

cles. Washington: U.S. Govt. Print. Off., 1974. (93rd Congress, 2d session. Senate. Document No. 93-82).

79. See, generally, Samuel J. Archibald. "The Freedom of Information Act Revisited," *Public Administration Review*, v. 39, July-August, 1979, pp. 311-318.

80. See, for example, *Environmental Protection Agency v. Mink, et. al.*, 410 U.S. 73 (1973) where the Supreme Court ruled that a claim of exemption under the national defense and foreign policy provision of the F.O.I. Act (5 U.S.C. 552(b) (1)) was satisfied by affidavit of the Government that the documents in question were classified properly, that Congress gave the Executive Branch the authority to determine if any information should be classified, and that Congress did not intend to subject the soundness of Executive Branch security classification decisions to judicial review — of which *in camera* inspection was a central aspect — at the insistence of any objecting citizens. The 1974 amendments to the F.O.I. Act overturned this interpretation by granting the courts the discretion to make *in camera* examinations of classified records, to question Executive Branch assertions that the documents at issue are classified properly, and to overrule the Executive Branch as to whether or not information is classified properly according to published rules and criteria.

Similarly, in *Administrator, Federal Aviation Administration v. Robertson*, 422 U.S. 255 (1975), the Supreme Court had ruled to the effect that the F.O.I. Act exemption allowing the withholding of records "specifically exempted from disclosure by statute" (5 U.S.C. 522(b)(3)) included within its ambit statutory provisions granting general discretionary authority to the head of an agency. Such provisions allow the withholding of information "not required in the public interest." This decision was overturned by an amendment to the Freedom of Information Act contained in the subsequently adopted Government in the Sunshine Act (90 Stat. 1241, 1247 at section 5). In brief, the provision for exemption from disclosure by intervening statute requires that such statutes specifically exempt information in a manner leaving no discretion on the issue or in terms of particular criteria or particular types of matters to be withheld.

81. For example, with regard to the difficulties of identifying what type of information constitutes a "trade secret," see James T. O'Reilly. "Government Disclosure of Private Secrets under the Freedom of Information Act," *The Business Lawyer*, v. 30, July, 1975, pp. 1125-1147.

82. The Attorney General's memorandum appears as U.S. Depart-

ment of Justice. *Attorney General's Memorandum on the Public Information Section of the Administrative Procedure Act.* Washington: U.S. Govt. Print. Off., June, 1967; for examples of judicial awareness of the weaknesses of this interpretative guide see *Consumers Union of the United States* v. *Veterans Administration*, 301 F. Supp. 796, 801 (1969); *Benson* v. *General Services Administration*, 289 F. Supp. 590, 595 (1968); *Soucie* v. *David*, 448 F. 2d. 1067, 1077 (1971); and *Getman* v. *National Labor Relations Board*, 450 F. 2d. 670 (1971).

83. See U.S. Congress. House. Committee on Government Operations. *U.S. Government Information Policies and Practices.* (Parts 4-9). Hearings, 92nd Congress, 2d session. Washington: U.S. Govt. Print. Off., 1972.

84. U.S. Congress. House. Committee on Government Operations. *Administration of the Freedom of Information Act.* Washington: U.S. Govt. Print. Off., 1972. (92nd Congress, 2d session. House. Report No. 92-1419), p. 8.

85. A general legislative history may be found in U.S. Congress. House. Committee on Government Operations. [and] Senate. Committee on the Judiciary. *Freedom of Information Act and Amendments of 1974 (P.L. 93–502) Source Book: Legislative History, Texts, and Other Documents.* Joint committee print, 94th Congress, 1st session. Washington: U.S. Govt. Print. Off., 1975; the F.O.I. Act was amended a second time in 1976 (see note 80).

86. Presumably this role was assumed—clearly, it was not assigned by Congress—as a consequence of the Justice Department's established leadership position in Administrative Procedure Act matters (the F.O.I. Act amended the A.P.A.) and responsibility for representing the Government in litigation, a prospect of definite portent under the Freedom of Information Act.

87. U.S. Commission on Federal Paperwork. *Confidentiality and Privacy.* Washington: U.S. Govt. Print. Off., July 29, 1977, p. 142.

88. When the Freedom of Information Act was amended in 1974 (88 Stat. 1561), the definition of "agency," indicating entities to which the statute would apply, was expanded to embrace almost every Executive Branch organization, including the Executive Office of the President, but not "the President's immediate personal staff or units in the Executive Office whose sole function is to advise and assist the President." See U.S. Congress. House. Committee of conference. *Freedom of Information Act Amend-*

ments. Washington: U.S. Govt. Print. Off., 1974. (93rd Congress, 2d session. House. Report No. 93-1380), p. 15.
89. *Ex Parte Milligan,* 71 U.S. (4 Wallace) 2, 125 (1866).

CHAPTER TWO NOTES

1. See Executive Office of the President. Office of Administration. "The Information Efficient Presidential Advisor." Washington, D.C., May 20, 1980 (draft), and Executive Office of the President. Office of Administration. "The Process of Development: Helping Senior Advisers become Information Efficient." Washington, D.C., June 9, 1980 (draft). Both papers are available to the public.

2. For instance, in 1977, the Information Systems Division of O.M.B. did not use a general purpose data base management system for application development.

3. The primary individuals were Richard Harden, then Special Assistant to the President for Organization and Management, and Frank Press, Assistant to the President for Science and Technology Policy.

4. See Executive Office of the President. Office of Science and Technology Policy. *Information Systems Needs in the Executive Office of the President: Final Report of the Advisory Group on White House Information Systems.* Washington: Executive Office of the President, Office of Science and Technology Policy, December, 1977.

5. See M. Zientra, "Presidential Office's DP Outlays Expected to Hit $10 Million in 1980," *Computerworld,* v. 15, June 9, 1980, p. 11.

6. See "A Model Office for Carter," *Business Week,* October 2, 1978, p. 40B.

7. See R. Ackoff, "Management Misinformation Systems," *Management Science,* v. 14, No. 4, 1967, pp. B147-B156.

8. For example, a system such as Bolt, Beraneck, and Newman's HERMES or Computer Corporation of America's COMIT with editing, message sending, message receiving, and filing capabilities.

9. See R. White, "The Prototype for the Automated Office," *Datamation,* v. 23, April, 1977, pp. 83-86, 88, 90.

10. L. Runyan, "A Trial Balloon," *Datamation,* v. 25, October, 1979, p. 55.

11. *Ibid.*
12. For instance, there is a need to have most of the user community on a system before the system can be an effective method of communication among them.
13. See "The Pahlavi Problem: A Superficial Diagnosis Brought the Shah into the United States," *Science*, v. 207, January 18, 1980, pp. 282-286.
14. Decision support systems differ from transaction processing systems in that they usually provide a model of some process, data about the process, and the ability to interact with the model in order to explore the consequences of different actions.

CHAPTER THREE NOTES

1. Woodrow Wilson. *Congressional Government*. Cleveland and New York: World Publishing Company, 1956; originally published 1885, p. 30.
2. An exception may be found, perhaps referentially, in the Freedom of Information Act; see *Federal Open Market Committee* v. *Merrill*, S.C. No. 77-1387 (June 28, 1979), p. 19 (slip opinion).
3. See *U. S.* v. *Burr*, 25 Fed. Cas. 30 (No. 14692d) (Cir. Ct. Va. 1807); 25 Fed. Cas. 55(No. 14693) (Cir. Ct. Va. 1807); 25 Fed. Cas. 187 (No. 14694) (Cir. Ct. Va. 1807).
4. 345 U.S. 1 (1952).
5. *U.S.* v. *Nixon*, 418 U.S. 683 (1974).
6. *Nixon* v. *Administrator of General Services*, 433 U.S. 425 (1977).
7. *Senate Select Committee on Presidential Campaign Activities* v. *Nixon*, 498 F. 2d 725 (C.A. D.C. 1974).
8. This case is discussed in Harold C. Relyea. "The Presidency and the People's Right to Know" in this volume.
9. However, see U.S. Congress. Senate. Committee on the Judiciary. *Refusals by the Executive Branch to Provide Information to the Congress 1964-1973*. Committee print, 93rd Congress, 2d session. Washington: U.S. Govt. Print. Off., 1974.
10. H. H. Gerth and C. Wright Mills, eds. *From Max Weber: Essays in Sociology*. New York: Oxford University Press, 1946, pp. 233-234.
11. See, generally, Raoul Berger. "Executive Privilege Vs. Congressional Inquiry," *U.C.L.A. Law Review*, v. 12, May, 1965, pp. 1044-1120, and August, 1965, pp. 1287-1364; _____. *Executive Privilege: A Constitutional Myth*. Cambridge: Harvard University Press, 1974; _____. "The Incarnation of

Executive Privilege," *U.C.L.A. Law Review*, v. 22, October, 1974, pp. 4-30; _____. "Executive Privilege In Light of U.S. v. Nixon," *Loyola of Los Angeles Law Review*, v. 9, December, 1975, pp. 20-33.

12. Bob Woodward and Scott Armstrong. *The Brethren*. New York: Simon and Schuster, 1979.
13. See *Ibid.*, pp. 287-347.
14. *Osborn* v. *Bank of U.S.*, 22 U.S. 737 (1824).
15. Ray Forrester. "Are We Ready for Truth in Judging?" *American Bar Association Journal*, v. 63, September, 1977, pp. 1212-1216.
16. 384 U.S. 436, 531-532.
17. *Marbury* v. *Madison*, 1 Cranch (5 U.S.) 137 (1803).
18. 2 Black (67 U.S.)635 (1863).
19. *Youngstown Sheet and Tube Co.* v. *Sawyer*, 343 U.S. 579 (1952).
20. 135 U.S. 1 (1890).
21. 158 U.S. 564 (1895).
22. *U.S.* v. *Midwest Oil Co.*, 236 U.S. 459 (1915).
23. 272 U.S. 52 (1926).
24. *Humphrey's Executor* v. *U.S.*, 295 U.S. 602 (1935).
25. *New York Times Co.* v. *U.S.*, 403 U.S. 713 (1971).
26. A more lasting statutory response may be found in the Presidential Records Act of 1978 (92 Stat. 2523; 44 U.S.C. 2201-2207).
27. See U.S. National Study commission on the Records and Documents of Federal Officials. *Final Report*. Washington: U.S. Govt. Print. Off., 1977; also see Arthur S. Miller and Henry Bartholomew Cox. "On the Need for a National Commission on Documentary Access," *George Washington Law Review*, v. 44, January, 1976, pp. 213-238.
28. *U.S.* v. *Nixon*, 418 U.S. 683, 705.
29. Carl J. Friedrich. *The Pathology of Politics*. New York: Harper and Row, 1972, p. 179.
30. Irving Janis. *Victims of Groupthink*. Boston: Houghton Mifflin Company, 1972.
31. *Goldwater* v. *Carter*, S.C. No. 79-856 (December 13, 1979).
32. J. A. G. Griffith. *The Politics of the Judiciary*. Manchester: Manchester University Press, 1977.
33. See Alpheus T. Mason. *Harlan Fiske Stone: Piller of the Law*. New York: Viking Press, 1956.
34. 492 F. 2d 587 (C.A. D.C. 1974).
35. 4 Wallace (71 U.S.) 475 (1867).
36. Archibald Cox. "Executive Privilege," *University of Pennsylvania Law Review*, v. 122, June, 1974, pp. 1383-1439.
37. 17 Fed. Cas. 144 (No. 9487) (C.C.D. Md. 1861).

38. 6 Wheaton (19 U.S.) 204 (1821).
39. 273 U.S. 135 (1924).
40. 243 U.S. 521 (1917).
41. 294 U.S. 125 (1935).
42. 408 U.S. 606 (1972).
43. 421 U.S. 491 (1975).
44. 511 F. 2d 430 (C.A. D.C. 1974).
45. 366 F. Supp. 104 (D.C. D.C. 1973).
46. *McCulloch* v. *Maryland*, 4 Wheaton (17 U.S.) 316 (1819).
47. See Charles Black. "The Working Balance of the American Political Departments," *Hastings Constitutional Law Quarterly*, v. 1, Spring, 1974, pp. 13-21.
48. 418 U.S. 116 (1974).
49. 408 U.S. 665 (1972).
50. 354 U.S. 178 (1957).

CHAPTER FOUR NOTES

1. 345 U.S. 1 (1952).
2. See testimony of Morton H. Halperin before the Subcommittee on Legislation of the House Permanent Select Committee on Intelligence on H.R. 4736 and H.R. 4746, 96th Congress, 1st session (August 7, 1979).
3. U.S. Congress. House. Committee on Government Operations. *Clarifying and Protecting the Right of the Public to Information*. Washington: U.S. Govt. Print. Off., 1966. (89th Congress, 2d session. House. Report No. 1497), pp. 9-10; also see Christine M. Marwick, ed. *The 1980 Edition of Litigation Under the Federal Freedom of Information Act and Privacy Act*. Fifth edition. Washington: Center for National Security Studies, 1979, pp. 42-50.
4. 410 U.S. 73, 94 (1973).
5. See U.S. Congress. Senate. Committee on Government Operations [and] Committee on the Judiciary. *Executive Privilege, Secrecy in Government, Freedom of Information*. Hearings, 93rd Congress, 1st session. Washington: U.S. Govt. Print. Off., 1973; also see U.S. Congress. House. Committee on Government Operations. *U.S. Government Information Policies and Practices*. (Parts 4-9). Hearings, 92nd Congress, 2d session. Washington: U.S. Govt. Print. Off., 1972.
6. *Ray* v. *Turner*, 587 F. 2d 1187 (1978); *Halperin* v. *Dept. of State*,

565 F. 2d 699 (1977); *Phillippi* v. *C.I.A.*, 546 F. 2d 1009 (1976); also see *Hayden* v. *N.S.A.*, 78-1720 (D.C. Cir. Oct. 29, 1979).

7. See *Federal Register*, v. 43, July 3, 1978, pp. 28949-28962.

8. Reprinted with revisions from Morton H. Halperin. "A Balancing Test for Classified Information," *The Federal Bar Journal*, v. 38, Fall, 1979, pp. 134-140. (Reprinted with permission)

9. *Federal Register*, v. 43, July 3, 1978, pp. 46282-46283.

10. E.O. 12065, section 3-303.

11. 5 U.S.C. 552(b)(1); see *Ray* v. *Turner* and *Halperin* v. *Dept. of State* cited at note 6.

12. Morton H. Halperin and Daniel N. Hoffman. *Top Secret*. Washington: New Republic Books, 1977.

13. *Ibid.*, pp. 58-67.

14. *Ibid.*, pp. 58, 67-68, 72-73.

15. S. Res. 400, 94th Congress, 2d session. An identical provision is contained in H. Res. 658, 95th Congress, 1st session, establishing the House Permanent Select Committee of Intelligence.

16. Presidential Review Momorandum/NSC-29 (June 1, 1977).

17. This description of the process of drafting the Executive order is based on interviews with participants in the process.

18. Based upon text of draft Executive order as cited in *Access Reports*, v. 3, September 20, 1977, pp. 3-10 and a version appearing in U.S. Congress. Senate. Committee on the Judiciary. *Freedom of Information*. Hearings, 95th Congress, 1st session. Washington: U.S. Govt. Print. Off., 1978, pp. 458-467.

19. The full text of the letter, signed by representatives for nine civil liberties organizations, appears in U.S. Congress. Senate. Committee on the Judiciary. *Freedom of Information, op. cit.*, pp. 469-472.

20. *Weekly Compilation of Presidential Documents*, v. 14, July 3, 1978, pp. 1193-1194.

21. See Information Security Oversight Office Implementing Directive, section 3-B, appearing in *Federal Register*, v. 43, October 5, 1978, p. 46282.

22. Unpublished Brzezinski letter (November 30, 1978).

23. C.I.A. regulations attached to Government motion for summary judgment in various F.O.I. Act cases, including *Afshar* v. *Dept. of State*, 76-1421 (D.C. D.C. filed July 30, 1976).

24. See, for example, supplemental affidavit of Eloise Page in *Afshar* v. *Dept. of State*, 76-1421 (D.C. D.C. filed July 30, 1976).

25. See, generally, Halperin and Hoffman, *op. cit.*, pp. 27-32.

26. See Marwick, *op. cit.*, p. 94.

27. See *Halperin* v. *Dept. of State* cited at note 6.
28. See *Ray* v. *Turner* cited at note 6.

CHAPTER FIVE NOTES

1. *Weekly Compilation of Presidential Documents*, v. 10, September 16, 1974, pp. 1117–18.
2. U.S. Congress. Senate. Committee on Appropriations. *Treasury, Postal Service, and General Government Appropriations for Fiscal Year 1979*. Hearings, 95th Congress, 2nd session. Washington: U.S. Government Printing Office, 1978, p. 859.
3. Franklin D. Roosevelt Library, Hyde Park, N.Y., founded 1941; Holdings: 38,000 books; 59,000 pamphlets and serials; 20 million manuscripts; 90,000 photographs; 20,000 museum objects. Harry S Truman Library, Independence, Mo., founded 1957; Holdings: 41,843 books; 2,264 bound periodicals; 9,786,000 manuscripts on paper; 52,380 other printed matter; 146 oral history interviews; 14 VF drawers. Dwight D. Eisenhower Library, Abilene, Kan., founded 1962; Holdings: 25,880 books, 26,340 other printed items, 18,573,800 manuscripts pages, 102,560 photographs, 592,880 feet film, 2,360 sound recordings, 190,940 pages oral interviews. Herbert Hoover Library, West Branch, Ia., founded 1962. Holdings: 19,885 books; 855 bound periodicals; 19,983 unbound periodicals, 2,000 linear feet of manuscripts; 83,000 photographs; 2,295 sound recordings; 4,055 reels of microfilm; 588,830 feet of motion picture film. John F. Kennedy Library, Boston, Mass., opened 1979. Holdings: 16,000 volumes; 10 million manuscript papers; 2.2 million pages of records of the Democratic National Committee; 500,000 pages of collections of personal papers; 2,500 reels of records and papers; 65,000 still photos; 2,000 sound recordings; 1.5 million feet of motion picture film. Lyndon B. Johnson Library, Austin, Tex., founded 1972. Holdings: 3,122 books; 2,288 unbound periodicals; 4,926 Congressional hearings; 32,722,737 archives manuscript pages; 519,648 photos; 4,000 video-recordings; 8,176 sound recordings, 35,560 museum items, 519,640 feet of motion picture film. All of the foregoing are administered through the National Archives and Record Service. The seventh, the Gerald R. Ford Library on the campus of the University of Michigan at Ann Arbor has subsequently (April 1981) been opened. The eighth, the Rutherford B. Hayes Library in Fremont, Ohio, is privately supported.

4. See, U.S. Congress. House. Committee on Government Operations. *Presidential Records Act of 1978*. Washington: U.S. Government Printing Office, 1978. (95th Congress, 2nd session. House. Report No. 95-1487 Part I). Public Law 95-591, *Presidential Records Act of 1978*, November 4, 1978. See Robert L. Hardesty. "The President's Papers," *The New York Times*, April 29, 1979.

5. Cf., *New York Times*, December 11, 1938. Quoted in H.G. Jones. *The Records of a Nation*. New York: Atheneum, 1969, p. 145.

6. Cf., John McDonough, R. Gordon Hoxie, and Richard Jacobs. "Who Owns Presidential Papers?" *Manuscripts*, v. 27. Winter, 1975; Arthur Schlesinger, Jr. "Who Owns a President's Papers?" *Wall Street Journal*, February 26, 1975, p. 16; Buford Rowland. "The Papers of the Presidents," *American Archivist*, v. 13, July, 1950, pp. 195-211; James Rhoads. "Who Should Own the Documents of Public Officials?" *Prologue*, v. 7, Spring, 1975, pp. 32-35; Arnold Hirshon. "The Scope, Accessibility and History of Presidential Papers," *Government Publications Review*, v. 1, 1974, pp. 363-390; J. Frank Cook. "Private Papers of Public Officials," *American Archivist*, v. 38, July, 1975, pp. 299-324; David Horn. "Who Owns Our History?", *Library Journal*, v. 100, April 1, 1975, pp. 635-639; Russell Fridley. "Should Public Papers Be Private Property?" *Minnesota History*, v. 44, Spring, 1974, pp. 37-39; Warren Reed. "Public Papers of the Presidents," *American Archivist*, v. 25, October, 1962, pp. 435-439; Oliver W. Holmes. " 'Public Records'—Who Knows What They Are?" *American Archivist*, v. 14, January, 1960, pp. 3-26.

7. Cf., John C. Fitzpatrick, ed. *The Writings of George Washington from the Original Manuscript Sources*, 1745-1799. Washington: U.S. Government Printing Office, 1931-1940. v. 37, p. 284.

8. Leston Cappon. "Why Presidential Libraries?" *The Yale Review*, v. 48, October, 1978, pp. 14-15.

9. Ibid., p. 15.

10. Cf., J. Frank Cook, op. cit., p. 306.

11. Cf., Herbert Adams, ed. *The Life and Writings of Jared Sparks* 2 vols. Boston: Houghton, Mifflin, 1893; Jared Sparks, ed. *The Writings of George Washington*, 12 volumes. Boston: Little, Brown, 1855. Cook noted that "following fifteen months of negotiation and persuasion by Marshall and others, Washington agreed to the publication of his uncle's papers, after he, as heir, obtained the right to forbid the publication of any letters he deemed embarrassing or damaging" p. 306.

12. *Ibid.*, p. 306.
13. Cf. Sister Louise Lovely, C.H.M. "The Evolution of Presidential Libraries," *Government Publications Review*, v. 6, 1979, pp. 27-35; R. D. W. Connor. "The FDR Library," *American Archivist*, v. 3, April, 1940, pp. 83-92.
14. U.S. Congress. House. Committee on Government Operations. *To Provide for the Acceptance and Maintenance of Presidential Libraries and other Purposes.* Hearings, 84th Congress, 1st session. Washington: U.S. Government Printing Office, 1955, p. 394; Cf. Helen D. Bullock. "The Robert Todd Lincoln Collection of the Papers of Abraham Lincoln," *Library of Congress Quarterly Journal*, v. 5, November, 1947, pp. 3-9; Kenneth Duckett and Francis Russell. "The Harding Papers. How Some Were Burned . . . and Some Were Saved," *American Heritage*, v. 16, February, 1965, pp. 24-31.
15. Margaret Truman. *Harry S. Truman*. New York: William Morrow & Co., 1973.
16. James D. Richardson, ed. *A Compilation of the Messages and Papers of the Presidents*, 1787-1897, 10 vols. Washington: U.S. Government Printing Office, 1896-1898, vol. 8, p. 378. Cf. William Howard Taft. *Our Chief Magistrate and his Powers*, New York: Columbia University Press, 1916, p. 34.
17. Lester Cappon, op. cit., p. 16:
"Thus the checkered story of presidential papers, their status as private property strengthened by custom, runs through 150 years until 1939, a variegated record of conscientious preservation, of accidental or willful destruction, of crass commercialism, and of sheer indifference."
18. Cited in H.G. Jones. *The Records of a Nation*. New York: Atheneum, 1969, p. 146. The group included Charles Beard, Samuel Morrison, William Dodd, Randolph Adams, Frederic Passon, Julian Boyd, and Helen Taft Manning.
19. *Ibid.*, p. 145.
20. *Ibid.*, p. 147.
21. An advisory committee was soon established and included Waldo Leland, R. D. W. Conner, Robert Binkley, W. E. B. Dubois, Guy Stanton Ford, Douglas Southall Freeman, Edwin Gay, Monsignor Peter Guilday, Allan Nevins, Bessie Louis Perre and Walter Prescott Webb. Notes from this meeting can be located in "Minutes, First meeting of the Executive Committee," December 17, 1938, FDR Library File Box, Roosevelt Library.
22. Cf. Waldo Leland. "The Creation of the Franklin D. Roosevelt Library: A Personal Narrative," *American Archivist*, v. 18, Janu-

ary, 1955, pp. 11-29; R. D. W. Conner. "The Franklin D. Roosevelt Library," *American Archivist*, v. 3, April, 1940, pp. 81-92; Herman Kahn. "The Presidential Library — A New Institution," *Special Libraries*, v. 50, March, 1959, pp. 106-113; Herman Kahn. "The Long-Range Implications for historians and archivists of the charges against the Franklin D. Roosevelt Library." *American Archivist*, v. 34, July, 1971, pp. 265-275.

23. H.G. Jones, *op. cit.*, p. 147.

24. *Presidential Libraries Act*; Public Law 373, 84th Congress.; 69 Stat. 965-66.

25. J. Frank Cook, *op. cit.*, p. 311.

26. Cf. U.S. Congress. Senate. Committee on Appropriations. *Treasury, Postal Service, and General Government Appropriations for Fiscal Year 1979*. Hearings, 95th Congress, 2nd Session. Washington: U.S. Government Printing Office, 1978, pp. 825-830.

27. J. Frank Cook, op. cit., pp. 314-316.

28. Nixon-Sampson Agreement, September 6, 1974, in *Weekly Compilation of Presidential Documents*, v. 10, September 16, 1974, pp. 1104-5; Cf. Clement Vose. "Presidential Papers as a Political Science Concern," *PS*, v. 8, Winter, 1975, pp. 8-18.

29. J. Frank Cook, *op. cit.*, p. 134; Lester Cappon (*op. cit.*, p. 32) noted that "in view of all that had transpired during the previous two years, this was *reductio and absurdum* concerning the custom of private ownership of presidential records."

30. *Ibid.*, p. 315.

31. *Presidential Recordings and Materials Preservation Act*; 44 U.S.C. 2107; Public Law 93-526; 88 Stat. 1695.

32. See Sister Louise Lovely, *op. cit.*, pp. 30-31; also see Lester Cappon, *op. cit.*, pp. 33.

33. Membership on the Commission included Herbert Brownwell, (Chairman and former Attorney General of the United States), Philip Buchen (Special Counsel to President Ford), J. Edward Lumbard (Federal Judiciary), Gaylord Nelson (Senate), Lowell P. Weicher, Jr. (Senate), Allen Ertel (House), Robert Lagomarsino (House), John Thomas (State Department), David Cooke (Defense), James Rhoads (Archivist of the U.S.), Elizabeth Hamer Kegan (Library of Congress); William Leuchtenburg (American Historical Association), Ann Morgan Campbell (Society of American Archivists), Frank Freidel, Jr., (Organization of American Historians), Lucius Battle (COMSAT), Ernest May (Professor of History at Harvard, representing the public). CF. Sister Louis Lovely's analysis of the majority and minority reports

which revealed marked disagreement in some areas of the Commission's findings and recommendations; see Note 13, *supra*.

34. CF. Note 2, *supra*.
35. U.S. General Services Administration News Release, October 1, 1979.
36. Sister Louise Lovely, *op cit.*, p. 29.
37. Hugh Heclo. *Studying the Presidency: A Report to the Ford Foundation*. New York: The Ford Foundation, 1979.
38. Steven Puro. "Research in Presidential Libraries: The Soliciter General of the United States" paper presented at the Missouri Political Service Association meeting, 1979.
39. Forthcoming, the University of Texas Press, 1980.
40. Certainly this has been the case with regard to my own research at the Lyndon Johnson Library. I consider professionally trained archivists an invaluable asset in helping researchers identify relevant areas for inquiry.
41. Letter, Kermit Gordon to Bill Moyers, July 28, 1965, Executive/FG 11-1, Container #11, folder June 13, 1965-August 19, 1965.
42. Letter, John Steinbeck to Jack Valenti, January 14, 1968. Executive/PR 18, Container #362.
43. Memorandum, Mary R. to the President, June 5, 1968. Diary backup, June 5, 1968.
44. Memorandum, Robert Kintner to the President, Personal, July 28, 1966. Files of Harry McPherson, Container #18.
45. Memorandum, Harry McPherson to the President, November 2, 1967. Executive/FG 1 (16), November 2, 1967-January 5, 1968, Folder EX/FG 1, November 2, 1967-November 7, 1967.
46. Memorandum, Bill Moyers to MJDR, undated. Diary Backup File, Undated.
47. Hugh Heclo. *Studying the Presidency: Report to the Ford Foundation*. New York: The Ford Foundation, 1979.
48. *U.S. News & World Report*, June 18, 1979, p. 5.
49. See Note 2, *supra*.
50. *Ibid.*

CHAPTER SIX NOTES

1. *Code of Federal Regulations, 1976.* Title 41, chapter 101-11.401-3(d); *Federal Register*, v. 40, July 9, 1975, p. 28952.
2. U.S. Congress. House. Committee on House Administration. Subcommittee on Printing. *The "Public Documents Act."* Hear-

ings, 93rd Congress, 2d session. Washington: U.S. Government Printing Office, 1974, pp. 35, 41.

3. Arthur Schlesinger, Jr. "Who Owns a President's Papers?" *Wall Street Journal*, February 26, 1975.

4. National Study Commission on Records and Documents of Federal Officials. *Final Report*. Washington: General Services Administration, 1977; "The Records of Federal Officials," [Final Report of the Forty-Eighth American Assembly], *The American Archivist*, v. 38, July, 1975, pp. 329–336; Alonzo L. Hamby and Edward Weldon, eds. *Access to the Papers of Recent Public Figures: The New Harmony Conference*. Bloomington, Indiana: Organization of American Historians, 1977.

5. Walter Lippmann. "The Sale of Official Opinions," *New York Tribune*, March 3, 1938; M. B. Schnapper. "Public Papers and Private Gain," *The Nation*, v. 229, November 24, 1979, pp. 524–526.

6. U.S. Congress. House. Committee on Government Operations. Subcommittee on Government Information and Individual Rights. *Presidential Records Act of 1978*. Hearings, 95th Congress, 2d session. Washington: U.S. Government Printing Office, 1978, p. 82. Although the language that Congressman Ertel used in his bill was not followed precisely in the final text of the statute, it is clear from the subsequent legislative history that automatic public ownership of a President's political papers was to be virtually complete. The House report on the bill listed as private only those political acts of voting and making campaign contributions of less than $100. U.S. Congress. House. Committee on Government Operations. *Presidential Records Act of 1978*. Washington: U.S. Government Printing Office, 1978. (95th Congress, 2d session. House. Report No. 95-1487 Part I), pp. 11–12. The legislative report was later modified to limit what could be characterized as private political papers to those materials relating to a President's own election. *Congressional Record*, v. 124, October 5, 1978, pp. H11756-7. Subsequent debate in the House and Senate suggests an extremely narrow definition of those political papers that would remain under a President's control. See remarks of Congressman John Brademas, *Ibid.*, October 10,.1978, p. H11928; Senator Charles Percy, *Ibid.*, October 13, 1978, p. S19069; Senator Gaylord Nelson, *Ibid.*, p. S19070; and Congressman Jack Brooks, *Ibid.*, October 14, 1978, p. H13036.

7. U.S. Congress. House. Committee on Government Operations. *Presidential Records Act of 1978, op. cit.* (Hearings), p. 268.

8. *Ibid.*, p. 275.
9. See: Arthur Link. Remarks during Panel Discussion, "Presidential Papers—Public or Private," Ninetieth Annual Meeting of the American Historical Association, December 29, 1975; Edwin A. Weinstein, James William Anderson, and Arthur S. Link. "Woodrow Wilson's Political Personality: A Reappraisal," *Political Science Quarterly*, v. 93, Winter, 1978, pp. 585–598; Alexander L. George and Juliette L. George, "Dr. Weinstein's Interpretation of Woodrow Wilson: Some Preliminary Observations," *The Psychohistory Review*, v. 8, Summer-Fall, 1979, p. 72.
10. H. G. Jones. *The Records of A Nation*. New York: Atheneum, 1969, pp. 155, 161–163.
11. Anthony Lewis. "Who Really Owns the Papers of Departing Federal Officials?" *The New York Times*, February 6, 1977.
12. National Archives and Records Service. "Donation of Personal Papers to the Richard Nixon Library." November, 1972.
13. *Federal Register*, v. 41, November 19, 1976, p. 51149. Although this bulletin did not apply to Presidential papers, the Archivist urged Congress to make similar standards applicable to Presidents in the proposed Presidential records act; see U.S. Congress. House. Committee on Government Operations. *Presidential Records Act of 1978, op. cit.* (Hearings), p. 135.
14. Dean Rusk, Remarks, Annual Meeting of the American Historical Association, December 29, 1975.
15. A. J. P. Taylor, "Keeping It Dark," *Encounter*, v. 13, August, 1959, p. 43.
16. Gouverneur Morris to George Washington, April 6, 1792, George Washington Papers, Manuscript Division, Library of Congress; George Washington to Gouverneur Morris, June 21, 1792, Gouverneur Morris Papers, Columbia University Library. It is, perhaps, worth noting that Washington did not deposit or make copies of this correspondence for the State Department archives, although it was not an uncommon practice for him.

CHAPTER SEVEN NOTES

1. Daniel Patrick Moynihan, "The Presidency and the Press," *Commentary*, u.51, March, 1971, pp. 41–52. Sen. Moynihan, an aide in the Nixon White House, presents a blistering attack on the press for the problems it has caused Presidents. *New York Times* White House correspondent John Herbers described the contin-

ued manipulatability of reporters in his book, *No Thank You, Mr. President*. New York: W.W. Norton, 1976.

2. *The New York Times*, May 10, 1961, cited by Itazhak Galnoor (ed.) in *Government Secrecy in Democracies*. New York: Colophon Books, 1977, p. vii.

3. John Lengel, *Washington Post*, August 9, 1974, cited by William E. Porter in *Assault on the Media*. Ann Arbor: The University of Michigan Press, 1976, p. 192.

4. Herbert S. Parmet, *Eisenhower and the American Crusade*. New York: The Macmillan Company, 1972, pp. 552-558. Also R. Gordon Hoxie, *Command Decision and the Presidency*. New York, Reader's Digest Press, 1977, p. 258.

5. Ron Nessen, *It Sure Looks Different From the Inside*. Chicago: Playboy Press, 1978, p. 13.

6. "The character of the cabinet may be made a nice index of the theory of the presidential office, as well as the President's theory of party government; but the one view is, so far as I can see, as constitutional as the other." Woodrow Wilson, *Constitutional Government*. New York: Columbia University Press, 1908, p. 77.

7. Richard E. Neustadt, *Presidential Power: The Politics of Leadership from F. D. R. to Carter*. New York: John Wiley, 1980.

8. Interview with *Dennis Farney* (Washington, D.C.: MJK, June 27, 1979).

9 Interview with *Walt Rostow* (Austin, Texas: MJK, July 9, 1976).

10. Interview with *James Reston* (Washington, D.C.: MBG and MJK, January 28, 1977).

11. Background interview, (Washington, D.C.: MJK and MBG, December, 1976).

12. Interview with *Walt Rostow*, July 9, 1976.

13. Background interview, (Washington, D.C.: MJK and MBG, December, 1976).

14. Francis E. Rourke, *Secrecy and Publicity, Dilemmas of Democracy*. Baltimore Md.: The Johns Hopkins University Press, 1961, pp. 197-198.

Selected Reading List

FREEDOM OF INFORMATION ACT

Books

Ackerly, Robert L., and William J. Spriggs. Freedom of information: course manual. Washington, Federal Publications, Inc., 1979. var. pag.

Anderson, David A., and Brandon C. Janes, eds. Privacy and public disclosures under the Freedom of Information Act. Austin, Texas, Tarlton Law Library, University of Texas School of Law, 1976. 173 p. (Tarlton Law Library legal bibliography series; no. 11).

Cross, Harold L. The people's right to know — legal access to public records and proceedings. Morningside Heights, New York, Columbia University Press, 1953. 405 p.

Dorsen, Norman, and Stephen Gillers, eds. Government secrecy in America: none of your business. New York, The Viking Press, 1974. 362 p.

Galnoor, Itzhak, ed. Government secrecy in democracies. New York, New York University Press, 1977. 313 p.

Ladd, Bruce. Crisis in credibility. New York, New American Library, 1968. 247 p.

Levenson, Alan B., and Harvey L. Pitt. Government information: Freedom of Information Act, Sunshine Act, Privacy Act. New York City, Practicing Law Institute, c1978. 760 p.

Marwick, Christine, ed. The 1980 edition of litigation under the amended Federal Freedom of Information Act. 5th ed. Washington, The Center for National Security Studies, 1980: var. pag.

Mezines, Basil J., Jacob A. Stein, and Jules Gruff. Administrative law: acquisition, use and disclosure of government information; Freedom of Information, Privacy, Sunshine, and related Acts. v. 2. New York, Matthew Bender & Co., 1977; var. pag.

O'Reilly, James T. Federal information disclosure: procedures, forms, and the law. Colorado Springs, Colorado, Shepard's Inc. [and] New York, McGraw-Hill, 1979: 2 v. var. pag.

Rourke, Francis E. Secrecy and publicity: dilemmas of democracy. Baltimore, Johns Hopkins Press, 1961. 236 p.

Sherick, L. G. How to use the Freedom of Information Act (FOIA). New York, Arco Publishing Company, Inc., 1978. 138 p.

Steele, Fritz. The open organization: the impact of secrecy and disclosure on people and organizations. Reading, Addison-Wesley, 1975. 204 p.

Wiggins, James Russell. Freedom or secrecy. Rev. ed. New York, Oxford University Press, 1964. 289 p.

Articles

Adams, Greg. Freedom of Information Act — agency secrecy continues. Washington law review, v. 52, Nov. 1976: 121-141.

Adams, Wilsie H., Jr. The Freedom of Information Act and pretrial discovery. Military law review, v. 43, Jan. 1969: 1-35.

Adler, Mark S. National security information under the amended Freedom of Information Act: historical perspectives and analysis. Hofstra law review, v. 4, Spring 1976: 759-804.

Administrative Law — Freedom of Information Act — commercial or financial information "confidential" if disclosure would impare government access to information or harm competitive position of informant. Harvard law review, v. 88, Dec. 1974: 470-477.

— — —Courts must order agencies to disclose information unless it falls within specific exemptions. University of Illinois law forum, v. 1971, no. 2, 1971: 329-336.

— — —Department of Agriculture must disclose detentions of meat and poultry products and warning letters sent to processors. Harvard law review, v. 85, Feb. 1972: 861-870.

— — —Disclosure of service academy's honor and ethics code case summaries with identifying information deleted is permissible under act. Maryland law review, v. 34, no. 3, 1974: 429-441.

— — — Exemption 5 — information concerning grounds for some Renegotiation Board decisions made unavailable. Brigham Young University law review, v. 1976, no. 1, 1976: 269-280.

— — — Internal memoranda that contain statements of policy or interpretations adopted by an agency may be subject to disclosure. — Sterling Drug, Inc. v. F.T.C. Texas law review, v. 50, May 1972: 1006-1017.

— — —Freedom of Information Act — letters of warning and detention are identifiable records not within investigatory files exemption, and their disclosure is not a violation of due process. Fordham law review, v. 40, May 1972: 921-929.

— — —Private letter rulings issued by the Internal Revenue Service held disclosable as interpretations of the law adopted by the agency. Indiana law review, v. 7, no. 2, 1973: 416-432.

— — —Private letter rulings issued by the Internal Revenue Service to taxpayers are not exempt from disclosure under the Freedom of Information Act although Internal Revenue Service technical advice memoranda are so exempt. Georgia law review, v. 9, Winter 1975: 499-510.

— — —The processing of an unexpected deluge of FOIA requests on a first-in, first-out basis, except where the information seeker demonstrates exceptional need or urgency, is compliance with the Freedom of Information Act. Georgia law review, v. 11, Fall 1976: 241-250.

— — —Trial court's procedures must effectively place burden of justification on agency denying request for information. Harvard law review, v. 87, Feb. 1974: 854-865.

— — —Writ of mandamus granted requiring pesticide applicators' reports open to public inspection. University of Kansas law review, v. 20, Spring 1972: 525-538.

Albert, Jeffrey B. Freedom of information — court may permit withholding of information not exempted from disclosure under Freedom of Information Act: Consumers Union of United States, Inc. v. Veterans Administration. Harvard civil rights-civil liberties law review, v. 5, Jan. 1970: 121-133.

Amendment of the seventh exemption under the Freedom of Information Act. William and Mary law review, v. 16, Spring 1975: 697-715.

Amoroso, Frank. The Freedom of Information Act: shredding the paper curtain. St. John's law review, v. 47, May 1973: 694-724.

Andich, David W. The Freedom of Information Act, a challenge to the executive and the judiciary. John Marshall journal of practice and procedure, v. 7, Spring 1974: 293-334.

Archibald, Samuel J. Access to government information—the right before the First amendment. In The First amendment and the news media: final report. Cambridge, Mass., Roscoe-Pound-American Trial Lawyers Foundation, 1973: 64-76.

— — —The FOI Act goes to court. Columbia, School of Journalism, University of Missouri, 1972. 14 p. (Missouri. University. Freedom of Information Center. Report no. 280).

Arnold, Marc, and Andrew Kisseloff. An introduction to the Federal Privacy Act of 1974 and its effect on the Freedom of Information Act. New England law review, v. 11, Spring 1976: 463-496.

Asbill, Mac, Jr. Freedom of information and the IRS. Oil and Gas Institute, Southwestern Legal Foundation, v. 25, 1974: 487-528.

Asbill, Mac, Jr., and others. The Reach for information in tax cases. Twenty-ninth Annual Institute on Federal Taxation. University of So. California Law Center, v. 29, 1977: 655-705.

Atkinson, Clifford K. Administrative law—Freedom of Information Act: pre-FOIA statutes giving Federal agencies discretion in withholding agency information held valid under exemption 3. National resources journal, v. 16, Oct. 1976: 1027-1031.

Attorney General's memorandum on the public information section of the Administrative Procedure Act. Administrative law review, v. 20, Mar. 1968: 263-318.

Avery, Jane C. What are administrative staff manuals and instructions to staff that affect a member of the public that must be disclosed under the Freedom of Information Act. American law reports federal, v. 22. Rochester, N.Y., The Lawyers co-operative publishing co., 1975: 325-338.

— — —What constitutes "trade secrets and commercial or financial information obtained from a person and privileged or confidential," exempt from disclosure under Freedom of Information Act. American law reports federal, v. 21, Rochester, N.Y., The Lawyers co-operative publishing co., 1974: 224-247.

Baach, Martin R. Administrative law—Freedom of Information Act—classification of files pursuant to Executive Order is not subject to judicial review under the Freedom of Information Act. University of Cincinnati law review, v. 42, no. 3, 1973: 529–539.

Bagge, Carl E. The Federal Power Commission and freedom of information. Public utilities fortnightly, v. 86, Sept. 24, 1970: 72–75.

Barker, Carol. Freedom of Information Act and its declassification procedures. Government publications review, v. 1, Winter 1973: 147–150.

Barton, Ansley B. United States v. Nixon and the Freedom of Information Act: new impetus for agency disclosure? Emory law journal, v. 24, Spring 1975: 405–424.

Beaty, Gene R. Disclosure of the Air Force human factors investigation. Journal of air law and commence, v. 42, Spring 1976: 385–402.

Belair, Robert R. Agency implementation of the Privacy Act and the Freedom of Information Act: impact on the Government's collection, maintenance and dissemination of personally identifiable information. The John Marshall journal of practice and procedure, v. 10, Spring 1977: 465–512.

— — — Less Government secrecy and more personal privacy? Experience with the Freedom of Information and Privacy Acts. Civil liberties review, v. 4, May-June 1977: 10–18.

Bennett, Charles P. The Freedom of Information Act: is it a clear public records law? Brooklyn law review, v. 34, Fall 1967: 72–82.

Berner, Richard Olin. The effect of the 1976 amendment to exemption three of the Freedom of Information Act. Columbia law review, v. 76, Oct. 1976: 1029–1047.

Bertsch, Gene C. Vaughn v. Rosen: procedure and proof under the Freedom of Information Act. University of Pittsburgh law review, v. 35, Summer 1974: 850–863.

Betters, Robert C. Administrative law — Freedom of Information Act — IRS required to make available documents interpreting code sections, subject to its right to propose deletions for in camera review. Suffolk University law review, v. 10, Spring 1976: 610–622.

Black, Samuel H. Tax policymaking process: public access and judicial review. Tulane Tax Institute, v. 24, 1975: 227–253.

— — — The Freedom of Information Act and the Internal Revenue Service. New York University Institute on Federal Taxation, v. 33, 1975: 683–706.

Blanchard, Robert O. A history of the Federal records law. Columbia, School of Journalism, University of Missouri, 1967. 12 p. (Missouri. University. Freedom of Information Center. Report no. 189).

— — — A watchdog in decline. Columbia journalism review, v. 5, Summer 1966: 17–21.

— — — The Freedom of Information Act — disappointment and hope. Columbia journalism review, v. 6, Fall 1967: 16–20.

— — — Present at the creation: the media and the Moss committee. Journalism quarterly, v. 49, Summer 1972: 271–279.

— — — Remember the Freedom of Information Act? It's practically in mothballs today. Quill, v. 60, Aug. 1972: 16-18.

Bos, Gerald A. Administrative law — Freedom of Information Act — procedural requirements amended. Tulane law review, v. 49, Mar. 1975: 678-685.

Brant, Jonathan. A general introduction to privacy. Massachusetts law quarterly, v. 61, Mar. 1976: 10-18.

Brauer, Mary A. Administrative law — Freedom of Information Act — disclosure of IRS private letter rulings. Wisconsin law review, v. 1974, no. 1, 1974: 227-237.

Bretting, Denise. CAB decision — public disclosure — under the Freedom of Information Act the CAB must release foreign air transportation certificate decisions, which require Presidential approval, as soon as they are submitted to the President. Journal of air law and commerce, v. 42, Autumn 1976: 891-906.

Browne, Secor D. The Freedom of Information Act and the CAB. Public utilities fortnightly, v. 86, Sept. 24, 1970: 70-72.

Bryant, Roscoe. The history and background of Public Law 90-23, the Freedom of Information Act. North Carolina central law journal, v. 3, Spring 1972: 193-197.

Cabot, Stephen J. "Freedom of information" vs. the NLRB: conflicts and decisions. Personnel journal, v. 56, June 1977: 292-294, 312.

Campbell, Enid. Public access to government documents. Australian law journal, v. 41, July 1967: 73-89.

Campbell, Nancy Duff. Reverse Freedom of Information Act litigation: the need for congressional action. Georgetown law journal, v. 67, Oct. 1978: 103-205.

Caron, Arthur J., Jr. Federal procurement and the Freedom of Information Act. Federal bar journal, v. 28, Summer 1968: 271-286.

Cavanagh, John E. The Freedom of Information Act and government contractors — problems in protection of confidential information. Public contract law journal, v. 2, Jan. 1969: 225-235.

Chandler, Lucy J. Administrative law — attorney fees under the Freedom of Information Act — commercial interest and in propria persona appearances. Wayne law review, v. 24, Mar. 1978: 1045-1060.

Clark, Elias. Holding government accountable: the amended Freedom of Information Act. Yale law journal, v. 84, Mar. 1975: 741-769.

Clarke, Thomas H., Jr. Restraint of agency proceedings under the Freedom of Information Act. Washington and Lee law review, v. 32, Winter 1975: 191-213.

Clement, Daniel Gorham. The rights of submitters to prevent agency disclosure of confidential business information: the reverse Freedom of Information Act lawsuit. Texas law review, v. 55, Mar. 1977: 587-644.

Cohen, David S. The public's right of access to government information under the first amendment. Chicago-Kent law review, v. 51, Summer 1974: 164-185.

Colton, Douglas. Administrative law — Freedom of Information Act — the doctrine of executive privilege limits statutory access to information held within the Executive Office of the President. Soucie v. DuBridge, civil no. 1571-70 (D.D.C. Aug. 21, 1970). Texas law review, v. 49, Apr. 1971: 780-791.

Connolly, Walter B., and John C. Fox. Employer rights and access to documents under the Freedom of Information Act. Fordham law review, v. 46, Nov. 1977: 203-240.

Cox, Michael P. A walk through section 552 of the Administrative Procedure Act: the Freedom of Information Act, the Privacy Act; and the Government in the Sunshine Act. University of Cincinnati law review, v. 46, no. 4, 1978: 969-987.

Craft, Alice M. The National Environmental Policy Act, the Freedom of Information Act and the Atomic Energy Commission: the need for environmental information. Indiana law journal, v. 47, Summer 1972: 755-770.

Crist, Phyllis. Administrative law—the Freedom of Information Act and equitable discretion, 5 U.S.C. 552 (1970). Denver law journal, v. 51, no. 2, 1974: 263-274.

Davis, Kenneth Culp, et al. Public information act and interpretative and advisory rulings. Administrative law review, v. 20, Dec. 1967: 1-54.

Davis, Kenneth Culp. The Information Act; a preliminary analysis. University of Chicago law review, v. 34, Summer 1967: 761-816.

Davison, Laurie N. Access to broadcasters' financial statements filed with the FCC: the Freedom of Information Act alternative. George Washington law review, v. 42, Nov. 1973: 145-161.

Developments under the Freedom of Information Act—1971. Duke law journal, v. 1972, Apr. 1972: 136-158.

Developments under the Freedom of Information Act—1972. Duke law journal, v. 1973, Apr. 1973: 178-206.

Developments under the Freedom of Information Act—1973. Duke law journal, v. 1974, Apr. 1974: 251-296.

Developments under the Freedom of Information Act—1974. Duke law journal, 1975, May 1975: 416-456.

Developments under the Freedom of Information Act—1975. Duke law journal, v. 1976, May 1976: 366-408.

Developments under the Freedom of Information Act—1976. Duke law journal, v. 1977, May 1977: 532-564.

Developments under the Freedom of Information Act—1977. Duke law journal, v. 1978, Mar. 1978: 189-223.

Developments under the Freedom of Information Act—1978. Duke law journal, v. 1979, Feb. 1979: 327-354.

Dillingham, Del. The impact of the FOIA on NLRB discovery procedures. procedures. University of Michigan journal of law reform, v. 10, Spring 1977: 476-496.

Disclosure of union authorization cards under the Freedom of Information Act—interpreting the personal privacy exemptions. Minnesota law review, v. 62, June 1978: 949-986.

Dobkin, James A. The release of government-owned technical data under the freedom of information law: between Scylla and Charybdis. Villanova law review, v. 14, Fall 1968: 74–85.

Donohue, James P., Jr. Freedom of Information Act — renegotiation procedures will not be temporarily stayed while a controversy over the status of documents under the information act is settled. Fordham urban law journal, v. 3, Winter 1975: 359–374.

Drachsler, David A. The Freedom of Information Act and the "right" of nondisclosure. Administrative law review, v. 28, Winter 1976: 1–11.

Eaton, Berrien C., Jr., and Michael J. Lynch. Tax practice as affected by the Freedom of Information Act and the information retrieval system. Seventeenth Annual Tulane Tax Institute, 1968: 405–553.

Eclavea, Romualdo P. What constitutes "final opinion" or "order" of Federal administrative agency required to be made available for public inspection within meaning of Freedom of Information Act. American law reports federal, v. 20. Rochester, N.Y., The Lawyers co-operative publishing co., 1974: 400–404.

— — — What constitute investigatory files exempt from disclosure under Freedom of Information Act. American law reports federal, v. 17. Rochester, N.Y., The Lawyers co-operative publishing co., 1973: 522–548.

Epstein, Julius. Epstein v. Resor or the emasculation of the Freedom of Information Act. Lincoln law review, v. 7, Dec. 1971: 82–99.

Executive privilege and the Freedom of Information Act: the constitutional foundation of the amended national security exemption. Washington University law quarterly, v. 1976, Fall 1976: 609–666.

Fader, Carole. The FOI Act and the media. Columbia, School of Journalism, University of Missouri, 1973. 7 p. (Missouri. University. Freedom of Information Center. Report no. 303).

Federal administrative law developments — 1969: freedom of information. Duke law journal, v. 1970, Feb. 1970: 72–98.

Federal administrative law — 1970: freedom of information. Duke law journal, v. 1971, no. 1, 1971: 164–193.

The Federal Freedom of Information Act as an aid to discovery. Iowa law review, v. 54, Aug. 1968: 141–159.

Fellmeth, Robert C. The Freedom of Information Act and the Federal Trade Commission: a study in malfeasance. Harvard civil rights-civil liberties law review, v. 4, Spring 1969: 345–377.

File classified "Top Secret" is within national security exemption from the act and is not obtainable unless the classification is arbitrary and unreasonable. Epstein v. Resor, 296 F. Supp. 214 (N.D. Cal. 1969). Harvard law review, v. 83, Feb. 1970: 928–935.

Flaherty, Peter F. The Freedom of Information Act and the Privacy Act of 1974: a study in conflicts. Journal of legislation, v. 5, 1978: 26–35.

Flannery, John P. Commercial information brokers. Columbia human rights law review, v. 4, Winter 1972: 203–235.

Florsheim, B. L. Administrative law — aircraft accident investigation records — Freedom of Information Act. Journal of air law and commerce, v. 33, Summer 1967: 490-496.

Fox, William F., Jr. and Peter N. Weiss. The FOIA national security exemption and the new executive order. Federal Bar journal, v. 37, Fall 1978: 1-16.

Freedom of information and the individual's right to privacy: Department of the Air Force v. Rose, California Western law review, v. 14, no. 1, 1978: 183-203.

Freedom of Information, Sunshine, and Privacy Laws: impact on business. Proceedings ABA national institute, Dec. 9-10, 1977. Plaza Hotel, New York City. Business lawyer, v. 34, March 1979: whole issue.

Freedom of information: the statute and the regulations. Georgetown law journal, v. 56, Nov. 1967: 18-57.

Freedom of information — Supreme Court construes Freedom of Information Act exemption of "matters that are specifically exempted from disclosure by statute" to permit nondisclosure under all prior nondisclosure statutes. Temple law quarterly, v. 49. Fall 1975: 238-250.

The Freedom of Information Act: access to law. Fordham law review, v. 36, May 1968: 765-782.

— — — Labor law — an employer charged with an unfair labor practice is not entitled under the FOIA to NLRB files compiled pursuant to investigation of the charge when the enforcement proceeding is pending. George Washington law review, v. 45, Nov. 1976: 114-126.

— — — Regulations of the Food and Drug Administration . . . papers and discussion. Food and Drug Law Institute, Arlington, Va., March 12, 1975. Food drug cosmetic law journal, v. 30, June 1975: 311-380.

The Freedom of Information Act and the exemption for intra-agency memoranda. Harvard law review, v. 86, April 1973: 1047-1067.

Furby, Tommy E. The Freedom of Information Act: a survey of litigation under the exemptions, Mississippi law journal, v. 48, Sept. 1977: 784-817.

Fuselier, Louis A., and Armin J. Moeller Jr. NLRB investigatory records: disclosure under the Freedom of Information Act. University of Richmond law review, v. 10, Spring 1976: 541-555.

Garvey, Donald B. Prehearing discovery in NLRB proceedings. Labor law journal, v. 26, Nov. 1975: 710-723.

Giannella, Donald A. Agency procedures implementing the Freedom of Information Act: a proposal for uniform regulations. Administrative law review, v. 23, May 1971: 217-270.

Gibson, Charles H. What the Freedom of Information Act means to tax practice and practitioners. Taxation for accountants, v. 10, Apr. 1973: 204-206.

Gilbert, Alan R. Construction and application of Freedom of Information Act provision concerning award of attorney fees and other litigation costs. American law reports federal, v. 36. Rochester, N.Y., The Lawyers co-operative publishing co., 1978: 530-554.

Gilson, Roger P., Jr. Administrative disclosure of private business records under the Freedom of Information Act: an analysis of alternative methods of review. Syracuse law review, v. 28, Fall 1977: 923-980.

Goldberg, Stuart C., and Robert W. Wien. Facilitating discovery in civil securities actions: the 1975 amendments to the Freedom of Information Act of 1966. New York law forum, v. 21, Fall 1975: 277-289.

Goodale, James C. Senate bill no. 1 and the Freedom of Information Act: do they conflict? Administrative law review, v. 28, Summer 1976: 347-362.

Gorski, James M. Access to information? Exemptions from disclosure under the Freedom of Information Act and the Privacy Act of 1974. Willamette law journal, v. 13, Winter 1976: 135-171.

Government information and the rights of citizens: project. Michigan law review, v. 73, May-June 1975: whole issue.

Governmental investigations of the exercise of first amendment rights: citizens' rights and remedies. Minnesota law review, v. 60, June 1976: 1257-1288.

Graf, William S. Stern's victory over FBI shows FOI Act potential. Journalism quarterly, v. 52, Spring 1975: 131-134.

Greenberg, Ira N. The Freedom of Information Act: an historical examination of the first exemption in legislation and litigation. Journal of library and information science, v. 4, Apr. 1978: 1-13.

Hake, Theodore C. Administrative law — abuse of discretion — agency disclosure under FOIA — any disclosure of FOIA-exempt information without weighing benefit to the agency, harm to the public, and the possibility of compromise is an abuse of discretion. St. Mary's law journal, v. 8, no. 3, 1976: 543-550.

Hall, Stephen D. What is a record? Two approaches to the Freedom of Information Act's threshold requirement. Brigham Young University law review, v. 1978, no. 2, 1978: 408-435.

Hannigan, Michael J., and Francis J. Nealon. The Freedom of Information Act — the parameters of the exemptions. Georgetown law review, v. 62, Oct. 1973: 177-207.

Harader, William H. Interface of FOI and Privacy Acts. Columbia, School of Journalism, University of Missouri, 1977. 8 p. (Missouri. University. Freedom of Information Center. Report no. 371).

Hartman, Donal F., Jr. Departmental executive privilege: a bar to disclosure when dealing with the IRS. Gonzaga law review, v. 11, Spring 1976: 931-957.

Hassman, Phillip E. What matters are exempt from disclosure under Freedom of Information Act as "specifically authorized under criteria established by an executive order to be kept secret in the interest of national defense or foreign policy." American law reports federal, v. 29. Rochester, N.Y., The Lawyers co-operative publishing co., 1976: 606-619.

Hausen, Robert J. Administrative law — Freedom of Information Act — exemption 7(A) rejected as discovery tool in NLRB enforcement proceedings. St. John's law review, v. 51, Winter 1977: 251-269.

Hawker, Curtis. FOIA: what's a trade secret? Columbia, School of Journalism, University of Missouri, 1978. 6 p. (Missouri. University. Freedom of Information Center. Report no. 393).

Hayes, William R. Freedom of information — exemption three — SWAP reports are specifically exempt from disclosure by statute because FAA administrator issued a withholding order pursuant to discretionary authority. Journal of air law and commerce, v. 41, Spring 1975: 367-379.

Hennings, Thomas C., Jr. Constitutional law: the people' right to know. American Bar Association journal, v. 45, July 1959: 667-670, 768-770.

— — — A legislative measure to augment the free flow of public information. American University law review, v. 8, Jan. 1959: 19-27.

Hoerster, John K. The 1966 Freedom of Information Act — early judicial interpretations. Washington law review, v. 44, Spring 1969: 641-686.

Hoglund, John A. and Jonathan Kahan. Invasion of privacy and the Freedom of Information Act: Getman v. NLRB. George Washington law review, v. 40, March 1972: 527-541.

Holt, Robert G. Open America v. Watergate Special Prosecution Force: relief from the strict time limits of the Freedom of Information Act. Utah law review, v. 1976, no. 3, 1976: 603-615.

Horton, Frank. The public's right to know. Case and comment, v. 77, Jan.-Feb. 1972: 3-18.
    Reprinted in North Carolina Central law journal, v. 3, Spring 1972: 123-142.

Huard, Leo A. The 1966 public information act: an appraisal without enthusiasm. Public contract law journal, v. 2, Jan. 1969: 213-224.

Hudson, Robert V. FOI crusade in perspective: three victories for the press. Journalism quarterly, v. 50, Spring 1973: 118-124.

Hulett, Mary. Privacy and the Freedom of Information Act. Administrative law review, v. 27, Summer 1975: 275-294.

Hunter, J. Stewart. Freedom of Information Act: an appraisal. Bureaucrat, v. 1, Summer 1972: 131-135.

Ikowitz, Jay. The title guarantee theory and related decisions: are the courts interfering with exemption 7 of the FOIA? New York Law School law review, v. 23, no. 2, 1977: 275-306.

In camera inspection of national security files under the Freedom of Information Act. University of Kansas law review, v. 26, Summer 1978: 617-624.

The Information Act: judicial enforcement of the records provision. Virginia law review, v. 54, Apr. 1968: 466-490.

The "Investigatory files" exemption to the Freedom of Information Act. Washington University law quarterly, 1974, no. 3, 1974: 463-474.

Irons, Peter H. Government litigation files as a source of legal history. Law library journal, v. 69, No. 1976: 503-507.

Irving, John S., and Carol DeDeo. The right to privacy and freedom of information: the NLRB and issues under the Privacy Act and the Freedom of Information Act. Twenty-ninth annual New York University Conference on Labor, v. 29, 1976: 49-90.

Irving, John S., and Elinor Hadley Stillman. Interrelationship between the Freedom of Information Act and the National Labor Relations Act. Southwestern Legal Foundation, Institute on Law, Labor Law Developments, 1975: 181-243.

Johnson, James W. The Freedom of Information Act: its application in the Air Force. Air force law review, v. 16, Spring 1974: 54-64.

Johnson, Judy. Freedom of Information Act—stay of agency proceedings pending decision on disclosure of agency documents. Bannercraft Clothing Co. v. Renegotiation Board. Texas law review, v. 51, Apr. 1973: 757-767.

Johnstone, James J. The Freedom of Information Act and the FDA. Food durg cosmetic law journal, v. 25, June 1970: 296-306.

Jones, Richard H., and William E. Findler. The Freedom of Information act in military aircrash cases. Journal of air law and commerce, v. 43, 1977: 535-553.

Jordan, William, William Kehoe, and Ronald Schechter. The Freedom of Information Act — a potential alternative to conventional criminal discovery. American criminal law review, v. 14, Summer 1976: 73-161.

Kaczynski, Stephen J. "Reversing" the Freedom of Information Act: congressional intention or judicial intervention? St. John's law review, v. 51, Summer 1977: 734-758.

Kailer, W. Alan. The release of private information under open records laws. Texas law review, v. 55, May 1977: 911-927.

Kalo, Joseph J. Deterring misuse of confidential government information: a proposed citizens' action. Michigan law review, v. 72, Aug. 1974: 1577-1610.

Karem, Edward. The FOI Act gets teeth. Columbia, School of Journalism, University of Missouri, 1975. 8 p. (Missouri. University. Freedom of Information Center. Report no. 337).

Kass, Benny L. The new Freedom of Information Act. American Bar Association journal, v. 61, Mar. 1975: 366-367.

Katz, Joan M. The games bureaucrats play: hide and seek under the Freedom of Information Act. Texas law review, v. 48, Nov. 1970: 1261-1284.

Keller, James S. The investigatory files exemption to the FOIA: the D.C. circuit abandons Bristol-Myers. Geroge Washington law review, v. 42, May 1974: 869-893.

Kielbowicz, Richard B. The Freedom of Information Act and government's corporate information files. Journalism quarterly, v. 55, Autumn 1978: 481-486, 526.

Koch, Charles H., Jr. The Freedom of Information Act: suggestions for making information available to the public. Maryland law review, v. 32, no. 3, 1972: 189-225.

Kovach, Kenneth A. A retrospective look at the Privacy and Freedom of Information Acts. Labor law journal, v. 27, Sept. 1976: 548-564.

Kramer, Victor H., and David B. Weinberg. The Freedom of Information Act. Georgetown law journal, v. 63, Oct. 1974: 49-67.

Krause, Robert S., and Francis M. Gregory, Jr. Comments on proposed amendments to section 3 of the Administrative Procedure Act: the freedom of information bill. Notre Dame lawyer, v. 40, June 1965: 417-454.

Kruger, Gary I. A review of the fourth exemption of the Freedom of Information Act. Akron law review, v. 9, Spring 1976: 673-694.

Kuersteiner, Richard L., and Etta G. Herbach. Freedom of Information Act: an examination of the commercial or financial exemption. Santa Clara law review, v. 16, Spring 1976: 193-213.

Kutner, Luis. Freedom of information: due process of the right to know. Catholic Lawyer, v. 18, Winter 1972: 50-66.

Lacher, M. David. The Freedom of Information Act amendments of 1974: an analysis. Syracuse law review, v. 26, Summer 1975: 951-993.

Larman, Barry. Freedom of Information Act — personal information exempted from disclosure — Wine Hobby USA, Inc. v. IRS. Boston college industrial and commercial law review, v. 16, Jan. 1975: 240-254.

Lazenby, Beth. The right to information and the FOIA: shredding the paper curtain of secrecy. Houston law review, v. 11, Mar. 1974: 717-724.

Leahy, Ronald A. Four keys to information disclosure. Labor law journal, v. 29, July 1978: 420-424.

Levin, Ronald M. In camera inspections under the Freedom of Information Act. University of Chicago law review, v. 41, Spring, 1974: 557-581.

Levine, Jeffrey L. Judicial review of classified documents: amendments to the Freedom of Information Act. Harvard journal on legislation, v. 12, Apr. 1975: 415-446.

Linderman, Terrence G. Freedom of information — animal drug regulations. Food drug cosmetic law journal, v. 33, June 1978: 274-280.

Littman, Marion Katz. Freedom of Information Act — exemption (4) — research designs contained in grant applications. Boston college industrial and commercial law review, v. 17, Nov. 1975: 91-106.

Loveland, David C. Dept. of HEW implements the FOI Act. Columbia, School of Journalism, University of Missouri, 1971. 5 p. (Missouri. University. Freedom of Information Center. Report no. 273).

Machinery and Allied Products Institute. Freedom of Information Act — government contracts: proposed new Department of Defense Freedom-of-Information-Act regulations. Bulletin, no. 5624, Sept. 2, 1977. 6 p.

— — — Freedom of Information Act: important court decision. Third Circuit reverse FOIA decision limits: (1) applicability of statute prohibiting Federal employees from disclosing confidential business data and (2) scope of judicial review of an agency decision to disclose. Memorandum, G-95, Jan. 3, 1978. 14 p.

— — — Freedom of Information Act: important recent administrative and judicial developments affecting disclosure of confidential business information in government's hands; stringent burden of proof requirements for "reverse FOIA" plaintiffs discussed. Memorandum, G-93, July 8, 1977. 14 p.

— — —Freedom of Information Act: industrial relations: NLRB requests Supreme Court review of Fifth Circuit FOIA decision requiring disclosure of statements of witnesses to be called in unfair labor practice proceeding. Memorandum, G-97, Jan. 31, 1978. 4 p.

— — —Freedom of Information Act: Justice Department to defend FOIA actions for disclosure of exempt records only where disclosure would be "demonstrably harmful"; more active role by business in protecting its trade secrets and other confidential business information seen as necessary. Bulletin, no. 5588, May 27, 1977. 6 p.

— — —Freedom of Information Act: MAPI testifies before House Subcommittee; legislative record to be held open for 30 days to receive additional comments. Bulletin, no. 5636, Oct. 6, 1977. 10 p.

— — —Freedom of Information Act: MAPI testimony presented to Senate Subcommittee in FOIA oversight hearing. Bulletin, no. 5631, Sept. 16, 1977. 9 p.

— — —Freedom of Information Act: the requirement for government to disclose information in its possession and the implications for business, government, and the public. Memorandum, G-89, Mar. 1977. 58 p.

— — —The "Freedom of Information" Act: statutory intent and agency implementation reviewed from standpoint of industry's interest. Memorandum, G-39, Aug. 3, 1967. 26 p.

Madden, Terrence J. Freedom of Information Act — enjoining administrative proceedings pending a district court resolution of a demand for information — Bannercraft Clothing Company Inc. v. Renegotiation Board. University of Illinois law forum, v. 1973, no. 1, 1973: 180-192.

Malakoff, Louise Reiber. The First amendment and the public right to information. University of Pittsburgh law review, v. 35, Fall 1973: 93-114.

Malone, Susan Hileman. The corporate dilemma in "reverse" FOIA suits: Chrysler Corp. v. Schlesinger. University of Pittsburgh law review, v. 40, Fall 1978: 93-119.

Mamana, Joseph M. FDA's obligations under the 1966 public information act. Food drug cosmetic law journal, v. 22, Oct. 1967: 563-568.

Mankoff, Ronald M. The Freedom of Information Act as a taxpayer's tool. Tulane Tax Institute, 1974: 273-296.

Manso, Gary A. Administrative law — disclosure under the Freedom of Information Act — Rose v. Department of the Air Force. St. John's law review, v. 49, Winter 1975: 225-238.

Martin, Julian Clark, and Jack R. Springgate. Protection of a businessman's proprietary information. Louisiana law review, v. 32, June 1972: 497-541.

Martin, Robert. Disclosure v. privacy: competing policy goals within the context of the Freedom of Information Act. Forum, v. 13, Fall 1977: 142-153.

Mayer, Steven E. The Freedom of Information Act: a branch across the moat? Drake law review, v. 22, June 1973: 570-583.

McBrier, Frederick P. The EPA's proposed rule for Freedom of Information

Act disclosures: a model for orderly agency determinations. Utah law review, 1975, Winter 1975: 943-961.

McClain, Wallis. Implementing the amended FOI Act. Columbia, School of Journalism, University of Missouri, 1975. 10 p. (Missouri. University. Freedom of Information Center. Report no. 343).

McGinnis, Robert H. Freedom of Information Act: the expansion of exemption six. University of Florida law review, v. 27, Spring 1975: 848-855.

McGonegle, Timothy. Backdooring the NLRB: the use and abuse of the amended FOIA for administrative discovery. Loyola University law journal (Chicago), v. 8, Fall 1976: 145-185.

McKinnon, Mary Ann. Tax Analysts and Advocates v. the Internal Revenue Service: opening the information floodgates? Detroit College of Law review, v. 1975, no. 1, 1975: 145-160.

McMurray, Louise H. The Freedom of Information Act: 1974 amended time provisions interpreted. University of Miami law review, v. 32, Dec. 1977: 212-227.

Mead Data Central, Inc. v. United States Department of the Air Force: extending the FOIA's fifth exemption. William and Mary law review, v. 19, Winter 1977: 343-359.

Michaelson, Martin. Freedom of Information: up against the stone wall. Nation, v. 224, May 21, 1977: 624-618.

Miller, Judith. Getting the goods on the government. New republic, v. 165, Dec. 11, 1971: 13-15.

Mink, Patsy T. The Mink case: restoring the Freedom of Information Act. Pepperdine law review, v. 2, 1974: 8-27.

Mitchell, John J. Government secrecy in theory and practice: "rules and regulations" as an autonomous screen. Columbia law review, v. 58, Feb. 1958: 199-210.

Mitchell, W. G. Champion. Administrative law — needed — freedom of information. North Carolina law review, v. 52, Dec. 1973: 417-431.

Mitnick, Judith A. Judicial discretion and the Freedom of Information Act. Disclosure denied: Consumers Union v. Veterans Administration. Indiana law journal, v. 45, Spring 1970: 421-434.

Montgomery, David B., Anne H. Peters, and Charles B. Weinberg. The Freedom of Information Act: strategic opportunities and threats. Sloan management review, v. 19, Winter 1978: 1-13.

Moorehead, Donald V., and John D. Sharer. Reexamination of the rulings process — has the game changed? Thirty-sixth Annual Institute on Federal Taxation, New York University, 1978: 1207-1233.

Moss, John E., and Benny L. Kass. The spirit of freedom of information. In Symposium: the people's right to know. Trial, v. 8, Mar.-Apr. 1972: 14-15.

Murphy, James H. Seeking environmental information. Columbia, School of Journalism, University of Missouri, 1978. 5 p. (Missouri. University. Freedom of Information Center. Report no. 388).

Murphy, John F. Knowledge is power: foreign policy and information interchange among Congress, the executive branch, and the public. Tulane law review, v. 49, Mar. 1975: 505-554.

Murphy, Paul R. Administrative law—amendments to the Freedom of Information Act. Annual survey of American law, v. 1974/75, Summer 1975: 607-621.

Nader, Ralph. Freedom from information: the act and the agencies. Harvard civil rights-civil liberties law review, v. 5, Jan. 1970: 1-15.

Nathanson, Nathaniel L. Social science, administrative law, and the Information Act of 1966. Social problems, v. 21, Summer 1973: 21-37.

National security and the public's right to know: a new role for the courts under the Freedom of Information Act. University of Pennsylvania law review, v. 123, June 1975: 1438-1473.

Navazio, Bob, and Don Combs. Information disclosure at the Food and Drug Administration: in search of the public interest. Presented at the 1978 national conference of the American Society for Public Administration, Phoenix, Arizona. 30 p. + appendices.

1975-1976 annual survey of labor relations and employment discrimination law: NLRB obligations under the Freedom of Information Act: NLRB v. Sears. Boston College industrial and commercial law review, v. 17, Aug. 1976: 1114-1129.

Nyberg, Janet L. Testing the FOI Act. Columbia, School of Journalism, University of Missouri, 1974. 7 p. (Missouri. University. Freedom of Information Center. Report no. 318).

O'Brien, David M. Privacy and the right to access: purposes and paradoxes of information control. Administrative law review, v. 30, Winter 1978: 45-92.

O'Neill, James Richard. The Freedom of Information Act and its internal memoranda exemption: time for a practical approach. Southwestern law journal, v. 27, Dec. 1973: 806-836.

Open America v. Watergate Special Prosecution Force: judicial revision of FOIA time limits. Northwestern University law review, v. 71, Jan.-Feb. 1977: 805-817.

Oran, Stuart I. Public disclosure of Internal Revenue Service private letter rulings. University of Chicago law review, v. 40, Summer 1973: 832-853.

O'Reilly, James T. FOI and the 'Secret Seven' affair. Columbia, School of Journalism, University of Missouri, 1975. 5 p. (Missouri. University. Freedom of Information Center. Report no. 335).

— — —Government disclosure of private secrets under the Freedom of Information Act. Business lawyer, v. 30, July 1975: 1125-1247.

Oxman, Michelle. FOIA and Privacy Act interface: toward a resolution of statutory conflict. Loyola University law journal (Chicago), v. 8, Spring 1977: 570-593.

Panel discussion of Freedom of Information Act at midyear meeting New Orleans, Louisiana. Bulletin of the section of taxation, American Bar Association, v. 20, Apr. 1967: 43-58.

Pape, Stuart M. Meetings and correspondence, including FOI considerations. Food drug cosmetic law journal, v. 32, May 1977: 226-235.

Parks, Wallace. The open government principle: applying the right to know under the Constitution. George Washington law review, v. 26, Oct. 1957: 1-22.

——— Secrecy and the public interest in military affairs. George Washington law review, v. 26, Oct. 1957: 23-77.

Patten, Thomas L., and Kenneth W. Weinstein. Disclosure of business secrets under the Freedom of Information Act: suggested limitations. Administrative law review, v. 29, Spring 1977: 193-208.

Paul, Jack. Access to rules and records of Federal agencies: the Freedom of Information Act. Los Angeles bar bulletin, v. 42, Aug. 1967: 459-463, 482-484.

Pendergast, William R. The responsibility of the FDA to protect trade secrets and confidential data. Food drug cosmetic law journal, v. 27, June 1972: 366-375.

Phillips, William G. Freedom of Information Act: what it means to libraries. Government publications review, v. 1, Winter 1973: 141-146.

Piraino, Thomas A., Jr. Public disclosure of confidential business information under the Freedom of Information Act: toward a more objective standard. Cornell law review, v. 60, Nov. 1974: 109-130.

Plesser, Ronald. Freedom of Information Act: as applied to unclassified documents. Government publications review, v. 1. Winter 1973: 135-139.

——— The when and how of the Freedom of Information Act. Practical lawyer, v. 21, April 15, 1975: 61-68.

Post, Robert C. National security and the amended Freedom of Information Act. Yale law journal, v. 85, Jan. 1976: 401-422.

The Privacy Act of 1974: an overview and critique. Washington University law quarterly, v. 1976, Fall 1976: 667-718

Pomrenze, Seymour J. The Freedom of Information and Privacy Acts and the records manager — selected considerations. Records management quarterly, v. 10, July 1976: 5-9, 14.

Protection from government disclosure — the reverse-FOIA suit. Duke law journal, v. 1976, May 1976: 330-365.

Purver, Jonathan M. What are matters "related solely to the internal personnel rules and practices of an agency" exempted from disclosure under Freedom of Information Act. American law reports federal, v. 28. Rochester, N.Y., The Lawyers co-operative publishing co., 1976: 645-663.

——— What are matters "specifically exempted from disclosure by statute" under Freedom of Information Act. United States Supreme Court reports lawyers edition, v. 45. Rochester, N.Y., The Lawyers co-operative publishing co., 1976: 763-781.

Raisfeld, Ruth D. NLRB discovery after Robbins: more peril for private litigants. Fordham law review, v. 47, Dec. 1978: 393-417.

Recent cases reveal which IRS documents taxpayers may obtain under the FIA. Journal of taxation, v. 39, Sept. 1973: 180-181.

Redburn, Thomas. Open files: letting Exxon in. Washington monthly, v. 7, July-Aug. 1975: 18-25.

Reid, Thomas R. Public access to Internal Revenue Service rulings. George Washington law review, v. 41, Oct. 1972: 23-43.

Reitman, Alan. Freedom of information and privacy: the civil libertarian's dilemma. American archivist, v. 38, Oct. 1975: 501-508.

Relyea, Harold C., ed. The Freedom of Information Act a Decade Later. Public administration review, v. 39, July-Aug., 1979: 310-332.

Relyea, Harold C. Extending the freedom of information concept. Presidential studies quarterly, v. 8, Winter 1978: 96-98.

— — —Freedom of Information, Privacy, and Official Secrecy: The Evolution of Federal Government Information Policy Concepts. Social indicators research, v. 7, 1980: 137-156.

— — —The Freedom of Information Act: its evolution and operational status. Journalism quarterly, v. 54, Autumn 1977: 538-544.

— — —The Freedom of Information Act and Its Costs: A Brief Overview. International journal of public administration, v. 2, no. 1, 1980: 117-129.

— — —The provision of government information: the Federal Freedom of Information Act experience. Canadian public administration, v. 20, Summer 1977: 317-341.

Reverse-Freedom of Information Act suits: confidential information in search of protection. Northwestern University law review, v. 70, Jan.-Feb. 1976: 995-1019.

Rhoads, Gwendolyn R. Balancing the public's right to know with the individual's right to privacy. Marine Corps gazette, v. 62, June 1978: 49-54.

Rice, Richard E. Administrative law—Freedom of Information Act—in a suit under the Freedom of Information, Act, brought by government contractors involved in proceedings before the renegotiation board, a district court has jurisdiction to issue an injunction pendente lite to stay the board's proceedings. George Washington law review, v. 41, July 1973: 1072-1086.

The Right to disclosure of NLRB documents under the Freedom of Information Act. Fordham urban law journal, v. 5, Fall 1976: 119-130.

Rights in conflict—reconciling privacy with the public's right to know: a panel. Law library journal, v. 63, Nov. 1970: 551-563.

The rights of the public and the press to gather information. Harvard law review, v. 87, May 1974: 1505-1533.

Roberts, Sidney I. Private letter rulings: right to privacy vs. right to know. Tax notes, v. 4, Jan. 5, 1976: 3-15.

Robison, Proctor D. H. The plain meaning of the Freedom of Information

Act: NLRB v. Getman. Indiana law journal, v. 47, Spring 1972: 530-545.

Rodwin, Roger M. The Freedom of Information Act: public probing into (and) private production. Food drug cosmetic law journal, v. 28, Aug. 1973: 533-544.

Roffman, Howard. Freedom of information: judicial review of executive security classifications. University of Florida law review, v. 28, Winter 1976: 551-568.

Roman, Theodore, Jr. The Privacy Act and the Freedom of Information Act: where does GAO fit? The GAO review, v. 14, Winter 1979: 22-24.

Rosenberg, John. The FBI shreds its files: catch in the information act. Nation, v. 226, Feb. 4, 1978: 108-111.

— — The FBI would shred the past. Nation, v. 226, June 3, 1978: 653-655.

Rosenbloom, H. David. More IRS information may become public due to amended Freedom of Information Act. Journal of taxation, v. 45, Nov. 1976: 258-263.

Rosenfeld, Frank A. The freedom of Information Act's privacy exemption and the Privacy Act of 1974. Harvard civil rights-civil liberties law review, v. 11, Summer 1976: 596-631.

Rosenfeld, S. James. The FOIA and the SEC: the first six months. Securities regulation law journal, v. 4, Spring 1976: 3-44.

Rothchild, John. Finding the facts bureaucrats hide. Washington monthly, v. 3, Jan. 1972: 15-27.

Rourke, Francis E., ed. Administrative secrecy: a comparative perspective: a symposium. Public administration review, v. 35, Jan.-Feb. 1975: 1-42.

Rowat, Donald C. Freedom of information: the American experience. The Canadian forum, v. 58, Sept. 1978: 10-13.

Rowen, Theodore M. Administrative agency—Public Information Act—an agency may properly refuse to disclose agency documents in its possession when not properly identified or exempt within the act. University of Cincinnati law review, v. 38, Summer 1969: 570-575.

Rubin, Alfred P. A wholesome discretion. New York law forum, v. 20, Winter 1975: 569-616.

Rydstrom, Jean F. Scope of judicial review under Freedom of Information Act, of administrative agency's withholding of records. American law reports federal, v. 7. Rochester, N.Y., The Lawyers co-operative publishing co., 1971: 876-893.

— — What are interagency or intraagency memorandums or letters exempt from disclosure under the Freedom of Information Act. American law reports federal, v. 7. Rochester, N.Y., The Lawyers co-operative publishing co., 1971: 855-869.

Salomon, Kenneth D., and Lawrence H. Wechsler. The Freedom of Information Act: a critical review. George Washington law review, v. 38, Oct. 1969: 150–163.

Saloschin, Robert L. The work of the Freedom of Information Committee of the Department of Justice. Public utilities fortnightly, v. 86, Sept. 24, 1970: 75–77.

    Also appears in The Freedom of Information Act and the agencies. Administrative law review, v. 23, Mar. 1971: 147–151.

Samoff, Bernard, and Jeffrey C. Falkin. The Freedom of Information Act and the NLRB. Boston College industrial and commercial law review, v. 15, July 1974: 1267–1290.

Scher, Irving. Openness in government: protecting the informant's confidential information against discretionary release. Federal bar journal, v. 34, Fall 1975: 348–351.

Scher, Jacob. Access to information: recent legal problems. Journalism quarterly, v. 37, Winter, 1960: 41–52.

   – – –5 U.S.C. 1002 change discussed. Columbia, School of Journalism, University of Missouri, 1960. 4 p. (Missouri. University. Freedom of Information Center. Report no. 45).

Schick, Allen, ed. The short and sad history of freedom of information. Bureaucrat, v. 1, Summer 1972: 113–160.

Schmidt, Frank S. Freedom of Information Act and the Internal Revenue Service. Twentieth Annual Institute on Federal taxation. University of Southern California Law Center, 1968: 79–95.

Schultz, Franklin M. A primer on the public information act. Public contract law journal, v. 2, Jan. 1969: 208–212.

Scriven, Donald C. Freedom of Information Act — investigatory files exemption remains operative after investigation and law enforcement proceedings concluded. Tulane law review, v. 47, June 1973: 1136–1142.

The Secret law of the Immigration and Naturalization Service. Iowa law review, v. 56, Oct. 1970: 140–151.

Searcy, Seth S., III. Privacy and public records: the emerging conflict in values. Public affairs comment, v. 24, Nov. 1977: 1–5.

Segal, Morley. The Freedom of Information Act and political science research, PS, v. 2, Summer 1969: 315–320.

Sexton, John J. New law changes rules on what information IRS must disclose; confusion likely. Journal of taxation, v. 26, Feb. 1967: 120–122.

Sherwood, John T., Jr. The Freedom of Information Act: a compendium for the military lawyer. Military law review, v. 52, Spring 1971: 103–139.

Shiff, Anne L. The Freedom of Information Act — the use of equitable discretion to modify the act. Tulane law review, v. 44, June 1970: 800–805.

Sillyman, Michael Wayne. Response of the IRS to the Freedom of Information Act: an uphill battle for disclosure. Arizona State law journal, v. 1974, no. 3, 1974: 431–455.

Silverman, Barbara A. Freedom of Information Act requires disclosure of

IRS letter rulings. University of Miami law review, v. 29, Spring 1975: 610–616.

Sinovic, Dianna. Access to F.D.A. information. Columbia, School of Journalism, University of Missouri, 1978. 7 p. (Missouri. University. Freedom of Information Center. Report no. 392).

Sky, Theodore. Agency implementation of the Freedom of Information Act. Administrative law review, v. 20, June 1968: 445–457.

Smith, Richard B. The Freedom of Information Act and the agencies: SEC no-action letters. Public utilities fortnightly, v. 86, Sept. 24, 1970: 78–79.

Snyder, John L. Developments on Freedom of Information Act reveal trend toward greater disclosure. Journal of taxation, v. 50, Jan. 1979: 48–52.

Sobeloff, Jonathan. New Freedom of Information Act: what it means to tax practioners. Journal of taxation, v. 27, Sept. 1967: 130–134.

Sobol, Martin J. An example of judicial legislation: the Third Circuit's expansion of exemption 6 of the Freedom of Information Act to include union authorization cards. Villanova law review, v. 23, May 1978: 751–762.

Spanos, Peter R. Scope of disclosure of internal revenue communications and information files under the Freedom of Information Act. University of Michigan journal of law reform, v. 8, Winter 1975: 329–350.

Stein, Allen Jonathan. FOIA and FACA: freedom of information in the "fifth branch"? Administrative law review, v. 27, Winter 1975: 31–81.

Steinberg, Marc I. The 1974 amendments to the Freedom of Information Act: the safety valve provision 552(a)(6)(C) excusing agency compliance with statutory time limits—a proposed interpretation. Notre Dame lawyer, v. 52, Dec. 1976: 235–260.

Sternal, Guy J. Informational privacy and public records. Pacific law journal, v. 8, Jan. 1977: 25–47.

Steward, Charles E., and C. Daniel Ward. F.T.C. discovery: depositions, the Freedom of Information Act and confidential informants. American Bar Association antitrust law journal, v. 37, no. 2, 1968: 248–260.

Survey on government and the freedom of information. Loyola law review (New Orleans), v. 20, no. 1, 1973–1974: 1–88.

Symposium: freedom of information vs. privacy: an information dilemma. Bulletin of the American Society for Information Science, v. 3, Oct. 1976: 13–21.

Symposium: the Freedom of Information Act and the agencies. Administrative law review, v. 23, Mar. 1971: 129–167.

Symposium on the 1974 amendments to the Freedom of Information Act. American University law review, v. 25, Fall 1975: 1–83.

Symposium: the people's right to know. Trial, v. 8, Mar.-Apr. 1972: 12–32.

Symposium: public access to information. Northwestern University law review, v. 68, May-June 1973. 285 p.

Taylor, George A. Freedom of Information Act—investigatory files exemption—the government may withhold investigatory materials compiled for a law enforcement proceeding which has been terminated. St. Mary's law journal, v. 4, Summer 1972: 219–226.

Theoharis, Athan. Bureaucrats above the law: double-entry intelligence files. Nation, v. 225, Oct. 22, 1977: 393–397.

— — — The problem of purging FBI files. USA today, v. 197, Nov. 1978: 48–50.

Thompson, Earl G. The disclosure of private rulings. Marquette law review, v. 59, no. 3, 529–550.

Tuoni, Gilda M. NEPA and the Freedom of Information Act: a prospect for disclosure. Environmental affairs, v. 4, Winter 1975: 179–201.

Unclassified documents physically connected with classified documents may not be withheld under the national security and foreign affairs secrets exemption. Vanderbilt law review, v. 25, Mar. 1972: 397–403.

Uretz, Lester R. Freedom of information and the IRS. Arkansas law review, v. 20, Winter 1967: 283–291.

Vaughn, Robert G. The Freedom of Information Act and Vaughn v. Rosen: some personal comments. American University law review, v. 23, Summer 1974: 865–879.

Vaughn v. Rosen (484 F 2d 820): toward true freedom of information. University of Pennsylvania law review, v. 122, Jan. 1974: 731–744.

Voight, Harry H. Public access to intra-agency documents: the International Paper case. Natural resources lawyer, v. 4, July 1971: 554–568.

Walker, Richard H. Vaughn v. Rosen (484 F 2d 820): new meaning for the Freedom of Information Act. Temple law quarterly, v. 47, Winter 1974: 390–402.

Wallace, James H., Jr. Proper disclosure and indecent exposure: protection of trade secrets and confidential commercial information supplied to the government. Federal bar journal, v. 34, Fall 1975: 295–300.

Wallace, Mark S. Discovery of government documents and the official information privilege. Columbia law review, v. 76, Jan. 1976: 142–174.

Walter, Douglas H. The battle for information: strategies of taxpayers and the IRS to compel (or resist) disclosure. Taxes, v. 56, Dec. 1978: 740–752.

Waples, Gregory L. Freedom of Information Act: a seven-year assessment. Columbia law review, v. 74, June 1974: 895–959.

Ward, Peter C. The public's access to government — Freedom of Information, Privacy and Sunshine Acts. Law library journal, v. 70, Nov. 1977: 509–517.

Warden, John B. Administrative law — Freedom of Information Act — investigatory files remain exempt from public disclosure even after agency proceedings have terminated. SEC v. Frankel. Texas law review, v. 51, Dec. 1972: 119–127.

Warren, John H. Administrative law — judicial review, State secrets, and the Freedom of Information Act. (Epstein v. Resor) South Carolina law review, v. 23, no. 2, 1971: 332–340.

Weinberg, Steve. Freedom of Information: you still need a can opener. Nation, v. 220, Apr. 19, 1975: 463–466.

Weidenbruch, Peter P., Jr. Disclosure of government tax information and action. National tax journal, v. 27, Sept. 1974: 395-411.

Whitaker, Meade. Ruling letters and technical advice: the disclosure crossroads. Taxes, v. 53, Dec. 1975: 712-718.

— — —Taxpayer privacy vs. freedom of information: proposals to amend sec. 6103. Tax adviser, v. 6, Apr. 1975: 198-204.

White, Peter. Freedom of information: a glance at the U.S. and a look at Canada. The Australian library journal, v. 27, June 16, 1978: 151-157.

Why many business secrets are now in danger. Nation's business, v. 63, Dec. 1975: 28-31.

Wiegmann, William J. Administrative law — the scope of the FOIA exemptions. Reverse-FOIA suits. Annual survey of American law, v. 1977, no. 1, 1977: 1-39.

Wildes, Leon. Nonpriority program of the Immigration and Naturalization Service goes public: the litigative use of the Freedom of Information Act. San Diego law review, v. 14, Dec. 1976: 42-75.

Wilkerson, Carl. Reconciling the conflicting goals of the right to know and the right to privacy under the Freedom of Information Act. Chitty's law journal, v. 25, no. 7, Sept. 1977: 217-228.

Wisniewski, Robert E. Administrative law — privacy, public interest and judicial equitable discretion within the Freedom of Information Act. University of Toledo law review, v. 6, Fall 1974: 215-237.

Wolfe, Robert H. FOIA — section 552(b)(7) of the Freedom of Information Act of 1970 precludes the disclosure of documents compiled as investigatory files and used for law enforcement purposes by a Federal agency even when enforcement proceedings have been terminated. George Washington law review, v. 41, Oct. 1972: 93-106.

Would Macy's tell Gimbel's: government-controlled business information and the Freedom of Information Act, forwards and backwards. Loyola University law journal (Chicago), v. 6, Summer 1975: 594-621.

Wozencraft, Frank M. The Freedom of Information Act — the first 36 days. Administrative law review, v. 20, Mar. 1968: 249-261.

Wright, L. Hart. Inadequacies of Freedom of Information Act as applied to IRS letter rulings. Oklahoma law review, v. 28, Fall 1975: 701-721.

Young, Anthony L. Recent developments under FOIA and FACA directly affecting the pharmaceutical industry. Food, drug, cosmetic law journal, v. 31, Sept. 1976: 507-520.

Zedalis, Rex J. Resurrection of Reynolds: 1974 amendment to national defense and foreign policy exemption. Pepperdine law review, v. 4, Spring 1977: 81-114.

Zuckerman, Herbert L. How far can tax men go in obtaining IRS materials under the FIA? Journal of taxation, v. 39, Oct. 1973: 194-200.

Documents

U.S. Commission on Federal Paperwork. Confidentiality and privacy: a report. Washington, U.S. Govt. Print. Off., 1977. 175 p.

U.S. Congress. Conference Committees, 1974. Freedom of Information Act amendments; conference report to accompany H.R. 12471. Washington, U.S. Govt. Print. Off., 1974. 15 p. (93d Congress, 2d sess. House. Report no. 93-1380).

Also appears as 93d Congress, 2d sess. Senate Report no. 93-1200.

U.S. Congress. House. Committee on Government Operations. Amending section 552 of title 5, United States code, known as the Freedom of Information Act. Washington, U.S. Govt. Print. Off., 1974. 29 p. (93rd Congress, 2d sess. House. Report no. 93-876).

— — —A citizen's guide on how to use the Freedom of Information Act and the Privacy Act in requesting government documents: thirteenth report. Washington, U.S. Govt. Print. Off., 1977. 59 p. (95th Congress, 1st sess. House. Report no. 95-793).

— — —Clarifying and protecting the right of the public to information. Washington, U.S. Govt. Print. Off., 1966. 14 p. (89th Congress, 2d sess. House. Report no. 1497).

— — — Executive classification of information — security classification problems involving exemption (b)(1) of the Freedom of Information Act (5 U.S.C. 552). Washington, U.S. Govt. Print. Off., 1973. 113 p. (93d Congress, 1st sess. House. Report no. 93-221).

— — —Freedom of Information Act requests for business data and reverse-FOIA lawsuits: twenty-fifth report. Washington, U.S. Govt. Print. Off., 1978. 67 p. (95th Congress, 2d sess. House. Report no. 95-1382.

— — —Freedom of information legislation during the 85th Congress. Washington, U.S. Govt. Print. Off., 1958. 24 p.

At head of title: Committee print. 85th Congress, 2d sess. House of Representatives.

— — —Lack of guidelines for Federal contract and grant data. Washington U.S. Govt. Print. Off., 1978. 27 p. (95th Congress, 2d sess. House. Report no. 95-1663).

— — —Replies from Federal agencies to questionnaire submitted by the Special Subcommittee on Government Information. Washington, U.S. Govt. Print. Off., 1955. 552 p.

At head of title: Committee print. 84th Congress, 1st sess. House of Representatives.

U.S. Congress. House. Committee on Government Operations. Foreign Operations and Government Information Subcommittee. Administration of the Freedom of Information Act. Washington, U.S. Govt. Print. Off., 1972. 89 p. (92d Congress, 2d sess. House. Report no. 1419).

— — —Availability of information to Congress. Hearings, 93rd Congress, 1st sess. on H.R. 4938, H.R. 4893, and H.R. 6438. Apr. 3, 4, and 19, 1973. Washington, U.S. Govt. Print. Off., 1973. 361 p.

— — —Federal public records law. Hearings, 89th Congress, 1st sess. Mar. 30-Apr. 5, 1965. Washington, U.S. Govt. Print. Off., 1965. 528 p.

— — —Freedom of Information Act (compilation and analysis of departmental regulations implementing 5 U.S.C. 552). Washington, U.S. Govt. Print. Off., 1968. 314 p.

At head of title: 90th Congress, 2d sess. House. Committee print.

— — — The Freedom of Information Act. Hearings, 93d Congress, 1st sess. Washington, U.S. Govt. Print. Off., 1973. 412 p.

— — — Sale or distribution of mailing lists by Federal agencies. Hearings, 92nd Congress, 2d sess. June 13 and 15, 1972. Washington, U.S. Govt. Print. Off., 1972. 362 p.

— — — U.S. Government information policies and practices (various parts with titles). Hearings, 92d Congress, 1st and 2d sess. Washington, U.S. Govt. Print. Off., 1971–1972. 3758 p.

U.S. Congress. House. Committee on Government Operations. Government Information and Individual Rights Subcommittee. Business record exemption of the Freedom of Information Act. Hearings, 95th Congress, 1st sess. Oct. 3-4, 1977. Washington, U.S. Govt. Print. Off., 1977. 356 p.

— — — FBI compliance with the Freedom of Information Act. Hearing, 95th Congress, 2d sess. Apr. 10, 1978. Washington, U.S. Govt. Print. Off., 1978. 78 p.

— — — Freedom of Information Act and amendments of 1974 (P.L. 93-502): source book: legislative history, texts, and other documents. Committee on Government Operations, U.S. House of Representatives, Subcommittee on Government Information and Individual Rights: Committee on the Judiciary, U.S. Senate, Subcommittee on Administrative Practice and Procedure. Washington, U.S. Govt. Print. Off., 1975. 571 p.

At head of title: 94th Congress, 1st sess. Joint committee print.

— — — Information policy issues relating to contractor data and administrative markings. Hearing, 95th Congress, 2d sess. Sept. 18, 1978. Washington, U.S. Govt. Print. Off., 1979. 224 p.

U.S. Congress. House. Committee on Government Operations. Special Subcommittee on Government Information. Availability of information from Federal departments and agencies (various parts with subtitles). Hearings, 84th through 86th Congresses. Washington, U.S. Govt. Print. Off., 1956–1959. 4260 p.

— — — Availability of information from Federal departments and agencies (periodic progress reports). Washington, U.S. Govt. Print. Off., 1958–1961. (85th Congress, 2d sess. House. Report no. 1884) 295 p.; (85th Congress, 2d sess. House. Report no. 2578) 243 p.; (86th Congress, 2d sess. House. Report no. 2084) 222 p.; (87th Congress, 1st sess., House. Report no. 818) 197 p.

U.S. Congress. House. Committee on the Judiciary. Subcommittee on Civil and Constitutional Rights. FBI oversight. Hearings, 94th Congress, 1st and 2d sess. Oct. 21-Dec. 12, 1975; Feb. 11-Sept. 29, 1976. Part 3. Washington, U.S. Govt. Print. Off., 1976. 628 p.

— — — FBI oversight. Hearings, 95th Congress, 1st sess. June 6, 27, and Nov. 9, 1977. Part 1. Washington, U.S. Govt. Print. Off. 1978. 239 p.

U.S. Congress. Senate. Committee on Government Operations. Subcommittee on Intergovernmental Relations [and] Committee on the Judiciary. Subcommittees on Separation of Powers and Administrative Practice and Procedure. Executive privilege, secrecy in government, freedom of information. Hearings, 93rd Congress, 1st sess. Apr. 10-June 26, 1973. Washington, U.S. Govt. Print. Off., 1973. 1482 p.

U.S. Congress. Senate. Committee on Interior and Insular Affairs. Subcommittee on Indian Affairs. Indian amendment to Freedom of Information Act. Hearing, 94th Congress, 2d sess. May 17, 1976. Washington, U.S. Govt. Print. Off., 1976. 165 p.

U.S. Congress. Senate. Committee on the Judiciary. Amending the Freedom of Information Act. Washington, U.S. Govt. Print. Off., 1974. 64 p. (93rd Congress, 2d sess. Senate. Report no. 93-854).

— — —Clarifying and protecting the right of the public to information, and for other purposes. Washington, U.S. Govt. Print. Off., 1964. 17 p. (88th Congress, 2d sess. Senate. Report no. 1219).

— — —Clarifying and protecting the right of the public to information, and for other purposes. Washington, U.S. Govt. Print. Off., 1965. 10 p. (89th Congress, 1st sess. Senate. Report no. 813).

U.S. Congress. Senate. Committee on the Judiciary. Subcommittee on Administrative Practice and Procedure. Administrative procedure act. Hearings, 89th Congress, 1st sess. May 12-21. 1965. Washington, U.S. Govt. Print. Off., 1965. 572 p.

— — —Federal Employee Disclosure Act of 1975, S. 1210. Hearings, 94th Congress, 1st sess. Apr. 28; June 12, 18, 19,5. Washington, U.S. Govt. Print. Off., 1976. 301 p.

— — —Freedom of information. Hearings, 88th Congress, 1st sess., on S. 1666 . . . and S. 1663 (in part) . . . Oct. 28-31, 1963. Washington, U.S. Govt. Print. Off., 1964. 322 p.

— — —Freedom of Information Act. Hearings, 95th Congress, 1st sess. Sept. 15-Nov. 10, 1977. Washington, U.S. Govt. Print. Off., 1978. 1042 p.

— — —The Freedom of Information Act, ten months review. Washington, U.S. Govt. Print. Off., 1968. 314 p.

At head of Title: 90th Congress, 2d sess. Committee print.

— — —Freedom of Information Act source book: legislative materials, cases, articles. Washington, U.S. Govt. Print. Off., 1974. 432 p. (93d Congress, 2d sess. Senate. Document no. 93-82).

U.S. Congress. Senate. Committee on the Judiciary. Subcommittee on Criminal Laws and Procedures. The erosion of law enforcement intelligence [—capabilities—] and its impact on the public security. Hearings, 95th Congress, 1st and 2d sess. Washington, U.S. Govt. Print. Off., 1977, 1978. 8 pts.

— — —The erosion of law enforcement intelligence and its impact on the public security. Washington, U.S. Govt. Print. Off., 1978. 179 p.

At head of title: 95th Congress, 2d sess. Committee print.

U.S. Department of the Army. The Adjutant General Center. Records Management Division. The Freedom of Information Act: summaries of cases, 1967-1974. Washington, Oct.4, 1974. 119 p.

— — —Freedom of Information Act case summaries: 1975 and 1976. Washington, n.d. 93 p.

U.S. Dept. of Justice. Attorney General's memorandum on the 1974 amendments to the Freedom of Information Act. Washington, U.S. Dept. of Justice, 1975. 65 p.

— — —Attorney General's memorandum on the public information section of the Administrative Procedure Act: a memorandum for the executive departments and agencies concerning Section 3 of the Administrative Procedure Act as revised effective July 4, 1967. Washington, U.S. Govt. Print. Off., 1967. 47 p.

U.S. Dept. of Justice. Office of Legal Counsel. Freedom of Information Committee. Freedom of information case list. (various years.) Washington, issued periodically.

U.S. General Accounting Office. Data on Privacy Act and Freedom of Information Act provided by Federal law enforcement agencies: report by the Comptroller General of the United States. [Washington] 1978. 23 p.

— — —Government field offices should better implement the Freedom of Information Act: report by the Comptroller General of the United States. [Washington] 1978. 47 p.

— — —Impact of the Freedom of Information and Privacy Acts on law enforcement agencies: report by the Comptroller General of the United States. [Washington] 1978. 36 p.

U.S. General Accounting Office. Timeliness and completeness of FBI responses to requests under the Freedom of Information and Privacy Acts have improved: report to the Congress by the Comptroller General of the United States. [Washington] 1978. 93 p.

U.S. President, 1974-1977 (Ford). Vetoing H.R. 12471, amend Freedom of Information Act: message. Washington, U.S. Govt. Print. Off., 1974. 5 p. (93d Congress, 2d sess. House. Document no. 93-383).

EXECUTIVE PRIVILEGE

Books

Ball, Howard. No pledge of privacy. Port Washington, Kennikat Press, 1977. 144 p.

Berger, Raoul. Executive privilege: a constitutional myth. Cambridge, Harvard University Press, 1974. 430 p.

Breckenridge, Adam Carlyle. The executive privilege: Presidential control over information. Lincoln, University of Nebraska Press, 1974. 188 p.

Essays on executive privilege. Chicago, American Bar Foundation, 1974. 35 p.

Guido, Kenneth J., Jr. The right of the House Judiciary Committe to all Presidential documents it deems necessary for its impeachment inquiry. Washington, Common cause, 1974. 34 p. (Samuel Pool Weaver Constitutional Law series no. 1).

Orman, John M. Secrecy, accountability and Presidential power: the case of Gerald R. Ford. Prepared for delivery at the 1977 annual meeting of the Midwest Political Science Association. The Pick-Congress Hotel, Chicago, Illinois, Apr. 21-23, 1977. 51 p.

Sofaer, Abraham D. War, foreign affairs, and constitutional power. Cambridge, Mass., Ballinger Publishing Co., 1976. 506 p.

Ungar, Sanford J. The papers and the papers: an account of the legal and political battle over the Pentagon papers. New York, E. P. Dutton Co., 1972. 319 p.

Wiggins, James Russell. Freedom or secrecy. Revised edition. New York, Oxford University Press, 1964. 289 p.

Articles

Archibald, Samuel, and Harold C. Relyea. The present limits of executive privilege. In remarks of William S. Moorehead. Congressional Record [daily ed.] v. 119, Mar. 28, 1973: H2243-H2246.
　　Reprinted in Raoul Berger, Executive privilege: a constitutional myth. 373-386.

Association of the Bar of the City of New York. Committee on Civil Rights. Executive privilege: analysis and recommendations for congressional legislation. Record of the Association of the Bar of the City of New York, v. 29, Feb. 1974: 177-208.

Baldwin, Gordon B. Congressional power to demand disclosure of foreign intelligence agreements. Brooklyn journal of international law, v. 3, Fall 1976: 1-30.

— — — The foreign affairs advice privilege. Wisconsin law review. v. 1976: no. 1, 16-46.

Barton, Ansley B. United States v. Nixon and the Freedom of Information Act: new impetus for agency disclosure? Emory law journal, v. 24, Spring 1975: 405-424.

Berger, Margaret A. How the privilege for governmental information met its Watergate. Case Western Reserve law review, v. 25, Summer 1975: 747-795.

Berger, Raoul. Congressional subpoenas to executive officials. Columbia law review, v. 75, June 1975: 865-896.

— — — Executive privilege v. congressional inquiry. UCLA law review, v. 12, May 1965: 1044-1120 and Aug. 1965: 1287-1364.

— — — The grand inquest of the nation. Harper's magazine, v. 247, Oct. 1973: 12-13, 18, 20-23.

— — — The incarnation of executive privilege. UCLA law review, v. 22, Oct. 1974: 4-29.

— — — The President, Congress, and the courts. Yale law journal, v. 83, May 1974: 1111-1155.

Berger, Raoul, and Abe Krash. Government immunity from discovery. Yale law journal, v. 59, Dec. 1950: 1451-1466.

Bernstein, Barton J. The road to Watergate and beyond: the growth and abuse of executive authority since 1940. Law and contemporary problems, v. 40, Spring 1976: 58-86.

Bishop, Joseph W., Jr. The executive's right of privacy: an unresolved constitutional question. Yale law journal, v. 66, Feb. 1957: 477-491.

Borman, Keith. Policing the executive privilege. University of Michigan journal of law reform, v. 5, Spring 1972: 568-580.

Cappelletti, Mauro, and C. J. Golden, Jr. Crown privilege and executive privilege: a British response to an American controversy. Stanford law review, v. 25, June 1973: 836-844.

Carrow, Milton M. Governmental nondisclosure in judicial proceedings. University of Pennsylvania law review, v. 107, Dec. 1958: 166-198.

Clary, Everett B. "Each branch shall be independent": the Burr-Watergate syndrome. California State Bar journal, v. 59, Jan.-Feb. 1974: 17-18, 20, 22-23, 78-81.

Cleveland, Harlan, and Stuart Gerry Brown. The limits of obsession: fencing in the "national security" claim. Administrative law review, v. 28, Summer 1976: 327-346.

Collins, P. R. Power of congressional committees of investigation to obtain information from the executive branch: the argument for the legislative branch. Georgia law journal, v. 39, May 1951: 563-598.

Colton, Douglas. Administrative law — Freedom of Information Act — the doctrine of executive privilege limits statutory access to information held within the Executive Office of the President. Texas law review, v. 49, Apr. 1971: 780-791.

Cox, Archibald. Executive privilege. University of Pennsylvania law review, v. 122, June 1974: 1383-1438.

Dixon, Robert G., Jr. Congress, shared administration, and executive privilege. In Congress against the President. New York, Academy of political cal science, 1975. Proceedings, v. 32, no. 1, 1975: 125-140.

Dorsen, Norman, and John H. F. Shattuck. Executive privilege, the Congress and the courts. Ohio State law journal, v. 35, no. 1, 1974: 1-40.

Egan, Jack. Executive privilege: it's the real thing. New York, v. 12, Dec. 25, 1978-Jan. 1, 1979: 16, 18, 21.

Ehrmann, Henry W. The duty of disclosure in parliamentary investigation: a comparative study. University of Chicago law review, v. 11, Dec. 1943: 1-25 and Feb. 1944: 117-153.

Ervin, Sam J., Jr. Controlling executive privilege. Loyola law review (New Orleans), v. 20, no. 1, 1974: 11-31.

— — —Executive privilege: the need for congressional action. Case and comment, v. 79, Jan.-Feb. 1974: 39-43, 45-48.

— — —Executive privilege: secrecy in a free society. Nation, v. 213, Nov. 8, 1971: 454-457.

Evans, Thomas E., III. Executive privilege and the Congress: perspectives and recommendations. De Paul law review, v. 23, Winter 1974: 692-736.

Evidence — executive immunity from disclosure — documents in possession of the F.B.I. Minnesota law review v. 35, May 1951: 586-590.

The Executive evidential privilege in suits against the government. Northwestern University law review, v. 47, May-June 1952: 259-269.

Executive privilege and the Freedom of Information Act: the constitutional foundation of the amended national security exemption. Washington University law quarterly, v. 1976, Fall 1976: 609-666.

Executive privilege — the President does not have an absolute privilege to withhold evidence from a grand jury. Harvard law review, v. 87, May 1974: 1557-1568.

Extension of absolute privilege to government officials of less than cabinet rank. Minnesota law review, v. 44, Jn. 1960: 547-555.

Farber, Daniel. Executive privilege at the state level. University of Illinois law forum, v. 1974, no. 4, 1974: 631-648.

Ford, William D., and Daniel H. Pollitt. Who owns the tapes? North Carolina central law journal, v. 6, Spring 1975: 197-203.

Freund, Paul A. On Presidential privilege. Harvard law review, v. 88, Nov. 1974: 13-39.

Frohmayer, David B. An essay on executive privilege. In remarks of Bob Packwood. Congressional Record [daily ed.] v. 120, Apr. 30, 1974: S6603-S6607.

Goldwater, Barry M. The President's constitutional primacy in foreign relations and national defense. Virginia journal of international law, v. 13, Summer 1973: 463-489.

Government privilege against disclosure of official documents. Yale law journal, v. 58, May 1949: 993-998.

Government information and the rights of citizens. Michigan law review, v. 73, May-June 1975: whole issue.

Gunther, Gerald. Judicial hegemony and legislative autonomy: the Nixon case and the impeachment process. UCLA law review, v. 22, Oct. 1974: 30-39.

Hardin, Paul, III. Executive privilege in the Federal courts. Yale law journal, v. 71, Apr. 1962: 879-905.

Henkin, Louis. Executive privilege: Mr. Nixon loses but the Presidency largely prevails. UCLA law review, v. 22, Oct. 1974: 40-46.

— — — The right to know and the duty to withhold: the case of the Pentagon papers. University of Pennsylvania law review, v. 120, Dec. 1971: 271-280.

Horton, Frank. The public's right to know. Case and comment, v. 77, Jan.-Feb. 1972: 3-18.

Reprinted in North Carolina central law journal, v. 3, Spring 1972: 123-142.

Hruska, Roman L. Executive records in congressional investigations — duty to disclose — duty to withhold. Nebraska law review, v. 35, Jan. 1956: 310-316.

Hurtgen, James R. The case for Presidential perogative. University of Toledo law review, v. 7, Fall 1975: 59-85.

Ivester, David Mitchell. The constitutional right to know. Hastings constitutional law quarterly, v. 4, Winter 1977: 109-163.

Kalijarvi, June D.W., and Don Wallace, Jr. Executive authority to impose prior restraint upon publication of information concerning national security affairs: a constitutional power. California Western law review, v. 9, Spring 1973: 468-496.

Karst, Kenneth L., and Harold W. Horowitz. Presidential prerogative and judicial review. UCLA law review, v. 22, Oct. 1974: 47-67.

Kramer, Donald T. Executive privilege with respect to Presidential papers and recordings. American law reports Federal, v. 19. Rochester, N.Y., The Lawyers co-operative publishing co., 1974: 472-484.

Kramer, Robert and Herman Marcuse. Executive privilege — a study of the period 1953-1960. George Washington law review, v. 29, Apr. 1961: 623-717 and June, 1961; 827-916.

Kurland, Philip B. United States v. Nixon: who killed Cock Robin? UCLA law review, v. 22, Oct. 1974: 68-75.

Kutner, Luis. Executive privilege . . . growth of power over a declining Congress. Loyola law review (New Orleans), v. 20, no. 1, 1974: 33-44.

— — —Nixon v. Cox: due process of executive authority. St. John's law review, v. 48, Mar. 1974: 441-460.

Lee, Rex E. Executive privilege, congressional subpoena power, and judicial review: three branches, three powers, and some relationships. Brigham Young University law review, v. 1978, no. 2, 1978: 231-297.

Lentz, William W. Executive privilege to withhold information from Congress: constitutional or political doctrine? University of Missouri at Kansas City law review, v. 42, Spring 1974: 372-389.

Lewin, Nathan. The Supreme Court and the Watergate tapes. New Republic, v. 170, June 22, 1974: 13-16.

Lim-chun, Lily Yau. U.S. v. Nixon and executive privilege. Columbia, School of Journalism, University of Missouri, 1975. 8 p. (Missouri. University. Freedom of Information Center. Report no. 345).

Luscombe, Mark A. Congressional control of agency privilege. University of Michigan journal of law reform, v. 9, Winter 1976: 348-374.

McAllister, Dale. Executive or judicial determination of privilege of government documents? Journal of criminal law, criminology and police science, v. 41, Sept.-Oct. 1950: 330-335.

McGlaughon, H. King, Jr. Constitutional law — executive privilege: tilting the scales in favor of secrecy. North Carolina law review, v. 53, Dec. 1974: 419-430.

Max, R. A. A judicial interpretation of the Nixon Presidency. Cumberland law review, v. 6, Spring 1975: 213-242.

Miller, Arthur Selwin. "Executive privilege": its dubious constitutionality. Bureaucrat, v. 1, Summer 1972: 136-141.

Mishkin, Paul J. Great cases and soft law: a comment on United States v. Nixon. UCLA law review, v. 22, Oct. 1974: 76–91.

Mone, Mary C. Federal procedure — "executive privilege" — certain police reports held privileged in civil rights action. Fordham law review, v. 42, Mar. 1974: 675–688.

Moore, John Norton. Contemporary issues in an ongoing debate: the roles of Congress and the President in foreign affairs. International lawyer, v. 7, Oct. 1973: 733–745.

Murphy, John F. Knowledge is power: foreign policy and information interchange among Congress, the executive branch, and the public. Tulane law review, v. 49, Mar. 1975: 504–554.

O'Brien, Francis William. The dissenting opinions of Nixon v. Sirica: an argument for executive privilege in the White House tapes controversy. Southwestern law journal, v. 28, Spring 1974: 373–390.

Oster, Jon F. Extension of absolute privilege to executive officers of government agencies. Maryland law review, v. 20, Fall 1960: 368–373.

Osterman, Melvin H. Evidence: government privilege to refuse to disclose the contents of official documents in the Federal courts. Cornell law quarterly, v. 41, Summer 1956: 737–749.

Power of the executive to withhold information from congressional investigating committees. Georgia law journal, v. 43, June 1955: 643.

President and Congress — power of the President to refuse congressional demands for information. Stanford law review, v. 1, Jan. 1949: 256–262.

Privileged documents of a government agency. Chitty's law journal, v. 5, Dec. 1955: 254–261, 268.

Ramis, Timothy V. Executive privileges: what are the limits? Oregon law review, v. 54, no. 1, 1975: 81–103.

Randolph, Robert C., and Daniel C. Smith. Executive privilege and the congressional right of inquiry. Harvard journal on legislation, v. 10, June 1973: 621–671.

Ratner, Leonard G. Executive privilege, self incrimination, and the separation of powers illusion. UCLA law review, v. 22, Oct. 1974: 92–115.

Regulatory "executive privilege" to withhold information. Indiana law journal, v. 32, Spring 1957: 385–400.

Reich, Yaron Z. United States v. AT&T: judicially supervised negotiations and political questions. Columbia law review, v. 77, Apr. 1977: 466–494.

Reinstein, Robert J. An early view of executive powers and privilege: the trial of Smith and Ogden. Hastings constitutional law quarterly, v. 2, Spring 1975: 309–340.

Rhodes, Irwin S. What really happened to the Jefferson subpoenas. American Bar Association journal, v. 60, Jan. 1974: 52–54.

The right of government employees to furnish information to Congress: statutory and constitutional aspects. Virginia law review, v. 57, June 1971: 885–919.

Rogers. William P. Constitutional law: the papers of the executive branch.

American Bar Association journal, v. 44, Oct. 1958: 941-944, 1007-1014.

Rosenthal, Paul C., and Robert S. Grossman. Congressional access to confidential information collected by Federal agencies. Harvard journal on legislation, v. 15, Dec. 1977: 74-118.

Rourke, Francis E. Administrative secrecy: a congressional dilemma. American political science review, v. 54, Sept. 1960: 684-694.

Rubin, Alfred P. A wholesome discretion. New York law forum, v. 20, Winter 1975: 569-616.

Rubin, Richard Alan. Foreign policy, secrecy, and the first amendment: the Pentagon papers in retrospect. Howard law journal, v. 17, no. 3, 1972: 579-612.

Sanford, William V. Evidentiary privileges against production of data within control of executive departments. Vanderbilt law review, v. 3, Dec. 1949: 73-98.

Schwartz, Bernard. A reply to Mr. Rogers: the papers of the executive branch. American Bar Association journal, v. 45, May 1959: 467-470, 525-526.

— — — Bad Presidents make hard law: Richard M. Nixon in the Supreme Court. Rutgers law review, v. 31, May 1978: 22-38.

— — — Executive privilege and congressional investigatory power. California law review, v. 47, Mar. 1959: 3-50.

Separation of powers and executive privilege: the Watergate briefs. Political science quarterly, v. 88, Dec. 1973: 582-654.

Shah, Chandrakant C. Executive privilege to withhold information from the judicial branch — a comparative study. (U.S. and U.K.) Texas Bar journal, v. 30, Jan. 1967: 15-16, 46-51.

Sofaer, Abraham D. Executive power and the control of information: practice under the framers. Duke law journal, v. 1977, Mar. 1977: 1-57.

— — — Executive privilege: an historical note. Columbia law review, v. 75, Nov. 1975: 1318-1321.

Spencer, Patricia L. Separation of powers — bills of attainder — Presidential papers — Chief Executive's right to privacy. Akron law review, v. 11, Fall 1977: 373-386.

Sternstein, Alan B. The justiciability of confrontation: executive secrecy and the political question doctrine. Arizona law review, v. 16, no. 1, 1974: 140-166.

Survey on government and the freedom of information. Loyola law review (New Orleans), v. 20, no. 1, 1973-1974: 1-88.

Symposium: executive privilege: public's right to know and public interest. Federal Bar journal, v. 19, Jan. 1959: vii-84.

Symposium: United States v. Nixon: an historical perspective. Loyola of Los Angeles law review, v. 9, Dec. 1975: 11-66.

Taubeneck, T. D., and John J. Sexton. Executive privilege and court's right to know — discovery against the United States in civil actions in Federal district courts. Georgetown law journal, v. 48, Spring 1960: 486-529.

Thatcher, C. Marshall. United States v. Nixon: what price unanimity? Ohio Northern law review, v. 2, no. 2, 1974: 303-317.

Van Alstyne, William. A political and constitutional review of United States v. Nixon. UCLA law review, v. 22, Oct. 1974: 116-140.

— — — President Nixon: toughing it out with the law. American Bar Association journal, v. 59, Dec. 19733: 1398-1402.

— — — The role of Congress in determining incidental powers of the President and the Federal courts: a comment on the horizontal effect of the sweeping clause. Law and contemporary problems, v. 40, Spring 1976: 102-134.

— — — The third impeachment article: congressional bootstrapping. American Bar Association journal, v. 60, Oct. 1974: 1199-1202.

Wallace, Mark S. Discovery of government documents and the official information privilege. Columbia law review, v. 76, Jan. 1976: 142-174.

Wolkinson, Herman. Demands of congressional committees for executive papers. Federal Bar journal, v. 10, Apr. 1949: 103-150; July: 223-259; Oct. 1949: 319-350.

Wood, Brenda M. Executive privilege may not be asserted as a defense to an action for damages for deprivation of constitutional rights without showing probable cause. Howard law journal, v. 18, no. 2, 1974: 477-490.

Younger, Irving. Congressional investigations and executive secrecy: a study in the separation of powers. University of Pittsburgh law review, v. 20, June, 1959: 755-784.

Documents

U.S. Congress. House. Committee on Expenditures in the Executive Departments. Directing all executive departments and agencies of the Federal Government to make available to any and all standing, special, or select committees of the House of Representatives and the Senate, information which may be deemed necessary to enable them to properly perform the duties delegated to them by the Congress. Parts 1 and 2. Washington, U.S. Govt. Print. Off., 1948. 34 p. (80th Congress, 2d sess. House. Report no. 1595).

U.S. Congress. House. Committee on Government Operations. Access of service secretaries to military information. Washington, U.S. Govt. Print. Off., 1976. 22 p. (94th Congress, 2d sess. House. Report no. 94-952).

— — — Amending the Freedom of Information Act to require that information be made available to Congress. Washington, U.S. Govt. Print. Off., 1974. 41 p. (93d Congress, 2d sess. House. Report no. 93-990).

— — — Executive branch practices in withholding information from congressional committees. Hearings, 86th Congress, 2d sess. June 28, 1960. Washington, U.S. Govt. Print. Off., 1960. 48 p.

— — — The right of Congress to obtain information from the executive and from other agencies of the Federal Government: study by the staff. Washington, U.S. Govt. Print. Off., 1956. 26 p.

At head of title: Committee print. 84th Congress, 2d sess. House of Representatives.

— — —U.S. Government information policies and practices—problems of Congress in obtaining information from the executive branch. Hearings, 92d Congress, 2d sess. May 12–June 1, 1972. Washington, U.S. Govt. Print. Off., 1972. 374 p.

U.S. Congress. House. Committee on Government Operations. Foreign Operations and Government Information Subcommittee. Access by the Congress to information from regulatory boards and commissions. Washington, U.S. Govt. Print. Off., 1970. 41 p.

At head of title: 91st Cong., 2d sess. House. Committee print.

— — —Availability of information to Congress. Hearings, 93d Congress, 1st sess. April 3–19, 1973. Washington, U.S. Govt. Print. Off., 1973. 361 p.

U.S. Congress. House. Committee on Government Operations. Subcommittee on Legislation and National security. Access of service secretaries to military information. Hearing, 94th Congress, 1st sess. Sept. 10, 1975. Washington, U.S. Govt. Print. Off., 1975. 40 p.

U.S. Congress. Joint Committee on Congressional Operations. Constitutional immunity of members of Congress. Hearings, 93d Congress, 1st sess. Mar. 21–July 19, 1973. Washington, U.S. Govt. Print. Off., 1973. 2 v.

— — —The constitutional immunity of members of Congress. Washington, U.S. Govt. Print. Off., 1974. 58 p. (93d Congress, 2d sess. Senate. Report no. 93–896).

— — —Special report: United States v. John Mitchell, et al. and United States v. Richard M. Nixon, et al. and Richard M. Nixon v. United States. Washington, U.S. Govt. Print. Off., 1974. 566 p.

At head of title: 93rd Congress, 2d sess. Committee print.

U.S. Congress. Senate. Committee on Foreign Relations. Congressional inquiry into military affairs. Washington, U.S. Govt. Print. Off., 1968. 8 p.

At head of title: 90th Congress, 2d sess. Committee print.

— — —National Security Act amendment. Hearings , 92d Congress, 2d sess., on S.2224. Mar. 28–Apr. 24, 1972. Washington, U.S. Govt. Print. Off., 1972. 139 p.

U.S. Congress. Senate. Committee on Government Operations. Congressional Right to Information Act. Washington, U.S. Govt. Print. Off., 1973. 24 p. (93d Congress, 2d sess. Senate. Report no. 93–612).

U.S. Congress. Senate. Committee on Government Operations. Preservation, protection, and public access with respect to certain tape recordings and other materials: report to accompany S. 4016. Washington, U.S. Govt. Print. Off., 1974. 10 p. (93d Congress, 2d sess. Senate. Report no. 93–1181).

U.S. Congress. Senate. Committee on Government Operations. Subcommittee on Intergovernmental Relations. Executive privilege—secrecy in government. Hearings, 94th Congress, 1st sess., on S. 2170, S. 2378,

S. 2420. Sept. 29, and Oct. 23, 1975. Washington, U.S. Govt. Print. Off., 1976. 647 p.

— — —Keeping the Congress informed and Joint Funding Simplification Act of 1973. Hearing, 93rd Congress, 1st sess. Sept. 11, 1973. Washington, U.S. Govt. Print. Off., 1973. 50 p.

U.S. Congress. Senate. Committee on Government Operations. Subcommittee on Intergovernmental Relations [and] Committee on the Judiciary. Subcommittees on Separation of Powers and Administrative Practice and Procedure. Executive privilege, secrecy in government, freedom of information. Hearings, 93rd Congress. 1st sess. Apr. 10–June 26, 1973. Washington, U.S. Govt. Print. Off., 1973. 1482 p.

U.S. Congress. Senate. Committee on the Judiciary. Subcommittee on Constitutional Rights. Executive privilege. Hearings, 86th Congress, 1st sess. Mar. 13–May 13, 1959. Washington, U.S. Govt. Print. Off., 1959. 2 pts. 365 p.

— — —Freedom of information and secrecy in government. Hearing, 86th Congress, 1st sess. Apr. 17, 1959. Washington, U.S. Govt. Print. Off., 1959. 64 p.

— — —The power of the President to withhold information from the Congress: memorandums of the Attorney General. Washington, U.S. Govt. Print. Off., 1958. 82 p.

At head of title: 85th Congress, 2d sess. Committee print.

— — —Withholding of information from Congress. Washington, U.S. Govt. Print. Off., 1961. 99 p.

At head of title: 86th Congress, 2d sess. Committee print.

U.S. Congress. Senate. Committee on the Judiciary. Subcommittee on Separation of Powers. Congressional access to and control and release of sensitive government information. Hearings, 94th Congress, 2d sess. Mar. 11 and 12, 1976. Washington, U.S. Govt. Print. Off., 1977. 121 p.

— — —Executive privilege: the withholding of information by the executive. Hearings, 92d Congress, 1st sess. July 27–Aug. 5, 1971. Washington, U.S. Govt. Print. Off., 1971. 635 p.

— — —Refusals by the executive branch to provide information to the Congress 1964–1973: a survey conducted . . . of instances in which executive agencies of the Government have withheld information from members and committees of the Congress and from the Comptroller General of the United States. Washington, U.S. Govt. Print. Off., 1974. 571 p.

At head of title: 93rd Congress., 2d sess. Committee print.

SECURITY CLASSIFICATION

Books

American Historical Association. Access to government documents, papers presented to a session of the American Historical Association, Dec. 1972. Manhattan, Kansas, Military Affairs, 1974. var. pag.

Barker, Carol M., and Matthew H. Fox. Classified files: the yellowing pages, a report on scholar's access to government documents. New York, The Twentieth Century Fund, 1972. 115 p.

Cox, Arthur Macy. The myths of national security. Boston, Beacon Press, 1975. 231 p.

Dorsen, Norman, and Stephen Gillers, eds. Government secrecy in America: none of your business. New York, The Viking Press, 1974. 362 p.

Franck, Thomas M., and Edward Weisband, eds. Secrecy and foreign policy. New York, Oxford University Press, 1974. 453 p.

Halperin, Morton H., and Daniel Hoffman. Freedom vs. national security. New York, Chelsea House Publishers, 1977. 592 p.

— — —Top secret. Washington, New Republic books, 1977. 158 p.

Irvine, Dallas. The origin of defense-information markings in the Army and former War Department. Washington, National Archives and records Service, General Services Administration, 1964. 49 p.

Leutze, James R., ed. The military in a democracy. Atlanta, Southern Newspaper Publishers Association Foundation, n.d. 111 p.

Mezines, Basil J., Jacob A. Stein, and Jules Gruff. Administrative law: acquisition, use and disclosure of government information; Freedom of Information, Privacy, Sunshine, and related Acts. v. 2. New York, Matthew Bender & Co., 1977. var. pag.

Schrag, Peter. Test of loyalty. New York, Simon and Schuster, 1974. 414 p.

Shapiro, Martin, ed. The pentagon papers and the courts. San Francisco, Chandler Publishing Company, 1972. 131 p.

Shils, Edward A. The torment of secrecy: the background and consequences of American security policies. Glencoe, Free Press of Glencoe, 1956. 238 p.

Summers, Robert E. Federal information controls in peacetime. New York, the H.W. Wilson Company, 1949. 301 p.

Ungar, Stanford J. The papers and the papers: an account of the legal and political battle over the pentagon papers. New York, E. P. Dutton Co., 1972. 319 p.

Wiggins, James Russell. Freedom or secrecy. Revised edition. New York, Oxford University Press, 1964. 289 p.

Periodicals

Atkins, Jeanni, and Belvel J. Boyd. Classification reexamined. Columbia, School of Journalism, University of Missouri, 1975. 11 p. (Missouri. University. Freedom of Information Center. Report no. 332).

Becker, Jerrold L. The Supreme court's recent "national security" decisions: which interests are being protected? Tennessee law review, v. 40, Fall 1972: 1-27.

Brown, William L. The Government's security declassification program. Federal Bar journal, v. 34, Fall 1975: 305-310.

Civil liberties and national security: a delicate balance. Northwestern University law review, v. 68, Nov.-Dec. 1973: 922-941.

Cleveland, Harlan, and Stuart Garry Brown. The limits of obsession: fencing in the "national security" claim. Administrative law review, v. 28, Summer 1976: 327–346.

Colby, William E. Intelligence secrecy and security in a free society. International security, v. 1, Fall 1976: 3–14.

Criley, Richard. Sneaking up on the press: Nixon's 'official secrets act'. Nation, v. 218, Mar. 2, 1974. 265–268.

Curtis, John W. Secrecy and national security: a program for congressional action and Presidential restraint. Ripon Forum, v. 9, November 1973: 1–24.

Dennis, Everette E. Purloined information as property: a new First Amendment challenge. Journalism quarterly, v. 50, Autumn 1973: 456–462, 474.

Diamond, Alan. Declassification of sensitive information: a comment on Executive Order 11652. George Washington law review, v. 41, July 1973: 1052–1071.

Dodge, John F., Jr. Evidence-privilege-maintaining action where the evidence may affect the national security. Michigan law review, v. 53, June 1955: 1187–1190.

Draper, Theodore. The classifiers of classified documents are breaking their own classification rules. New York Times magazine, Feb. 4, 1973: 10–11, 38, 46–47.

Eagle, Kenneth L. Prior restraint enforced against publication of classified material by CIA employee. North Carolina law review, v. 51, Mar. 1973: 865–874.

Edgar, Harold, and Benno C. Schmidt, Jr. The expionage statutes and publication of defense information. Columbia law review, v. 73, May 1973: 929–1087.

File classified "Top Secret" is within national security exemption from the act and is not obtainable unless the classification is arbitrary and unreasonable. — Epstein v. Resor, 296 F. Supp. 214 (N.D. Cal. 1969). Harvard law review, v. 83, Feb. 1970: 928–935.

Florence, William G., and Ruth Matthews. Executive secrecy: two perspectives. Columbia, School of Journalism, University of Missouri, 1975. 7 p. (Missouri. University. Freedom of Information Center. Report no. 336).

Fox, William F., Jr., and Peter N. Weiss. The FOIA national security exemption and the new executive order. Federal Bar journal, v. 37, Fall 1978: 1–16.

Gillers, Stephen. "Blueprint for tyranny": Congress overhauls the laws. Nation, v. 222, Feb. 14, 1976: 172–177.

Goodale, James C. Senate bill no. 1 and the Freedom of Information Act: do they conflict? Administrative law review, v. 28, Summer 1976: 347–362.

Government information and the rights of citizens: project. Michigan law review, v. 73, May-Juned 1975: whole issue.

Green, Harold P. Atomic energy information control. Chicago Bar record, v. 38, Nov. 1956: 55–62.

Halperin, Morton H., and Daniel N. Hoffman. Secrecy and the right to know. Law and contemporary problems, v. 40, Summer 1976: 132–165.

Haydock, Robert. Some evidentiary problems posed by atomic energy security requirements. Harvard law review, v. 61, Feb. 1948: 468–491.

Henkin, Louis. The right to know and the duty to withhold: the case of the pentagon papers. University of Pennsylvania law review, v. 120, Dec. 1971: 271–280.

In camera inspection of national security files under the Freedom of Information Act. University of Kansas law review, v. 26, Summer 1978: 617–624.

Johnston, Richard F., and Kay Marmorek. Access to government information and the classification process—is there a right to know? New York law forum, v. 17, no. 3, 1971: 814–840.

Kasdan, Ira T. Civil procedure—right to jury trial—defendant's need to introduce state secrets as evidence outweighs plaintiff's right to civil jury trial. Georgetown law journal, v. 66, Aug. 1978: 1575–1591.

Katz, Alan. Government information leaks and the First Amendment. California law review, v. 64, Jan. 1976: 108–145.

Kmet, Mary Alice. "Greater openness through classification reform." Security management, v. 22, Oct. 1978: 22–23, 27.

Levin, Ronald M. In camera inspections under the Freedom of Information Act. University of Chicago law review, v. 41, Spring: 1974: 557–581.

Levine, Jeffrey L. Judicial review of classified documents: amendments to the Freedom of Informaiton Act. Harvard journal of legislation, v. 12, Apr. 1975: 415–446.

Levings, Darryl, and Patricia Murphy. A U.S. "official secrets act"? Columbia, School of Journalism, University of Missouri, 1973. 6 p. (Missouri. University. Freedom of Information Center. Report no. 311).

Lewis, Herbert. Safeguarding classified information. Defense management journal, v. 9, Oct. 1973: 29–31, 62.

Max. R. A. A Judicial interpretation of the Nixon Presidency. Cumberland law review, v. 6, Spring 1975: 213–242.

National security and the public's right to know: a new role for the courts under the Freedom of Information Act. University of Pennsylvania law review, v. 123, June 1975: 1438–1473.

The national security interest and civil liberties. Harvard law review, v. 85, Apr. 1972: 1130–1326.

Nesson, Charles R. Aspects of the executive's power over national security matters: secrecy classifications and foreign intelligence wiretaps. Indiana law journal, v. 49, Spring 1974: 399–421.

Newman, James R. Control of information relating to atomic energy. Yale law journal, v. 56, May 1947: 769–802.

Nimmer, Melville B. National security secrets v. free speech: the issue left undecided in the Ellsburg case. Stanford law review, v. 26, Jan. 1974: 311–333.

Nufer, Harold F. Four momentous events in 1971–72: catalysts for reform of the national security classification system? Air University review, v. 28, July-Aug. 1977: 56-63.

O'Neill, James E. Secrecy and disclosure: the declassification program of the National Archives and Records Service. Prologue, v. 5, Spring 1973: 43-45.

— — — The security classification of records in the United States. Indian Archives, v. 22, Jan.-Dec. 1973: 35-45.

Palfrey, John Gorham. The problem of secrecy. Annals, v. 290, Nov. 1953: 90-99.

Post, Robert C. National security and the amended Freedom of Information Act. Yale law journal, v. 85, Jan. 1976: 401-422.

The question of stronger Federal laws to safeguard classified information: pros and cons. Congressional digest, v. 54, Nov. 1975: 257-288.

Reform in the classification and declassification of national security information: Nixon Executive Order 11,652. Iowa law review, v. 59, Oct. 1973: 110-143.

Roffman, Howard. Freedom of information: judicial review of executive security classifications. University of Florida law review, v. 28, Winter 1976: 551-568.

Rubin, Alfred P. A wholesome discretion. New York law forum, v. 20, Winter 1975: 569-616.

Ryan, David H. United States v. Marchetti and Alfred A. Knopf, Inc. v. Colby: secrecy 2; First amendment O. Hastings Constitutional law quarterly, v. 3, Fall 1976: 1073-1105.

Schmidt, Benno C. Jr., and Harold Edgar. S.1. Columbia journalism review, v. 14, Mar.-Apr. 1976: 18-21.

Sigal, Leon V. Official secrecy and informal communication in congressional bureaucratic relations. Political science quarterly, v. 90, Spring 1975: 71-92.

Spec, Milt. How to steal government secrets. Washington monthly, v. 10, Feb. 1979: 54-60.

Stevens, Jean. Classification: threat to democracy. Columbia, School of Journalism, University of Missouri, 1971. 10 p. (Missouri. University. Freedom of Information Center. Report no. 270).

Symposium on the 1974 amendments to the Freedom of Information Act. American University law review, v. 25, Fall 1975: 1-83.

Theoharis, Athan G. Classification restrictions and the public's right to know: a new look at the Alger Hiss case. Intellect, v. 104, Sept.-Oct. 1975: 86-89.

— — — Public or private papers?: the arrogance of the intelligence community. Intellect, v. 106, Oct. 1977: 118-120.

Thomason, Edwin A. Records declassification in the National Archives. Prologue, v. 7, Winter 1975: 235-238.

Unclassified documents physically connected with classified documents may not be withheld under the national security and foreign affairs secrets exemption. Vanderbilt law review, v. 25, Mar. 1972: 397-403.

Wallace, Mark S. Discovery of government documents and the official information privilege. Columbia law review, v. 76, Jan. 1976: 142-174.

Warnke, Paul C. National security and the public's right to know. Federal Bar journal, v. 34, Fall 1975: 301-304.

Welch, Edwin W. Classified information and the courts. Federal Bar journal, v. 31, Fall 1972: 360-377.

Wise, David. The new secrecy. Inquiry (San Francisco), v. 1, Oct. 16, 1978: 20-23.

— — — Toward an official secrets act. Inquiry (San Francisco), v. 1, Feb. 1978: 16-20.

Young, David M. Security and the right to know. Military review, v. 64, Aug. 1974: 46-53.

Young, David R. Secrecy and disclosure: braking the classification machine. Prologue, v. 5, Spring 1973: 41-42.

Zedalis, Rex J. Resurrection of Reynolds: 1974 amendment to national defense and foreign policy exemption. Pepperdine law review, v. 4, Spring 1977: 81-114.

Documents

U.S. Commission on Government Security. Report pursuant to Public Law 304, 84th Congress, as amended. 85th Congress, 1st sess. (Senate. Document no. 64). Washington, U.S. Govt. Print. Off., 1957, 807 p.

U.S. Congress. House. Committee on Armed Services. Full committee consideration of the inquiry into matters regarding classified testimony taken on April 22, 1974, concerning the CIA and Chile. Hearings, 94th Congress, 1st sess. Washington, U.S. Govt. Print. Off., 1975. 30 p.

— — — Report to the full committee on access by members of Congress to classified material. Washington, U.S. Govt. Print. Off., 1975. 19 p.

— — — Alleged purchase of classified information by a member of Congress: report. Washington, U.S. Govt. Print. Off., 1973. 10 p.

A head of title: 93d Congress, 1st sess. Committee print.

— — — Hearings on investigation of national defense establishment; study of regulations and procedures, classification and dissemination of information. Special Subcommittee No. 6 of the Committee on Armed Services, House of Representatives, 85th Congress, 2d sess. Mar. 10-July 9, 1958. Washington, U.S. Govt. Print. Off., 1958. 1144 p. 85th Congress, 2d sess.

U.S. Congress. House. Committee on Armed Services. Armed Services Investigating Subcommittee. Alleged purchase of classified information by a member of Congress. Hearings, 93rd Congress, 1st sess. Mar. 27, 1973. Washington, U.S. Govt. Print. Off., 1973: 56 p.

U.S. Congress. House. Committee on Armed Services. Special Subcommittee on Intelligence. Hearings on the proper classification and handling of government information involving the National Security and H.R. 9853, a related bill. Hearings, 92d Congress, 2d sess. Mar. 8-May 9, 1972. Washington, U.S. Govt. Print. Off., 1972. 353 p.

———Inquiry into matters regarding classified testimony taken on April 22, 1974, concerning the CIA and Chile. Hearing, 93rd Congress, 2d sess. Sept. 25, 1974. Washington, U.S. Govt. Print. Off., 1975. 38 p.

U.S. Congress. House. Committee on Government Operations. Access of service secretaries to military information. Washington, U.S. Govt. Print. Off., 1976. 22 p. (94th Cong., 2d sess. House. Report no. 94-952).

———Executive classification of information—security classification problems involving exemption (b)(1) of the Freedom of Information Act (5 U.S.C. 552). Washington, U.S. Govt. Print. Off., 1973. 113 p. (93rd Congress, 1st sess. House. Report no. 93-221).

———Safeguarding official information in the interests of the defense of the United States; The status of Executive Order 10501. Washington, U.S. Govt. Print. Off., 1962. 48 p. (87th Congress, 2d sess. House. Report no. 2456).

U.S. Congress. House. Committee on Government Operations. Foreign Operations and Government Information Subcommittee. Security classification reform. Hearings, 93rd Congress, 2d sess. July 11-Aug. 1, 1974. Washington, U.S. Govt. Print. Off., 1974. 756 p.

———U.S. government information policies and practices—security classification problems involving subsection (b)(1) of the Freedom of Information Act. Hearings, 92d Congress, 2d session. May 1-11, 1972. Washington, U.S. Govt. Print. Off., 1972. 654 p.

U.S. Congress. House. Committee on Government Operations. Subcommittee on Government Information and Individual Rights. Justice Department handling of cases involving classified data and claims of national security. Hearing, 95th Congress, 2d sess. Sept. 19, 1978. Washington, U.S. Govt. Print. Off., 1979. 221 p.

———Justice Department treatment of criminal cases involving CIA personnel and claims of national security. Hearings, 94th Congress, 1st sess. July 22-Aug. 1, 1975. Washington, U.S. Govt. Print. Off., 1975. 431 p.

———National Archives—security classification problems involving Warren Commission files and other records. Hearing, 94th Congress, 1st sess. Nov. 11, 1975. Washington, U.S. Govt. Print. Off., 1975. 99 p.

———Security classification exemption to the Freedom of Information Act. Hearings, 95th Congress, 1st session. Sept. 20, 1977. Washington, U.S. Govt. Print. Off., 1979. 118 p.

U.S. Congress. House. Committee on Government Operations. Subcommittee on Legislation and National Security. Access of service secretaries to military information. Hearing, 94th Congress, 1st sess. Sept. 10, 1975. Washington, U.S. Govt. Print. Off., 1975. 40 p.

U.S. Congress. House. Committee on Un-American Activities. Protection of classified information released to U.S. industry and defense contractors. Washington, U.S. Govt. Print. Off., 1962. 66 p. (87th Congress, 2d sess. House. Report no. 1945).

U.S. Congress. House. Permanent Select Committee on Intelligence. Disclosure of funds for intelligence activities. Hearings, 95th Congress, 2d sess. Jan. 24, 25, 1978. Washington, U.S. Govt. Print. Off., 1978. 185 p.

U.S. Congress. Joint Committee on Congressional Operations. Constitutional immunity of members of Congress. Hearings, 93d Congress, 1st sess. Mar. 21–July 19, 1973. Washington, U.S. Govt. Print. Off., 1973. 2 v.

— — —The constitutional immunity of members of Congress. Washington, U.S. Govt. Print. Off., 1974. 58 p. (93d Congress, 2d sess. Senate. Report no. 93–896).

U.S. Congress. Senate. Committee on Armed Services. Transmittal of documents from the National Security Council to the chairman of the Joint Chiefs of Staff. Hearings, 93d Congress, 2d sess. 3 parts. Washington, U.S. Govt. Print. Off., 1974. 354 p.

— — —Unauthorized disclosures and transmittal of classified documents: report. Washington, U.S. Govt. Print. Off., 1974. 11 p.

At head of title: 93rd Congress, 2d sess. Committee print.

U.S. Congress. Senate. Committee on Foreign Relations. Security classification as a problem in the congressional role in foreign policy. Washington, U.S. Govt. Print. Off., 1971. 41 p.

At head of title: 92d Congress, 1st sess. Committee print.

U.S. Congress. Senate. Committee on Government Operations. Subcommittee on Intergovernmental Relations. Government secrecy. Hearings, 93d Congress, 2d sess. May 22–June 10, 1974. Washington, U.S. Govt. Print. Off., 1974. 908 p.

— — —Legislation on government secrecy. Washington, U.S. Govt. Print. Off., 1974. 265 p.

At head of title: 93d Congress, 2d sess. Committee print.

U.S. Congress. Senate. Select Committee on Intelligence. National security secrets and the administration of justice. Washington, U.S. Govt. Print. Off., 1978. 51 p.

At head of title: 95th Congress, 2d sess. Committee print.

— — —Whether disclosure of funds authorized for intelligence activities is in the public interest. Hearings, 95th Congress, 1st sess. April 27 and 28, 1977. Washington, U.S. Govt. Print. Off., 1977. 475 p.

— — —Whether disclosure of funds for the intelligence activities of the United States is in the public interest. Washington, U.S. Govt. Print. Off., 1977. 18 p. (95th Congress, 1st sess. Senate. Report no. 95–274).

U.S. Congress. Senate. Select Committee on Intelligence. Subcommittee on Secrecy and Disclosure. The use of classified information in litigation. Hearings, 95th Congress, 2d sess. Mar. 1–6, 1978. Washington, U.S. Govt. Print. Off., 1978. 285 p.

U.S. Congress. Senate. Select Committee to Study Governmental Operations with Respect to Intelligence Activities. Government information security classification policy. [by Harold C. Relyea] In Supplementary reports on intelligence activities; book VI. Washington, U.S. Govt. Print. Off., 1976. p. 313-353. (94th Congress, 2d sess. Senate. Report no. 94-755).

U.S. Congress. Senate. Special Committee to Study Questions Related to Secret and Confidential Government Documents. Questions related to secret and confidential documents: report. Washington, U.S. Govt. Print.Off., 1973. 16 p. (93d Congress, 1st sess. Senate. Report no. 93-66).

U.S. Dept. of Defense. Office of the Defense Research and Engineering. Report of the Defense Science Board Task Force on Secrecy. Washington, Department of Defense, 1970. 12 p.

U.S. Dept. of Defense. Committee on Classified Information. Report to the Secretary of Defense by the Committee on Classified Information. Washington, Department of Defense, 1956. n.p.

U.S. Dept. of Defense. Office of the Secretary of Defense. Department of Defense, 1957. n.p.

— — —Defense implementation of Recommendations of Coolidge Committee on Classified Information (part 1). Defense implementation of Recommendations of Coolidge Committee on Classified Information (part 2). Washington, Department of Defense, 1957. n.p.

U.S. General Accounting Office. Continuing problems in DOD's classification of national security information; report to the Congress by the Comptroller General of the United States. Washington, 1979. 35 p.

U.S. General Accounting Office. Improved executive branch oversight needed for the government's national security information classification program: report by the Comptroller General. [Washington] 1979. 38 p.

U.S. Interagency Classification Review Committee. Progress report: implementation of Executive Order 11652 on classification and declassification of national security information and material. Washington. Issued annually, 1974-1978.

PRESIDENTIAL PAPERS, LIBRARIES AND INFORMATION MANAGEMENT

Books

Burnette, O. Lawrence, Jr. Beneath the footnote: a guide to the use and preservation of American historical sources. Madison, Wisconsin, State Historical Society of Wisconsin [1969]. 450 p.

Graebner, Norman A. The records of public officials. New York, The American assembly, Columbia University, 1975. 40 p.

Hamby, Alonzo, and Edward Weldon, eds. Access to the papers of recent public figures: the New Harmony conference. Bloomington, Organization of American historians, 1977. 107 p.

Jones, H. G. The records of a nation: their management, preservation, and use. New York Atheneum [1969] 309 p.

McCoy, Donald R. The National Archives: America's ministry of documents 1934-1968. Chapel Hill, University of North Carolina Press, 1978. 437 p.

Nelson, Anna Kasten, ed. The records of Federal officials: a selection of materials from the National Study Commission on Records and Documents of Federal officials. New York, Garland Publishing, Inc., 1978. 416. p.

Posner, Ernst. Archives and the public interest: selected essays. Washington, Public Affairs Press, 1967. 204 p.

Schmeckebier, Laurence F., and Roy B. Eastin. Government publications and their use. 2d rev. ed. Washington, The Brookings Institution, 1969. 502 p.

Articles

Aeschbacher, William D. Presidential libraries: new dimension in research facilities. Midwest quarterly, v. 6, Jan. 1965: 205-1635.

Album, Michael T. Government control of Richard Nixon's Presidential material. Yale law journal, v. 87, July 1978: 1601-1635.

American Assembly. The records of public officials: final report of the forty-eighth American assembly. American archivist, v. 38, July 1975: 329-336.

Bernstein, Barton J. Who owns history? Inquiry (San Francisco), v. 1, May 1, 1978: 6-8.

Brooks, Philip C. The Harry S. Truman library — plans and reality. American archivist, v. 25, Jan. 1962: 25-37.

— — — The selection of records for preservation. American archivist, v. 3, Oct. 1940: 221-234.

— — — Understanding the Presidency: the Harry S Truman library. Prologue, v. 1, Winter 1969: 3-12.

Cappon, Lester J. Why Presidential libraries? Yale review, v. 48, Oct. 1978: 11-34.

Cochrane, James L. The U.S. Presidential libraries and the history of political economy. History of political economy, v. 8, Fall 1976: 412-427.

Cole, Garold L. Presidential libraries. Journal of librarianship, v. 4, Apr. 1972: 115-129.

Cole, Virginia R. Presidential libraries. Special libraries, v. 59, Nov. 1968: 691-697.

Connor, R. D. W. The Franklin D. Roosevelt library. American archivist, v. 3, Apr. 1940: 81-92.

Cook, J. Frank. Papers of public officials: an analysis of the archivist's dilemma. In U.S. Congress. House. Committee on House Administration. Subcommittee on Printing. The "Public Documents Act." Hearings, 93d Congress, 2d session. Washington, U.S. Govt. Print. Off., 1974. pp. 61-72.

— — — "Private papers" of public officials. American Archivist, v. 38, July 1975: 299-324.

Drewry, Elizabeth B. The role of Presidential libraries. Midwest quarterly, v. 7, Autumn 1965: 53-65.

Eberhart, David C. The Federal register system: what to expect and how to find it. American Bar Association journal, v. 47, Nov. 1961: 1069-1073.

Elzy, Martin I. Scholarship versus economy: records appraisal at the National Archives. Prologue, v. 6, Fall 1974: 183-188.

Fairlie, John A. Administrative legislation. Michigan law review, v. 18, Jan. 1920: 181-200.

Flato, Linda. Automation at the White House. Datamation, v. 24, Jan. 1978: 190-193.

Ford, Frederick W. Some legal problems in preserving records for public use. American archivist, v. 20, Jan. 1957: 41-47.

Griswold, Erwin N. Government in ignorance of the law: a plea for better publication of executive legislation. Harvard law review, v. 48, Dec. 1934: 198-215.

Haight, David J., and George H. Curtis. Abilene, Kansas and the history of World War II: resources and research opportunities at the Dwight D. Eisenhower library. Military affairs, v. 41, Dec. 1977: 195-200.

Ham, F. Gerald. Public ownership of the papers of public officials. American archivist, v. 37, Apr. 1974: 357-360.

Herbert, Elsie S. How accessible are the records in government records centers? Journalism quarterly, v. 52, Spring 1975: 23-27, 60.

Hirshon, Arnold. The scope, accessability and history of Presidential papers. Government publications review, v. 1, Fall 1974: 363-390.

Horn, David E. Who owns our history? Library journal, v. 100, Apr. 1, 1975: 635-639.

Jones, H. G. Presidential libraries: is there a case for a national Presidential library? American archivist, v. 38, July 1975: 325-328.

Kahn, Herman. The Presidential library—a new institution. Special libraries, v. 50, Mar. 1959: 106-113.

Kirkendall, Richard S. Presidential libraries—one researcher's point of view. American archivist, v. 25, Oct. 1962: 441-448.

———A second look at Presidential libraries. American archivist, v. 29, July 1966: 371-386.

Leland, Waldo Gifford. The creation of the Franklin D. Roosevelt library: a personal narrative. American archivist, v. 18, Jan. 1955: 11-29.

Leopold, Richard W. The historian and the Federal Government. Journal of American History, v. 64, June 1977: 5-23.

Lewis, Finlay. Presidential papers: an attempt to own history. Nation, v. 219, Oct. 19, 1974: 366-369.

Lloyd, David D. The Harry S. Truman library. American archivist, v. 18, Apr. 1955: 99-110.

———Presidential papers and Presidential libraries. Manuscripts, v. 8, Fall 1955: 4-9.

McCoy, Donald R. The beginnings of the Franklin D. Roosevelt library. Prologue, v. 7, Fall 1975: 137-150.

McDonough, John, R. Gordon Hoxie, and Richard Jacobs. Who owns Presidential papers. Manuscripts, v. 27, Winter 1975: 2-11

Miller, Arthur Selwyn, and Henry Bartholomew Cox. On the need for a national commission on documentary access. George Washington law review, v. 44, Jan. 1976: 213-238.

Nelson, Anna K. Foreign policy records and papers: a case study of the preservation and accessibility of one group of documents. The Society for historians of American foreign relations newsletter, v. 8, June 1977: 14-26, Sept.: 18-32, and Dec.: 2-16.

— — —Government historical offices and public records. American archivist, v. 41, Oct. 1978: 405-412.

O'Neill, James E. Will success spoil the Presidential libraries? American archivist, v. 36, July 1973: 339-351.

Pinkett, Harold T. Accessioning public records: Anglo-American practices and possible improvements. American archivist, v. 41, Oct. 1978: 413-421.

Reid, Warren R. Public papers of the Presidents. American archivist, v. 25, Oct. 1962: 435-439.

Rhoads, James B. Who should own the documents of public officials? Prologue, v. 7, Spring 1975: 32-35.

Rowland, Buford. The papers of the Presidents. American archivist, v 13, July 1950: 195-211.

Schlesinger, Arthur M., Jr. Who owns a President's papers? Wall Street journal, Feb. 26, 1975: 16. Reprinted in Manuscripts, v. 27, Summer 1975: 178-182.

Shelley, Fred. The Presidential papers program of the Library of Congress. American archivist, v. 25, Oct. 1962: 429-433.

Sheppard, William F. Documents of American foreign policy: the case for earlier publication. World affairs, v. 134, Fall 1971: 125-131.

Spencer, Patricia L. Separation of powers — bills of attainder — Presidential papers—Chief executive's right to privacy. Akron law review, v. 11, Fall 1977: 373-386.

Stewart, William J. Opening closed material in the Roosevelt library, Prologue, v. 7, Winter 1975: 239-241.

The Presidency in the information age: new directions. Bulletin of the American Society for Information Science, v. 5, Dec. 1978: 13-27.

Tyler, John Edward. Access to Presidential materials. Columbia, School of Journalism, University of Missouri, 1975. 7 p. (Missouri. University. Freedom of Information Center. Report no. 346).

Vose, Clement E. Nixon's archival legacy. PS, v. 10, Fall 1977: 432-438.

— — —Presidential papers as a political science concern. PS, v. 8, Winter 1975: 8-18.

Documents

U.S. Commission on Federal Paperwork. Confidentiality and privacy: a report of the Commission on Federal Paperwork. Washington, U.S. Govt. Print. Off., 1977. 175 p.

U.S. Congress. House. Committee on Government Operations. Presidential libraries. Washington, U.S. Govt. Print. Off., 1955. 11 p. (84th Congress, 1st sess. House. Report no. 998, 2 parts).

— — — Presidential Records Act of 1978. Hearings, 95th Congress, 2d session. Feb. 23–Mar. 7, 1978. Washington, U.S. Govt. Print. Off., 1978. 896 p.

— — — Presidential Records Act of 1978: report to accompany H.R. 13500, including cost estimate of the Congressional Budget Office. Washington, U.S. Govt. Print. Off., 1978. 24 p. (95th Congress, 2d sess. House. Report no. 95–1487, part 1).

— — — To provide for the acceptance and maintenance of Presidential libraries, and for other purposes. Hearings, 84th Congress, 1st sess. June 13, 1955. Washington, U.S. Govt. Print. Off., 1955. 64 p.

U.S. Congress. House. Committee on House Administration. Disapproving certain regulations proposed by the General Services Administration implementing Section 104 of the Presidential Recordings and Materials Preservation Act. Washington, U.S. Govt. Print. Off., 1976. 27 p. (94th Congress, 2d sess. House. Report no. 94–1485).

— — — Disapproving regulations proposed by the General Services Administration implementing the Presidential Recordings and Materials Preservation Act. Washington, U.S. Govt. Print. Off., 1975. 69 p. (94th Congress, 1st sess. House. Report no. 94–560).

— — — Presidential Recordings and Materials Preservation Act; report to accompany S. 4016. Washington, U.S. Govt. Print. Off., 1974. 25 p. (93d Congress, 2d sess. House. Report no. 93–1507).

U.S. Congress. House. Committee on House Administration. Subcommittee on Printing. The Public Documents Act. Hearings, 93d Congress, 2d sess. on H.R. 16902 and related legislation. Sept. 30 [and] Oct. 4, 1974. Washington, U.S. Govt. Print. Off., 1974. 239 p.

— — — GSA regulations to implement title I of the Presidential Recordings and Materials Preservation Act. Hearings, 94th Congress, 1st sess. May 22–June 3, 1975. Washington, U.S. Govt. Print. Off., 1975. 576 p.

U.S. Congress. House. Committee to Inquire into State of Ancient Public Records and Archives of the United States. Report of the committee appointed to inquire into the state of the ancient public records and archives of the United States. Washington, printed by R. C. Weightman, 1810. 11 p.

U.S. Congress. Senate. Committee on Government Operations. Disapproving certain regulations proposed by the administrator of General Services under section 104 of the Presidentail Recordings and Materials Preservation Act. Washington, U.S. Govt. Print. Off., 1976. 24 p. (94th Congress, 2d sess. Senate. Report no. 94–748).

— — — Disapproving the regulations proposed by the General Services Administration implementing the Presidential Recordings and Materials Preservation Act; report to accompany S. Res. 244. Washington, U.S. Govt. Print. Off., 1975. 49 p. (94th Congress, 1st sess. Senate. Report no. 94–368).

— — —GSA regulations implementing Presidential Recordings and Materials Preservation Act. Hearing, 94th Cong., 1st sess. May 13, 1975. Washington, U.S. Govt. Print. Off., 1975. 457 p.

— — —Preservation, protection, and public access with respect to certain tape recordings and other materials; report to accompanys S. 4016. Washington, U.S. Govt. Print. Off., 1974. 10 p. (93d Congress, 2d sess. Senate. Report no. 93-1181).

— — —Providing for the acceptance and maintenance of Presidential libraries. Washington, U.S. Govt. Print. Off., 1955. 9 p. (84th Congress, 1st sess. Senate. Report no. 1189).

— — —The Presidential Records Act of 1978 — S. 3494. Hearing, 95th Congress, 2d sess. Sept. 15, 1978. Washington, U.S. Govt. Print. Off., 1979. 45 p.

U.S. Executive Office of the President. Office of Science and Technology Policy. Information systems needs in the Executive Office of the President: Final report of the Advisory Group on White House Information Systems. Washington, Executive Office of the President, 1977. 22 p.

U.S. National Study Commission on Records and Documents of Federal Officials. Final report. Washington, U.S. Govt. Print. Off., 1977. 137 p.

— — —Memoranda of law. Washington, U.S. Govt. Print. Off., 1977. 347 p.

— — —Memorandum of findings on existing custom or law, fact and opinion. Washington, U.S. Govt. Print. Off., 1977. 373 p.

— — —Public hearings background memorandum. Washington, U.S. Govt. Print. Off., n.d. 92 p.

— — —Study of the records of Supreme Court justices. Washington, U.S. Govt. Print. Off., 1977. 204 p.

THE PRESIDENT AND THE PRESS

Books

American Institute for Political Communication. The credibility problem. Washington, American Institute for Political Communication, 1972. 99 p.

Cornwell, Elmer E., Jr. The Presidency and the press. Morristown, N.J., General Learning Press, 1974. 32 p. (University Programs Modular Studies).

— — —Presidential leadership of public opinion. Bloomington, Indiana University Press, 1965. 370 p.

Deakin, James. Lyndon Johnson's credibility gap. Washington, Public Affairs Press, 1968. 65 p.

Kelley, S., Jr. Presidential public relations and political power. Baltimore, The Johns Hopkins University Press, 1956. 247 p.

Keogh, James. President Nixon and the press. New York, Funk and Wagnalls, 1972. 212 p.

Minow, Newton, John Bartlow Martin, and Lee M. Mitchell. Presidential television. New York, Basic Books, 1973. 232 p.

Pollard, James E. The Presidents and the press. New York, The Macmillan Company, 1947. 866 p.

— — — The Presidents and the press. Washington, Public Affairs Press, 1964. 125 p.

Stein, Meyer L. When Presidents meet the press. New York, Messner, 1969. 190 p.

White, Graham J. FDR and the press. Chicago and London, University of Chicago Press, 1979. 186 p.

Articles

Akamatsu, Muriel. Presidents v. press: F.D.R. to Nixon. Columbia, School of Journalism, University of Missouri, 1971. 7 p. (Missouri. University. Freedom of Information Center. Report no. 271).

Balutis, Alan P. The Presidency and the press. Presidential studies quarterly, v. 7, Fall 1977: 244-251.

Cater, Douglass. The President and the press. Annals, v. 307, Sept. 1956: 55-65.

Cornwell, Elmer E., Jr. The Presidential press conference: a study in institutionalization. Midwest journal of political science, v. 4, Nov. 1960: 370-389.

— — — The President and the press: phases in the relationship. Annals, v. 427, Sept. 1976: 53-64.

Grossman, Michael Baruch, and Francis E. Rourke. The media and the Presidency: an exchange analysis. Political science quarterly, v. 91, Fall 1976: 455-470.

Grossman, Michael Baruch, and Martha Joynt Kumar. The White House and the news media: the phases of their relationship. Political science quarterly, v. 94, Spring 1979: 37-53.

Kindsvatter, Peter S. Press relations: Carter's example. Columbia, School of Journalism, University of Missouri, 1980. 8 p. (Missouri. University. Freedom of Information Center. Report no 418).

Locander, Robert. The adversary relationship: a new look at an old idea. Presidential studies quarterly, v. 9, Summer 1979: 266-274.

— — — Carter and the press: the first two years. Presidential studies quarterly, v. 10, Winter 1980: 106-120.

— — — The President, the press, and the public: friends and enemies of democracy. Presidential studies quarterly, v. 8, Spring 1978: 140-150.

Moore, Susan E. Presidential press conferences. Columbia, School of Journalism, University of Missouri, 1975. 9 p. (Missouri. University. Freedom of Information Center. Report no. 339).

Reedy, George E. The President and the press: struggle for dominance. Annals, v. 427, Sept. 1976: 65-72.

Shibi, Haim. Presidential television. Columbia, School of Journalism, University of Missouri, 1976. 7 p. (Missouri. University. Freedom of Information Center. Report no. 347).

Index

DATE DUE

MAR 3 1990			
APR 2 0 1990			
MAY 2 1 1998			
MAY 2 5 2006			
1 6 MAR 2007			
2 4 MAY 2007			